What Ails the IAS and Why It Fails to Deliver

An Insider's View

Naresh Chandra Saxena

ATLANTIC
PUBLISHERS & DISTRIBUTORS (P) LTD

ATLANTIC
PUBLISHERS & DISTRIBUTORS (P) LTD
7/22, Ansari Road, Darya Ganj, New Delhi
Tel.: +91-11-4077 5252, 2327 3880
E-mail: orders@atlanticbooks.com
Web: www.atlanticbooks.com

Reprint 2026

Published by Atlantic Publishers & Distributors (P) Ltd.

Printed & bound in India by Atlantic Print Services

ADVANCE PRAISE

All over the world, relentless commodification has cynicized the behaviour of states. Even though India is no exception to that, before asking "What can be done", it is worth asking "What is Indian about this process?" because the formulaic answer is so often even less state. Dr Saxena, an IAS, gives us a book full of closely observed insights from his own working life and those of others about both inspiring successes and failures of system maintenance against the politicization of elite administrative culture, the penetration of private venality, and of caste, regional, religious and patriarchal identities into what he estimates is the wetter half of India's bureaucratic system. Even in the drier half, however, the result is poor development outcomes. He builds up to administrative reforms which include stability of tenure, domain expertise, pruning redundant positions, mid-career secondment for fresh experiences, lateral entry, shake-ups for accountability and M&E, especially of absenteeism. But they all need collective political backing. If you disagree, the ball is now in your court to mount an even better argument.

Barbara Harriss-White, *Emeritus Professor of Development Studies, Oxford University*

Hailed by some as India's steel frame and reviled by others as a relic of the colonial past, the Indian Administrative Service is an enigma for most. In this candid insider account of it, Naresh Saxena gives the IAS a human face and shares valuable ideas for administrative reform.

Jean Dreze, *Honorary Professor, Delhi School of Economics*

Dr Saxena is an immensely gifted and accomplished authority on the Indian Administrative Service. Here he draws on his unparalleled breadth of experience—in the ministries of rural development, environment and forests, and revenue; as Director of the Lal Bahadur Shastri National Academy of Administration; and on the Minorities Commission and the National Advisory Council. The result is a perceptive, compelling and deeply humane critique of the Service and its place in India's recent history.

James Manor, *School of Advanced Study, University of London*

A brutally frank and brilliant assessment by a very experienced civil servant of the failure of the IAS to deliver efficiently key services of health, forest rights, education and tribal rights and removal of hunger of the common man. Full of very interesting anecdotes on interface with politicians, self-introspection and suggestion on reforming the governance system. Emphasizes the need for administrative reforms including stable tenures, accountability, effective monitoring and information system and capacity building. A very compelling call for systemic change.

B. K. Chaturvedi, *Former Cabinet Secretary, Government of India*

A truly unusual and provocative book, written with candour, commitment and clarity. N. C. Saxena's superb account of the IAS places civil service reform in the context of a sharp and informed view of India's larger politics and society and the need for greater individual and collective initiatives together with strong political and administrative will to implement systemic reforms. This impressive work will appeal to those with an interest in making the state more outcome oriented and accountable to the people.

Zoya Hasan, *Professor Emerita, Jawaharlal Nehru University*

To

Naomi, Jhilmil and my grandsons,
Andrew, Sean, Ethan and Liam

CONTENTS

FOREWORD

India's Rusted and Debilitated Steel Frame

It is a formidable privilege for me to be invited to write the foreword of a book by a person who has straddled, as an intellectual colossus, India's higher civil services, for decades. Dr NC Saxena represents the best traditions of what has become in recent decades a very rare breed—a scholar administrator. He is one who has competently worked in the system at senior levels and contributed very significantly to social justice policymaking, and at the same time is able to critically reflect on the inner workings of this system, diagnosing its flaws while always mindful of its promise and potential.

This book, I have no doubt, is destined to be a reference point for decades to come for understanding this elite club of the Indian Administrative Service, to enter which millions of India's fine young people continue to aspire and which several more million criticize for betraying the trust that the nation places in it.

I have had the privilege of working closely with Dr Saxena when he was the Director of the Lal Bahadur Shastri National Academy of Administration in Mussoorie, where I was posted as a faculty, when I came to develop enormous respect and affection for him. Later, this only deepened as a colleague in the National Advisory Council of the United Progressive Alliance Government. Dr Saxena is gifted with a razor-sharp intelligence and intellectual curiosity. His intellectual grasp is boundless. He is uncompromising in his commitment to evidence-based scrutiny. He is never afraid of taking unpopular positions. I observe sometimes he takes an almost adolescent-like delight in arousing intellectual controversy. He combines all of this with a deeply felt allegiance to social justice, to the vision and values of the Indian Constitution, to the sacred task of nation-building—of building a country which is just and fair to even the last and most vulnerable of its citizens.

He brings all these gifts to bear on his acute forensic scrutiny of the civil services in which for decades he worked, as part of which he trained and inspired several generations of civil servant recruits; and which, as a scholar, he studied and challenged, sometimes driven to publicly lament what he saw as its betrayals. Therefore, when he told me that he was at work on a book on the IAS, I looked forward to it (but also worried secretly about how many of his peers and juniors in the service would receive it). I knew it would be definitive, provocative and insightful. The book does not disappoint. It carries all the hallmarks of his intellectual breadth and originality; his willingness to unsettle settled beliefs and, if necessary, to annoy his colleagues; his integrity, his sardonic humour, and, in the end, his profound commitment to social justice. The book is not a dry read. Unlike much of his more conventional academic writing, Dr Saxena spices his book with delightful and often funny anecdotes and stories, which brings to life what goes into governing (or not governing) this vast, diverse and maddeningly complex land.

During the two decades that I served in the Indian Administrative Service, I often would wonder why our country's founding fathers and mothers chose to retain in democratic India the permanent civil services, patterned closely after the colonial civil services, preserving also its grand trappings of large colonial bungalows and liveried staff. The puzzle was greater in the districts, in which the District Collector functions virtually as the head of a district government. When the country was boldly willing to rely on governments elected through a universal adult franchise at the union and state levels, why have we opted for unelected functionaries selected through a merit-based system to run the district government? After all, this was the level of government closest to the large mass of people—the working classes, farmers and homemakers.

Why, indeed, did the newly independent India not cast away a civil service established by our colonial masters? Sardar Patel famously described the Indian Administrative Service as India's 'steel frame'. India accomplished freedom amidst fearsome violence based on religious strife. In this fledging nation there were other myriad potential fractures of language, ethnicity, caste, class and many others. The expectation was that a great deal of this could tear apart India and that its multiple ruptures could be aggravated by competitive politics. It was a small band of carefully selected civil servants who would be expected to hold the country together, with fairness, firmness, integrity, independence and compassion. This was to be India's steel frame. At senior levels of government, power would vest with the elected executive, as it should. But here again, it was the higher civil services that were expected to fearlessly offer independent advice to their ministers. Sardar Patel said to his officers,

> Today my Secretary can write a note opposed to my views. I have given that freedom to all my secretaries. I have told them, 'If you do not give your honest opinion for fear that it will displease your Minister, please then you had better go'. I will never be displeased over a frank expression of opinion.

In Dr Saxena's review of the history of the Indian Administrative Service, he observes that it maintained its reputation for independence and integrity in the early decades after Independence, and prime ministers, chief ministers and senior ministers respected and supported officers even when they dissented with them. When and why did all of this change?

According to Dr Saxena, first, we should not paint the early decades of the civil services uncritically in halcyon colours. He believes that if we had asked poor people to evaluate these officers, they would not give them more than 3 marks out of 10, because despite being honest and independent, they did little to improve the lives of disadvantaged people.

But early young recruits to the civil service, he observes, were nurtured by their seniors and could look forward to the future with confidence and hope. Politicians respected their officers. He tells a classic story about Morarji Desai who as a Chief Minister detested his Chief Secretary, yet he supported him to the hilt. When asked why he did this, he replied, 'What has liking to do with the business of governance?'

And in these times, seniors assured their younger colleagues 'If you get into trouble, I will bail you out. Do what is right, and do it fearlessly'.

Dr Saxena believes that it was in the mid-1960s that political pressures started eroding administrative autonomy. New values emerged, which emphasized political loyalty and 'flexibility'. The reward structure benefited those who compromised with their constitutional duties.

Among the reasons that he sees for these changes is the rise of coalition governments after 1967, which increased the bargaining power of individual MLAs. Second, regional parties emerged, which focused more on the local than the national interest. Third, a whole army of intermediaries emerged, to help villagers mediate a police station, government hospital, land office or bank. Finally, he talks about the invasion of the political system by criminals and the growing nexus between criminal gangs, police, bureaucrats and politicians in many parts of the country.

He illustrates this decline of the civil services with numerous stories which describe vividly the nature and extent of the growing rot. But fortunately, there are also enough stories of officers who bravely resist. He also empathizes with the difficulties that bright men and women face who join the service confront an adverse work environment, constant political interference, frequent and often meaningless transfers, and often runaway corruption above and below them—all of which combine to erode sometimes quite quickly their idealism.

Dr Saxena suggests a host of imaginative reforms to address this near-terminal decline of the civil services. These include measures to ensure greater stability of tenure, encouraging high professionalism and the building of domain knowledge, giving high value to departments which are important for the poor such as health, education, labour and child welfare, weeding out officers who fail to upgrade themselves or show a decline in moral and financial integrity, lateral entry and encouraging systems for independent third-party evaluations which allow the performance of officers to be judged by their outcomes rather than simply budget utilizations.

These are all worthy reforms and must be encouraged. But my worry is whether they go far enough, to reach the core of the decline of the civil services, which I am convinced is at its core a moral decline. Looking back to the past 70 years, it should be evident to all that the higher civil services have failed to live up to the lofty faith that the country's founding fathers and mothers had placed on them. There have indeed been several civil servants who have contributed valuably to public service and nation building. But taken collectively, there can be no doubt that India's higher civil services, as a tribe, have let the country down at moments in our history when it was needed the most: during the emergency, during communal massacres such as in Nellie in 1983, Delhi in 1984, Gujarat in 2002, and indeed the rising tide of mob lynching in current times, when the Babri Masjid was demolished, during caste massacres, in implementing land reforms, in building a robust set of public services of education and health care for all citizens, and in designing and implementing programmes to combat poverty, to name a few.

For the civil services to fulfil the mandate that the country has placed on their shoulders, we require women and men of courage, conviction, integrity, compassion, with a deep sense of justice, convinced about the equality of castes and genders, untainted by communal, caste and patriarchal prejudice, and imbued with a deep sense of public service.

There is admittedly nothing in the present mode of recruitment of civil servants that tests any of these qualities. What the UPSC examinations test is not even high academic merit, but academic stamina and perseverance. But the distinction of this selection process, unmatched by any other in the public sector, is its integrity. It is untainted by nepotism, subjective bias and prejudice, and individual likes and dislikes. Recent reforms proposed by Prime Minister Modi may erode even this, and must be revisited, because a government should not pack the civil services with persons committed to their ideological world-view, in this case 'the RSS'.

We also need to think about training. Under Dr Saxena's leadership in the Lal Bahadur Shastri National Academy of Administration, I was a member of the faculty which ran these courses for three years, between 1993 and 1996. We were free to design our training programmes. In our time, we believed that the early training of the young officers should encourage young civil servants to reflect, question, dissent; to imbibe the values of the constitution and of public service; to understand the country's problems, their causes and possible solutions; to combat bigotry and patriarchy; to nurture their idealism; and to encourage integrity, courage, empathy, truth and a sense of justice. These are difficult goals, and our success was at best partial.

But none of these reforms go far enough into the core of the crisis that we find ourselves today. The crisis and failures of the civil service—to be fair, to be compassionate, to be just and to be honest—is part of a much larger civilizational crisis in which we find ourselves today. I believe that these are a result of our historical legacies of caste, gender and class, with the old injustices becoming transformed and even more entrenched with market fundamentalism, and all of this combined with the dangerous toxins of rising majoritarianism.

Dr Saxena concludes on a dejected note—that the IAS serves the state, but the state structure is increasingly getting divorced from public interest. What 'reforms' then could help rescue the very institution that was crafted by our leaders like Sardar Patel and Jawaharlal Nehru to hold this country together? What can prevent the rusted and debilitated steel frame from collapse, and will India lie in even greater danger after its falling apart?

The solutions, I am convinced, cannot be confined to changes in just the civil services. Solutions lie entirely in the realm of political economy. These would involve recognizing and addressing the depth of our civilizational crisis, the long distance we have travelled as a society, straying away from the constitutional vision and pledges of justice, liberty, equality and fraternity.

Harsh Mander

Activist, works with survivors of mass violence and street children and an ex-IAS officer

ACKNOWLEDGEMENTS

This book would not have been written without the encouragement of Namarita Kathait, who noticed my article, 'Has the IAS failed the nation? An insider view', published in the Economic and Political Weekly in 2018, and its summary in The Print, and exhorted me to convert the article into a book with real-life experiences. My friends in the IAS found the article critical of the IAS, and I hope they will change their opinion after reading the book, which primarily explains the enigma about why their undisputed individual competence does not get translated into collective outcomes, especially for disadvantaged groups. I am indebted to a large number of my colleagues in the IAS, some of them have been quoted in this book, either anonymously or by name, who have helped me shape my views over the decades.

I am grateful to Harsh Mander, who took time off from his extremely busy schedule to write the foreword for the book. I am also grateful to Barbara Harriss-White, Zoya Hasan, Jean Dreze, James Manor, and B.K. Chaturvedi for writing endorsements for the book. I thank my colleagues Wajahat Habibullah, Siraj Hussain, Noor Mohammad, and Sajjad Hassan for offering their valuable comments on one particular section of the book.

My most profound thanks to my wife, Naomi, who was the epitome of patience while I was working on this book.

LIST OF ABBREVIATIONS

B.Ed	Bachelor of Education
BDO	Block Development Officer
BIMAROU	Bihar, Madhya Pradesh ,Rajasthan, Odisha, Uttar Pradesh
BJP	Bhartiya Janata Party
BSP	Bahujan Samaj Party
BSUP	Basic Services to the Urban Poor
CAG	Comptroller and Auditor General
CAPART	Council for the Advancement of Peoples Action and Rural Technology
CBI	Central Bureau of Investigation
CHCs	Community Health Centre
CM	Chief Minister
CPI(M)	Communist Party of India (Marxist)
D.Ed	Doctor of Education
DCT	direct cash transfer
DDA	Delhi Development Authority
Deptt	Department
DFID	Department for International Development
DG	Director General
DM	District Magisrate
DRDAs	District Rural Development Agencies
EC	Essential Commodities

EAS	Employment Assurance Scheme
EWS	economically weaker sections
FCI	Food Corporation of India
FIR	First Information Report
FRA	Forests Rights Act
FY	fiscal year
GAD	General Administrative Department
GDP	Gross Domestic Product
GOI	Government of India
Govt	Government
HDI	Human Development Index
HHs	households
HIG	high income group
HP	Himachal Pradesh
I.G.	Inspector General
IAS	Indian Administrative Service
IAY	Indira Awas Yojana
ICDS	Integrated Child Development Services
ICS	Indian Civil Service
IG	Inspector General
IMR	Infant Mortality Rate
IPS	Indian Police Service
JFM	Joint Forest Management
KL	kendu leaves
LIC	Life Insurance Corporation
LIG	low-income group
M&E	Monitoring and Evaluation
MBA	Master of Business Administration
MDGs	Millennium Development Goals
MFPs	Minor Forest Products
MGNREGA	Mahatma Gandhi National Rural Employment Guarantee Act

MGNREGS	Mahatma Gandhi National Rural Employment Guarantee Scheme
MHRD	Ministry of Human Resource Development
MLA	Member of Legislative Assembly
MMR	Maternal Mortality Rate
MOS(IC)	Minister of State (Incharge)
MOTA	Ministry of Tribal Affairs
MP	Member of Parliament
MP	Madhya Pradesh
MSP	minimum support price
MT	million tonnes
MWCD	Ministry of Women and Child Development
NAC	National Advisory Council
NDA	National Democratic Alliance
NDC	National Development Council
NGOs	Non-Government Organisations
NHM	National Health Mission
Noida	New Okhla Industrial Development Authority
NREGA	National Rural Employment Guarantee Act
NSSO	National Sample Survey Office
OBC	Other Backward Class
OECD	Organisation for Economic Co-operation and Development
PAC	Provincial Armed Constabulary
PHCs	Primary Health Centre
PM	Prime Minister
PWD	Public Works Department
RSBY	Rashtriya Swasth Bima Yojana
RTI	Right to Information
SBM	Swachh Bharat Mission
SCs	Scheduled Castes
SDGs	Sustainable Development Goals

SDM	Sub-Divisional Magistrate
SIDA	Swedish International Development Agency
SP	Samajwadi Party
SP	Superintendent of Police
SSA	Sarva Shiksha Abhiyan
Std	Standard
STs	Scheduled Tribes
TDCC	Tribal Development Cooperative Corporation
UP	Uttar Pradesh
UPSC	Union Public Service Commission
ZALR	Zamindari Abolition and Land Reforms Act

Chapter 1

WHAT IS THIS BOOK ABOUT?

Bureaucracy the world over plays a vital role in providing public goods, such as defence, public order, property rights, macro-economic management, basic education, primary health care, disaster relief, protection of environment and coordinating private sector activity. In many developing countries including India, bureaucracy is also responsible for implementing social protection programmes to promote inclusive development, reduce poverty, and facilitate people's participation in economic life. India, despite high economic growth, has unfortunately not done well in social sector programmes, and could not achieve the International Millennium Development Goals (MDGs) in hunger, health, malnutrition, sanitation, and gender. Some decades back, one used to compare India with China and Sri Lanka, but these countries have left India far behind. On social indicators India does worse than countries even poorer than India, such as Bangladesh and Vietnam.

Interestingly, India has done quite well in improving physical infrastructure, where contractors are involved, such as road transport and power transmission. However, it does poorly in programmes that require active involvement of grassroots bureaucracy without contractors: whether it is quality of education, medical care, maintenance of land records, selection of beneficiaries, redressal of public grievances, groundwater management, crime control, timely payment of salaries to contractual workers or pensions to the poor and so on. Many welfare programmes are either not well designed or fail to reach a large number of marginalized and disadvantaged people, such as Scheduled Tribes (STs), Muslims and women, resulting in increased interstate and inter-class inequalities.

As is well known, officers of the Indian Administrative Service (IAS) are responsible for designing major development programmes in the Central Ministries, and their counterparts at the state and district levels implement them. When in a recent article (Has the IAS failed the nation? An insider view, Economic and Political Weekly, 23 June 2018, and its summary in *The Print*[1]), I argued that they must share the blame if the outcomes are dismal, my friends in the IAS jumped to defend the service and condemned my analysis. A recently retired Secretary to the Government of India (GOI) wrote to me,

> “Must confess that I was a trifle surprised at article written by you in 'The Print'. I have had the occasion to work with a large number of IAS officers in the recent past and I beg to disagree with you in the context of their competence and commitment. Coal, RSBY[2] and project clearances would not have happened but for these officers. Yes, there are a few exceptions but to say that IAS officers evolve as incompetent and arrogant may not be correct. Coming from you it puts a stamp on 'untruth'. The whole world seems to be baying for our blood. You have provided them with cannon fodder. There is indeed a lot to introspect but make a public statement about the 'incompetence' and 'arrogance' by an officer who is revered by large number of us is very surprising. I had always believed in handling the problems in the family within the family and not go to town with it.

Another one reprimanded me:

> “Completely disagree. There is a great deal of condescension here which seems to think that the officers of today because of cut throat competition and inability to acquire professional skills in specific domains are incompetent, and worse arrogant with nothing to contribute for their bloated sense of entitlement. This is not just unfair, it suggests that we who are casting this

1. https://theprint.in/opinion/ias-officers-see-tremendous-growth-in-two-areas-ignorance-and-arrogance/83474/ (accessed on 10 July 2019)
2. Rashtriya Swasth Bima Yojana (Central Health Insurance Scheme)

> critical eye were somehow superior and governed by a different 'esprit de corps'. As members of the service we are together in this forum because we share the extraordinary experience the IAS gave us. It seems to be politically correct and fashionable to run ourselves down, but that is reverse snobbery of a particular kind.

Although I did not criticize the younger generation specifically, some readers thought that I am glorifying the past and talking disparagingly of the present lot. I was reminded by another bright officer:

> '[W]hen I go to the districts and see some of the work being done, I come back inspired, officers are today fighting, trying to do their best caught between a venal polity and their conscience and desire to contribute. Senior officers have failed in mentoring and they fight their battles alone. The worst thing is the postretirement sinecures ... that is what is compromising our integrity!

How does one reconcile the analysis presented in this book with the above critical, but significant, observations? My friends are looking at the individual traits of the IAS officer, and they are right in their assessment. Most IAS officers are brilliant, hard working and honest. Many of them also try to remain distant from unscrupulous politicians. But people are more interested in the outcomes that the system is responsible for, rather than in their personal qualities. Are teachers and doctors present in their place of postings and providing quality services? Are widows and disabled receiving their pensions regularly in time? Are programmes being evaluated, timely and objectively? Do land records reflect the ground reality and are updated without bribes? Are entrepreneurs able to set up new ventures without undue hurdles? Are outcomes being measured and reported honestly, so that corrective action can be taken to improve delivery?

I am afraid the answer to these questions is in the negative. The system does not perform well, though people at the top are world class. US academic Lant Pritchett (2009) has an interesting explanation for why things go so shockingly awry in India, and why it is incapable of implementing programmes and policies. About the IAS, Pritchett comments:

> Because of the incredibly spectacular intelligence, cleverness, and competence of the top tiers of the Indian government—in particular the national services such as the Indian Administrative Service—it has managed to project the myth that India is just another regular modern state, with a growing economy, a democratic politics, a functional civil service, and making progress on social issues.

However, outcomes are dismal and he calls this the flailing state syndrome, 'a nation state in which the head, that is elite institutions at the national (and in some states) level remain sound and functional but that this head is no longer reliably connected via nerves and sinews to its own limbs...'. As a result, nothing works, because field-level agents of the state, from health workers to teachers and engineers, are increasingly beyond the control of the government, at the state and national levels. 'In police, tax collection, education, health, power, water supply—in nearly every routine service—there is rampant absenteeism, indifference, incompetence and corruption. As this is true of even relatively routine services, even more so for more sophisticated ones like networked irrigation or groundwater management.'

My initiatives fell flat

I am often asked why I did not change the system when I was in top policy positions. This book describes in detail what I tried to do and why I failed. Surprisingly, I did not find politicians averse to radical policy changes. As Revenue Secretary, I could issue a large number of circulars promoting land reforms and preventing tribal land alienation. According to the Section 211 of the Zamindari Abolition & Land Reforms Act (initiated by me in 1980) in Uttar Pradesh (UP), the encroacher on tribal land could be removed through executive action without going to any court. As a Joint Secretary, Ministry of Environment and Forests, I could initiate a new pro-tribal Forest Policy that was 180 degrees different from the old pro-industry and plantation-oriented policy. As a Joint Secretary, Minorities Commission, I exposed communal bias of district administration in handling riots. As Secretary, Rural Development, I tried to promote community awareness about the usage of toilets by drastically reducing the amount of subsidy and increasing funds for publicity. As member of the National Advisory Council (NAC), I succeeded in bringing in a new legislation to promote gender equality in matters of inheritance of agricultural land.

Unfortunately, none of these initiatives resulted in any sustained systemic improvement. Not a single acre of land was restored to the tribals in the UP tarai, now under Uttarakhand. State Forest Secretaries remained indifferent to the new Forest Policy, 1988. I was punished for bringing to light how police killed innocent Muslim women and children. With reduction in subsidy, the construction of new toilets came down by more than 20 per cent. States took no interest in making women landowners despite the law.

Did I not have qualities of leadership to inspire the field machinery? Was my tenure too short to make long-lasting changes? Was I not popular with my peer group? Was the field staff too busy with routine matters to implement new policies? Or, is the system too complex to respond to isolated initiatives?

I do admit that I made mistakes. For instance, my hard-hitting letter to the Chief Secretary of Bihar in 1998 about the collapse of administration during Lalu days had the opposite effect. Rather than inspiring the Bihar cadre IAS officers to push for development, it totally demotivated them and demolished their self-esteem. Bihar continued to be 'an area of darkness' for another seven years till a change occurred at the political level.

In the ultimate analysis, it appears that stand-alone bureaucratic initiatives have little lasting value unless supported by strong political ownership. When both coalesce, such as in construction and usage of toilets under the outstanding leadership of the Secretary Param Iyer in the Swachh Bharat Mission during the Modi regime, the results are for everyone to see. With the change in political leadership in 2005, Bihar became the fastest-growing Indian state despite the lack of internal resources. Though Hindi -speaking states are considered to be suffering from weak administrative capacity, Chhattisgarh under Raman Singh's leadership could ensure effective delivery of subsidized rice to the entitled households with negligible leakages. Improving water management by the Chief Minister (CM) in Madhya Pradesh could triple wheat production in just about a decade.

Who is the boss?

These examples challenge the public perception that civil servants are the real rulers, and they, therefore, are failing the country in not stemming the administrative rot that seems to have set in. Bihar's turnaround after 2005, discussed in detail in Chapter 8, tends to confirm the contrary viewpoint generally held by civil servants that it is the political culture that largely determines the nature of the civil service and the ends to which it would be put, and therefore civil servants should not be blamed for failure to achieve outcomes.

This book takes a somewhat middle-of-the-road position between the two extremes. Granted that radical reforms cannot succeed in isolation without political support, non-performing administration leaves little choice to the politicians but to resort to populist rhetoric and sectarian strategies. As Chidambaram put it, 'Civil servants design the projects and programmes, they make cost and time estimates, and they are directly responsible for implementation; yet, many programmes have failed completely and many others have yielded unsatisfactory results'. If the administrative processes can be streamlined, even routine administration with average leadership should suffice to produce results. The kind of successes we have discussed above and also in Chapters 3 and 11 need exceptional energies for outcomes to be sustained over a long period. Our aim should be to be able to replicate successes widely, which would need collective efforts and not only individual excellence.

The IAS officers feel that they are doing a fine job and nothing could be better. The citizen feels otherwise:

> Indeed, its infirmities are so widely known that the Indian bureaucracy is the subject of unstinting pop culture mockery. From Ji Mantriji, an adaption of the BBC series Yes Minister that made light of political will meeting administrative intransigence, to 'Office Office', a long-running sitcom about a hapless common man stymied by a corrupt, labyrinthine state, the Indian administrative apparatus has not fared well in terms of popular perception (Vaishnav and Khosla 2016).

The International agencies too have not rated us in complimentary terms. According to a survey of 12 Asian economies done by the Hong Kong-based Political and Economic Risk Consultancy in 2011, India's 'suffocating bureaucracy' was ranked the least efficient, and working with the country's civil servants was described as a 'slow and painful' process. 'They are a power centre in their own right at both the national and state levels, and are extremely resistant to reform that affects them or the way they go about their duties,' the report said.

To members of the IAS 'mutual admiration club' I would like to pose the following ten questions:

1. Is selection of beneficiaries for government programmes reasonably free from errors of inclusion and exclusion?
2. Are land records in ex-zamindari states and tribal areas updated regularly and reflect the ground reality?[3] If so, how is it that nearly two-thirds of all pending cases in Indian courts are related to property disputes which take an average of 20 years to settle?
3. Do IAS officers know why Bangladesh does better than us on social indicators?
4. Are the state governments honestly reporting data on hunger deaths, malnutrition, usage of toilets, and the number of poor who could not get jobs under National Rural Employment Guarantee Act (NREGA) for the statutory 100 days? If so, why does the wide gap between evaluated and reported data continue to persist?
5. Have the state Training Institutions evolved comprehensive training modules to reduce hatred and bias against minorities? If so, have such modules been evaluated for their effectiveness?
6. Are the IAS officers quite keen to serve in backward districts, or on posts where good administration is needed most, such as Tribal Development, Administrative Reforms, Training Institutions, Evaluation Directorates and so on?
7. Why is the quality of education in government schools declining over the years? What steps have the IAS Secretaries

3. A World Bank report (2013) on India concluded that 'spatial records are virtually non-existent in urban and often outdated in rural areas'. The Hindi film *Khosla Ka Ghosla* provides brilliant insights into the damage done by dysfunctional land titles.

posted in the Education departments taken to arrest the decline?

8. Why are many state governments not able to ensure regular monthly payment of honorarium to the contractual staff, such as para teachers, Rozgar Sahayaks, AWWs (Anganwadi workers) and cooks in mid-day meals (MDM)?
9. Can a farmer set up an industrial unit on his land without needing permission for change in land use?
10. Are controls imposed by the state governments under powers vested to them in the Essential Commodities Act, Indian Forest Act[4] and the Mandi Act helping to reduce corruption and enhance productivity?

It is not enough to know the answers to these vexing questions; there has to be both individual and collective desire as well as capacity to apply correctives. Besides, we need political and administrative will to implement systemic reforms, discussed in the last chapter of the book.

4. see chapter 8 for a case study from Odisha

2 Chapter

TUSSLE FOR POWER: BUREAUCRATS VERSUS POLITICIANS

The Early Phase

The Westminster-style permanent bureaucracy has a long history in India. The Indian Civil Service (ICS) was created as an all-India service through the GOI Act of 1858, with about 50 per cent of all officers in the districts as Collectors. Often referred to as the steel frame of the British Raj, the ICS remained a small organization and numbered 1,032 officials[1] at its peak in 1931 out of an overall bureaucracy of about 1 million officials ruling over an undivided India totalling approximately 350 million people. ICS officers in the pre-war period were amongst the best-paid bureaucrats in the world; in 1935, an ICS secretary to the GOI earned 6,666 rupees per month, while the US secretary of the treasury earned just half as much (Vaishnav and Khosla 2016).

Indians started joining the ICS from 1922 onwards, and were almost half of the total cadre at the time of Independence. Though as civil servants they carried out the orders of their imperial masters, they were generally admired by the educated Indians for being conscientious, hard-working and incorruptible. As is well known, Sardar Vallabhbhai Patel (1875–1950), India's first Home Minister, campaigned vigorously for their continuity. He reasoned that India,

1. The approximate number of IAS officers in position today would be around 3,500 with only 20 per cent in districts.

because of its diversity, its multiple languages, religions, ethnicity and its past history of regional fights in the medieval period, had strong centrifugal forces which, unless countered, could lead to the breakup of the union. He, therefore, advocated the creation of countervailing centripetal forces, which could both create a strain of national unity and hold the union together when under pressure from breakaway forces (Buch 2005). He saw the importance of having a uniform administrative structure and wanted to organize it on a nationwide basis with the central government having a considerable control over it, to counterbalance the emergence of centrifugal forces that could lead to the disintegration of the Indian Union. In his speech to the Constituent Assembly in October 1949, Sardar Patel said, 'You will not have a united India if you do not have a good All-India Service which has independence to speak out its mind' (Chaturvedi 2014).

What the IAS used to stand for

Though the name of the service was changed to IAS, its essential ingredients remained unaltered. More than half of them were to serve in a state other than their home state; they would have a national, rather than parochial, outlook; they would attract the best nationwide talent; and that such a group would possess an ingrained sense of independence and impartiality. Speaking at a provincial premiers' conference in 1946 to decide the future of the All-India Services, Patel stated that ICS officers were 'useful instruments' that would 'also serve as a liaison between the Provinces and the GOI and introduce a certain amount of brashness and vigour in the administration both of the Centre and the Provinces.' The ICS and IAS were thus mandated to play a critical role in holding together India's highly divided federal polity.

During the first two decades after Independence morale and motivation amongst members of the IAS was quite high. State-level and district-level politicians were generally in awe of the high calibre and incorruptibility of the IAS officers, and left their management by and large to the Service itself. Their interference and patronage seeking activities were mostly confined to officials at the sub-district level, such as Police and Revenue Inspectors.

It is worth noting that the performance of any organization, including the public service, is deeply influenced by its operating culture, which in turn is often set in place and shaped by the beliefs, values and assumptions of its seniors of several generations. Entering a profession with ideals, exercising enormous power from the beginning, the young IAS officer was also blessed by an extraordinary combination of trust and support from those above him or her. This trust between a junior and his or her senior was not confined to the districts. What Collectors enjoyed from Commissioners, Deputy Secretaries did from Secretaries and Secretaries from Chief Secretaries. Total trust, and the promise of support in case you fumbled or failed, generated enormous courage and initiative, making heroes of men. This sense of belonging was continued in the training the probationer received in the district. Collectors who were to train young civil servants were handpicked, and the Assistant Collector would often become a member of the Collector's household. The young officer could then look forward to the future with confidence, hope and optimism. There was cohesion, loyalty and attitudinal homogeneity within the administrative fraternity. Common educational background, followed by deliberate efforts to make the probationer feel that entry into service was induction into a privileged group, who lived, thought and acted together, gave the gawky probationer, in a very short span of time, extraordinary confidence.

Founding Values of the IAS

'I agree with the Chief Secretary'

Over time, these founding values were internalized by the civil service and stood as guiding principles for its policies and programmes. Many civil servants demonstrated a profound sense of duty and idealism in their work in those days.

A few examples of interaction between the civil servants and politicians would be in order here.

In early 1964, the then Collector of Betul district of Madhya Pradesh was asked by his Chief Secretary, the legendary R.C.V.P. Noronha of the ICS, to make preparations for setting up refugee camps. The instructions consisted of just one sentence that he was required to make all arrangements and that he was free to take such action as he deemed fit. The Collector probably broke all the rules in the book, plus a number of rules not yet invented, but he set up his camps within one week. After the refugees had been received and settled, by which time the audit people had started to sit up and take notice of irregularities, the Collector visited Bhopal and met the Chief Secretary. Mr Noronha asked him to give a summary of the action taken by him in one typed page. The Chief Secretary's note on the Collector's report read, 'Collector, Betul, has carried out my orders in taking the above action. CM may approve'. D. P. Mishra was the CM, and he wrote, 'I agree with the Chief Secretary'. This one single page covered everything that the Collector had done.

It is on such mutual trust that Government was run those days, which unfortunately does not exist today.

> 'The whole kit-and-caboodle of spies and counterspies, vigilance people and people who spy on vigilance people, enquiry followed by enquiry, has so vitiated the system that the civil services have reached almost the point of no return in the matter of efficiency, decision making and effectiveness' (Buch 2005).

'What has liking to do with business of government?'

The role of civil servants at the very senior level is not only to advise government but also to provide guidance and support to their juniors. One outstanding example is that of the late V.K.B.Pillai, the then Chief Secretary, Bihar. The PWD Minister, in a fit of pique, reverted the chief engineer on extremely flimsy grounds. Shri Pillai had the gumption to meet the CM and hand him the collective resignation of all the secretaries to the Bihar government. The reversion order was withdrawn post-haste and the Minister duly hauled up. The Chief Secretary was prepared to quit on an issue concerning one of his juniors, and the CM was magnanimous enough to accept the correctness of his Chief Secretary's stand.

There is another inspiring story of Morarji Desai, who was the CM of Bombay during 1957–1962, and Rasiklal Parikh, who was his revenue minister after the merger of Saurashtra into Bombay. D. S. Bakhle of the ICS was the Chief Secretary and D. S. Joshi was the Revenue Secretary. Parikh went to Desai and asked for the transfer of Joshi. Desai insisted on consulting Bakhle (incidentally Desai and Bakhle were at logger-heads over prohibition), who advised against the transfer. Desai agreed with Bakhle. At this, Parikh threw a tantrum and said that he did not want Joshi as he did not like him. Morarji Desai's reply is a classic. he said,'I detest Bakhle, but he is my Chief Secretary. What has liking got to do with the business of government?'

'If you get into trouble, I will bail you out'

Arun Ghosh, who served GOI in various capacities, such as Economic Adviser to the Ministry of Commerce and Industry, Special Secretary Industrial Development, Special Secretary Company Affairs, Chairman, Bureau of Industrial Costs and Prices and Member Planning Commission, described the immense power and confidence that the earlier civil servants enjoyed in the following story (Ghosh 1998):

> "At an early stage of my career (in government), I was suddenly entrusted with a special assignment, with enormous consequences. The then Secretary to the Government of India—he was not the person to have chosen me for the assignment; his joint secretary had done so—called me and gave me three bits of advice. I think they are worth repeating. 'Look', he said, 'you have been given this task; you have to succeed, and your responsibility is enormous, I would give you three bits of advice. First, you will find all manner of government rules which you may need to flout in order to succeed in your task. Remember, I want you to succeed, not come and tell me that government rules stood in your way. Secondly, and I want you to note this, if you get into trouble, breaking rules, I will bail you out. So, don't be afraid, get the job done. Thirdly, and this is the last point, remember, if I have to bail you out, this is the last assignment you have from me. You must know how to get a job done without getting into trouble.'

Which civil servant today would explicitly tell a junior officer: 'if you get into trouble, I will bail you out?'

Bureaucracy, a Part of Our State System

Even in those days, the state-level politicians and Ministers took little interest in policy issues; these were relegated to the civil servants, whereas their interest in administration was largely confined to establishment matters and contracts. A prime example of this is a case which occurred in Madhya Pradesh, when the Fourth Five-Year Plan (1969–1974) was under formulation, the Deputy Secretary in the Industries Department responsible for plan formulation prepared a draft of the plan for the industry. When the file was sent to the minister, it was returned with the remark that he did not want to see it. When the Deputy Secretary personally took the file to the Minister and requested that he might at least try and see whether all his policy objectives were met by the plan, he was told brusquely that the Minister was not interested. As the Deputy Secretary was leaving the room in disgust, the Minister called him back and asked him whether the transfer of a particular inspector had been affected.

> This story illustrates the real malaise of Indian administration at the sub-national level: bureaucrats formulate long-term policy and politicians responsible for higher-level government decide postings and transfers. This is an utter perversion of the system, and the fact that it is now universal, makes the pill no sweeter. (Buch 2005)

How policies made without political involvement fail to make impact is described later in this Chapter.

Bureaucracy is not an isolated phenomenon. It is a part of our state system. P. N. Haksar, who worked with Mrs Indira Gandhi for a long period, compared the state to a ship, where the political leadership is the captain of the ship and bureaucracy is the engine room. Both of them have to work together to make the ship move in a particular direction. The direction is set by the political leadership, with advice from the crew as to how to reach there. The inspiring of confidence, gaining of mutual trust, is perhaps the most crucial and critical element in the running of any state system; more specially, if it is done through a political process (Haksar 2005). Many civil servants learn these peculiarities of the democratic system quite early in their careers and adjust accordingly.

B. G. Deshmukh, who retired as Cabinet Secretary in 1989, describes in the following (Deshmukh 2004) how he had to accommodate political pressures while trying to follow rules and procedures:

> "I was Deputy Secretary, GAD, in Maharashtra in the 1960s. As a Deputy Secretary, I was looking after the allotment of fiat cars. At that time, fiat car was a real boon. If I remember right, our quarterly quota was 90. When I took up the job, I found that a register was being maintained for applicants on the waiting list. When the file with the first 90 names in the waiting list went to the Chief Minister, he just kept the list aside and sent his own list back. I told the Chief Minister that a regular waiting list was being maintained and there was nothing wrong in going by the waiting list. He said, 'Mr Deshmukh, you don't know. As a politician I have some compulsions. I have to allot cars even out of turn to some people. What is wrong in it?' I said, 'Alright, how many cars would you require?' 'Give me about 20 cars', he said. Hence, next time, while preparing the allotment gist, I kept the first 20 names blank and from 21 to 90 went strictly according to the waiting list. This worked. Thus, it is important to understand how the politicians work.

Erosion of administrative autonomy after 1967

However, with the passage of time, political pressures started eroding administrative autonomy, and the control over district administration passed on from the civil servants to their political bosses. The difference between then and now is that previously civil servants had clear ideas about the type of behaviour that would be rewarded or punished. Furthermore, as a retired chief secretary put it, 'control over that, judgements about it, were in the hands of the civil service itself.' Now, increasingly, these standards for reward or punishment can no longer be identified—lip service is still paid to the old conventions and values, but they no longer provide working criteria. New values have entered in from outside, and civil servants can no longer define what acceptable and unacceptable behaviour is. Newer values emphasize political loyalty, flexibility and also merit, but merit is only one amongst others. Uncertainty centres on the reward structure (Potter 1986). Such uncertainty about service norms has been the principal reason for low morale and lack of initiative amongst senior civil servants.

Political structure in India started witnessing several changes after the general elections in 1967. First, many states had coalition governments which increased the bargaining power of the individual MLAs, and their demands for interference in administration such as transfers and postings of IAS officers could not be ignored. Second, several regional parties became powerful who were guided more by local rather than national interests. Third, a whole army of intermediaries and political fixers developed between the ordinary citizen and the MLA, who make it their business to get the villagers' businesses transacted with diverse government agencies, with banks, insurance companies and other such operations. Few villagers would, for instance, go to a police station or government hospital without first trying to get the support of someone with inside access (Krishna 2006).

The political system in many states has also been invaded by criminals. Antisocial forces are used for the mobilization of party funds, for management of election, organizing meetings and conference and even recruiting workers at lower levels from amongst antisocial elements, which has increased manifold since last two decades (Dab et al. 2014).

Consequent to the bomb blasts in Bombay in March 1993 instigated by the Dawood Ibrahim gang in which more than 250 people died, the GOI set up a Committee headed by the then Home Secretary, N.N. Vohra, in October 1993 to study the problem of the criminalization of politics and of the nexus amongst criminals, politicians and bureaucrats in India. The Committee found a strong nexus amongst the criminal gangs, police, bureaucracy and politicians in various parts of the country. It revealed that criminal gangs enjoyed not only the patronage of politicians, of all parties, but also the protection of government functionaries. Over the years, criminals had been elected to local bodies, State Assemblies and Parliament. The existing criminal justice system, which was essentially designed to deal with the individual offences/crimes, is unable to deal with the activities of the Mafia; the provisions of law in regard to economic offences are weak.

The expansion of State functions during the period 1970–1990 in India considerably increased bureaucratic control over the various means and processes of production and distribution. Thus, this period was characterized by both enhanced role of the state and enhanced control of politicians over bureaucracy. The ambitious IAS individuals who wanted to 'feel powerful' and share the spoils and patronage were often willing to pay a price in terms of obeisance to political bosses, and 'look after' their interests. A 1952 batch IAS officer, Gill (1999) writes how two IAS officers, though honest themselves, helped the ruling political party in defence deals. One was rewarded with the post of the Governor of a state, and the Prime Minister helped the other to be elected as head of a UN agency, and later as Governor of a north-eastern state. 'There is always the hope of a suitable reward for the service rendered to the Big Boss.' Loyalty seldom goes unrewarded.

Today, the postings of Collectors and Superintendents of Police in a district are not decided by the Chief Secretary or DGP but by the CM or those who are close to him. Often there are political compulsions, dictated by vested interests of mafia gangs, organized criminals, builders' lobby, contractors and other such category of people who control local politics, which cannot be ignored, resulting in the surrender of professionalism or objective criteria for reward and punishment. The degree of politicization may be less for Audit and Accounts or the Foreign Service, but it is quite high in the three all-India Services, where transfers and postings are controlled by the State governments. This erodes the credibility of the government not only in the eyes of the people, but also for civil servants who think that the government is not a level-playing field; one cannot expect fairness from government and one has to approach the politicians with offers of bribes and right kind of contacts for favours, whether due or undue.

This is not to suggest that ministers should have no role in administration; even members of parliament (MPs) and members of legislative assembly (MLAs)[2] should keep a watch over the performance of the services. Political pressure can be healthy if it results in greater demand on the administration for efficiency and better services to the people. Pressures that are properly regulated and wisely tempered improve the spirit of administration and

2. The collapse of legislatures is discussed in Chapter 4.

help to keep it on an even keel (Mathur 2019). Unfortunately, the main problem today is that the politics of the country has itself become divorced from public welfare and is more concerned with narrow sectarian interests. An impression exists, especially at the State and district levels, that people have low expectations from political processes (except in purely caste and communal terms), as their economic interests are to be taken care of by the market forces. This impression is more prevalent with the State-level politicians who can always blame the GOI for price rise, unemployment, lack of resources and so on. Therefore, as far as they are concerned, the state machinery can be milked dry through rent-seeking behaviour without any harm to their political interests of getting re-elected. Politicians think that electoral behaviour can be manipulated through precipitating caste or other populist wave at the time of elections, which does not require sustained work in the constituency. At the same time elections require funds which have to come through the looting of the government treasury.

The imposition of Emergency in 1975 led the Indian state to be treated as a private property of those who were at the top, and this culture of using executive power for private gains has become a norm since then. A vast gap exists between stated and unstated objectives of the government. On paper, the avowed objective of the government is to give clean administration, but in some departments and States, many posts are auctioned to the highest bidder. People have, unfortunately, accepted the position as *fait accompli* and have resigned themselves to their fate. They too tend to seek shortcuts and exploit the system by breaking rules or approaching mafia gangs and politicians for favours.

There is a growing belief widely shared amongst the politicians that there is nothing wrong in using power and public office for private ends.[3] Often state-level politicians have little inclination for process reforms that would yield results only in the long run. A paper brought out by the Department of Administrative Reforms for a conference on the occasion of Civil Services Day observed:

3. An important political leader was shown on the Indian TV in March 2003 openly asking the party MLAs and MPs to contribute money towards party coffers from the government fund that they get for local works in their constituencies. The distinction between public funds, private gains and party funds is blurred in the minds of the political class.

> For a variety of reasons, elections as an instrument for external accountability have some well known weaknesses. In India, these weaknesses are exacerbated by the particular nature of the evolution of Indian democracy. Politics in India is marked by a conception of competition where to hold the state accountable is to gain access to its power and the goods it provides. Clientelism and patronage are rife and voters are mobilized more on the politics of caste, regional or religious identity than on the politics of accountability and initiatives that bring long term benefits to the public as a whole. Consequently, the state and its apparatus, including the bureaucracy are treated not so much as a means of generating public goods but as a means of generating benefits for the particular group that controls the state. (GOI 2009)

The state resources are the most valued prize for both politicians and their constituencies, which leads to a client–patron relationship between the holders of state power and those seeking favours. Patronage is controlled by individuals, not established institutions bound to follow set procedures. Where power is highly personalized and weakly institutionalized, the decision-making process is replaced by arbitrary and behind-the-scene transactions. In such an environment, exercise of power for its clients demands fudging of rules, dependence upon corrupt civil servants, plundering of the public treasury and decay of governance. When the fence starts eating the field, there is little chance of development reaching the poor.

Winston Churchill, on the eve of India's Independence, had said,

> Power will go to the hands of rascals, rogues and freebooters. All Indian leaders will be of low calibre and men of straw. They will have sweet tongues and silly hearts. They will fight among themselves for power and India will be lost in political squabbles.

What appeared as a scandalous outburst then may be called an understatement now!

An IAS officer's predicaments

In almost all states, people see the bureaucracy as wooden, disinterested in public welfare and corrupt. Bright men and women join the IAS, but adverse work environment, constant political interference, frequent and often meaningless transfers and corruption below and above them all lead to the erosion of idealism and encourage at least some of them to misuse their authority. Disillusionment and greed, and not need, is the driving force behind graft amongst some civil servants.

India's own Second Administrative Reforms Commission (2008) is no less scathing in its criticism:

> "The state apparatus is generally perceived to be largely inefficient with most functionaries serving no useful purpose. The bureaucracy is generally seen to be tardy, inefficient and unresponsive. Corruption is all-pervasive, eating into the vitals of our system, undermining economic growth, distorting competition and disproportionately hurting the poor and marginalized citizens. Criminalization of politics continues unchecked, with money and muscle power playing a large role in elections. In general there is a high degree of volatility in society on account of unfulfilled expectations and poor delivery. Abuse of authority at all levels in all organs of state has become the bane of our democracy.

The IAS serves the state, but the state structure is itself getting increasingly divorced from public interest. In some north Indian states parallel authority structures and Mafia gangs have emerged. Tribal regions in central and north-east India are out of bounds for normal administration. In such a situation, it is no surprise if the bureaucracy, too, is in bad shape.

Politicization of Bureaucracy

Over the years, whatever little virtues the IAS possessed—integrity, political neutrality, courage and high morale—all are showing signs of decay. Some civil servants are deeply involved in partisan politics: they are preoccupied with it, penetrated by it, and now participate individually and collectively in it. This is understandable, though unfortunate, because between expression of the will of the State (represented by politicians) and the execution of that will (through the administrators) there cannot be any long-term dichotomy. In other words, a model in which politicians would be casteist, corrupt and will harbour criminals, whereas civil servants will continue to be efficient, responsive to public needs and change-agents cannot be sustained indefinitely.[4] In the long run, administrative and political values have to coincide. The civil servant needs the political leader for posting, transfer and appointment to a creamy post, and the politician needs him for diverting and manipulating governmental funds to the private coffer of the politician. Madhu Koda, the ex-CM of Jharkhand, could amass ₹ 4,000 crore only with the help of friendly civil servants (Sharma 2012). Obviously, politicization of bureaucracy in some states in now widespread.

The symbiotic relationship between the politician and the civil servant has been captured by Subramanian (2004), a retired Cabinet Secretary, in his book, quoted below.

> “In my four decades of public service, I have come across thousands of politicians, small and large, operating at the district or village or state or national level. I have worked closely with hundreds of them in one context or another. I am saddened to say that I have come across only a handful of honest politicians.

And how does the ‘neta’ himself view the ‘babu’?

He quotes the UP CM, Mulayam Singh Yadav, addressing a conclave of IAS officers:

> “You all have such excellent minds and education; some of you are scholars; some of you have Nobel Prize minds; you will all succeed in any walk of life, wherever you turn your attention to; you have good jobs; you can educate your children well; and you are all respected by society; (and then, the clincher, raising his voice) Why do you

4. Though theoretically it is a strong argument that the political and administrative cultures would coalesce with the passage of time, it has surprisingly not happened in India so far and not engulfed the entire IAS, for reasons described later in this chapter.

> come and touch my feet? Why do you come and lick my shoes? Why do you come to me for personal favours? When you do, I will do as you desire and then extract my price from you.

Subramanian adds, 'It was an amazing statement because it succinctly summed up the situation and pinpointed the reason for the collapse of the steel frame.'

While defending the continuation of the all-India Services, Sardar Patel had said, 'they are as good as we are'. At that time, it was taken as a compliment that the civil service was being compared with statesmen who had won freedom for the country. One does not know how many civil servants will like to be told today that they are like politicians. But things have moved a full circle, and perhaps some of them do behave like politicians—the English-speaking politicians![5]

According to Sanjeev Ahluwalia,[6] who resigned from the IAS and now works for the Observer Research Foundation,

> What the zenana was to the Great Mughals, the IAS is to our political leaders at the Centre and in the states. Curiously, even the numbers match. Both the IAS and Emperor Akbar's zenana—the largest—are around 5,000 strong. The only difference is that, unlike the zenana, the IAS is predominantly male.

B.G. Deshmukh, a retired Cabinet Secretary, seems to agree with Sanjeev's description of the system. While commenting on his colleague, Seshan, he wrote:

> So far as Seshan's work as Secretary (Security) is con cerned, it is a fact that he did immensely improve the efficiency of the security machinery, but unfortunately he used it purely for personal reasons for advancing his own interest and career. He managed to have a tremendous hold over Rajiv Gandhi and flaunted his easy access to

5. This is how I described the Bihar IAS officials in a letter to the Chief Secretary in 1998, which raised a huge storm, see Chapter 8 for details.
6. www.asianage.com/opinion/oped/180618/govts-lateral-hiring-great-idea-bad-timing.html (accessed on 10 July 2019).

> the PM. One must also remember that in the Moghul Darbar-like atmosphere of Delhi where a courtier, who seems to have close and easy access to the Emperor (PM), is not only feared but courted by many. (Deshmukh 2004)

Interestingly, despite these constraints, the lure of the IAS amongst the youth aspirants is still strong, and quite likely, stronger than before. Almost all of the one million who appear for the Union Public Service Commission (UPSC) test give IAS as their first choice in preference to Foreign Service, Police, or Income Tax. Amongst the IAS recruited between 2001 and 2005, only one-third were arts graduates, 13 per cent science graduates, the majority holding a professional degree, with 25 per cent engineers, 15 per cent medical doctors, 8 per cent managers (MBAs) and 6 per cent lawyers (Benbabaali 2008). Some highly paid young professionals even quit their jobs to join the IAS. As one of them stated:

> Even if I become the CEO of my company, I am still a nobody in the eyes of the public, I have no social recognition on a large scale. When I go out, I am anonymous. But as an IAS, if I go to visit a village, the whole population will be out to welcome me.

Rajasthan, Odisha, UP and Bihar are relatively poor states but are over-represented in the IAS, because in these feudal states the prestige of the civil service is very high. Unlike Pakistan, where reservation in the civil service is on a regional basis so as to give adequate representation to provinces other than Punjab, in India there has never been any demand from backward states for quota in the all-India Services, because these states are already over-represented!

In India, it is widely believed that IAS officers occupy the highest position on the dowry market. Forty per cent of the interviewed officers declared that they were offered more than ₹ 10 crore as a dowry, especially in the form of immovable property, but only half of them admitted that they actually took it. The dowry they get is sometimes so huge that they can recycle part of it to marry their sisters to good matches, and thus elevate the position of the whole family. Dowry is in a way the first bribe that a male IAS gets in his career. Between 2001 and 2005, amongst 170 IAS officers on whom marriage data could be collected, 45 per cent had a typical arranged marriage, within the caste, and generally with dowry. Forty per cent chose a love marriage, most of the time without dowry, and without consideration of caste, creed or region. This proportion is much higher than the national average, since in India the majority of marriages are arranged by the families within the same caste. IAS women usually do not give dowry, so marriages between officers are either love marriages or cadre-based marriages (Benbabaali 2008).

Silver Linings

Though there has certainly been a perceptible decline in the moral fibre of the IAS, one should not jump to the conclusion that all IAS officers are corrupt or indulge in politicking to win favours from politicians. There are still a significant number, it may be more than half of the total, reaching up to 75 per cent in certain states (this includes even some BIMAROU states such as Rajasthan and Madhya Pradesh), who stay clean both in respect of personal integrity and political aloofness, and yet are not sidelined, at least not forever. If one looks at the officers who donned the highest post of Cabinet Secretary in the last 30 years, one can assert with confidence that almost all of them had a strong reputation for integrity, uprightness and capability. The same could be said for many Secretaries to GOI.

Why has the demon of corruption or politicization not engulfed the entire Service? There are several countervailing forces which keep the cautious IAS officers away from money and dirty politics. First, unlike many state Public Service Commissions, whose reputation for selection is not above board, the UPSC, which is in charge of the recruitment of the IAS, has an unblemished reputation for integrity and professionalism. A rigorous process of recruitment for the higher civil services ensures that the best talent available in society joins the civil service in India. 'Jugaad'[7] does not work here. As an institution, over the decades the UPSC has acquired a reputation for transparency, independence and credibility.[8] It would have been difficult for the IAS trainees to retain their idealism had

7. Indian trait for manipulation through approach or bribes.
8. In 1962, a candidate closely related to the Prime Minister Pandit Nehru qualified in the IAS written examination, but was rejected by the Interview Board of the UPSC.

they joined the service through bribery or approach. Second, for the first 10 years of their career, all IAS officers follow a similar path of serving in the districts, and since two-thirds of them are from outside the state, there are little heart burnings about who got posted where. Third, most IAS officers aspire to come to GOI and serve in the central Ministries. Here the selection at the level of Joint Secretary and above follows a rigorous process, and much depends on the performance record of the officers. An officer who has been consistently ranked as average by his superiors in the last 10 years has little chance of being picked up by the Centre; though once selected, posting to Ministries is susceptible to pressures and pulls.

Fourth, many officers feel quite comfortable working in Ministries which have low political priorities, such as elementary education, agriculture, or health in GOI, as they see bright career prospects if they acquire domain knowledge in these sectors. The fact that the Joint Secretary in GOI has a stable tenure of five years gives him ample time to specialize, interact with the best professionals in these subjects, and build networks with the United Nations and donors. Thus, in contrast to the IPS,[9] there is a wider range of desirable jobs in the IAS, including posting at the Mussoorie academy, although at the State level most training institutions are in disarray and considered a punishment posting. Fifth, salaries have become quite decent after 1997. Sixth, with the number of Central Bureau of Investigation (CBI) enquiries against IAS officers working in 'wet' Ministries swelling every year, risk-averse officers feel quite safe and happy in contributing their skills to the cause of the 'common man or woman' in 'dry' Ministries. Whereas the economic Ministries in GOI are often mired with rumours of grand corruption, the social sector Ministries, such as Rural Development, Elementary Education[10], etc, despite their colossal budgets, hardly face bribery charges as almost the entire budget is passed on to the

9. An IPS officer who is not dealing with crime and law and order considers himself sidelined.
10. The list of 'clean' ministries also included the Planning Commission, which used to handle a budget of more than ₹ 1.5 lakh crores (roughly US$20 billion) a year. The Modi government in January 2015 replaced the commission with a think tank called NITI Aayog (means Policy Commission), which is a purely advisory body with no executive functions.

States. And lastly, political culture in many states has become more professional and outcome oriented in the last two decades, a subject that we will discuss in Chapter 4.

To sum up, it would be highly oversimplistic to conclude that 'corrupt bureaucrats are despised but thrive; the honest are respected but do not rise; and idealists end up in the boondocks' (Vaishnav and Khosla 2016). There are no watertight categories, and many of us (as the example of B. G. Deshmukh dealing with Fiat quota shows) learn to combine integrity and outcome orientation with pragmatism. For the majority of us, wielding authority being treated deferentially and enjoying 'official' perks is sufficient to keep us away from making money. Mr Seshan once said, 'the number of bureaucrats who would confront a politician is going down fast because everyone is trying to feather his own nest. Unless a man is mentally off he would not try and confront a politician.' Again this denigration of the entire service can easily be challenged by looking at the careers of many officers, who did well, despite remaining apolitical and having some pinpricks with their political (or administrative) bosses.

I fought and failed

A few personal examples from my own career would not be out of place here.

In the case study (given as annexure to this chapter) on my experience as revenue[11] secretary, I have described in detail my tussle with both, Ministers and civil servants. Some readers may conclude that the Revenue Secretary (that is me) was an irresponsible maverick who had little faith in following set government procedures, and he should consider himself lucky to have escaped government's wrath. Perhaps you are right. Luckily, the prevailing administrative culture in UP in those days was magnanimous enough to tolerate such irreverent and non-conformist behaviour. Though there were policy differences between me and the Chief Secretary, it did not

11. This department in the states looks after rural land related issues, including land reforms. In UP, this is not considered to be a high priority department, as the revenue secretary has no control over field staff, does not deal with transfers and postings, and land revenue is no longer an important source of state revenues.

degenerate into personal acrimony, and both continued to maintain mutual respect for each other.

One of the reasons for failure of policies being pursued by the Revenue Secretary in the case study seems to be the total absence of pressure from below, from the poor and tribals, on the political system. This important issue would be further discussed in a subsequent chapter on programmes for the poor. Many civil servants were convinced that appropriation of land from the enterprising farmers amounted to an attack on the legitimacy of private property and it went against the principle of income earned through commercial drive of medium and big farmers. After some time, the Government orders which were issued by the revenue department became a source of amusement to the field staff. Such circulars were seen by them not as Government orders but as arising out of the personal whims of Saxena, the Revenue Secretary. He was seen to be attempting a 'Marxist revolution' not through peoples' uprising, but through government circulars. Their indifference to the new circulars was not only due to intellectual conviction against the so-called outdated concept of land reforms, but also because neither local politicians nor their own superiors ever questioned them about the non-implementation of the pro-poor government orders of the Revenue Department. Unlike other State Secretaries, the Revenue Secretary, unfortunately, does not control the field-level officials such as Tahsildars, and hence he could not ensure that his circulars were even read, what to say of being acted upon. Individual initiative without collective consensus does not result in systemic change. More examples of my failures are discussed in chapter 11.

Vajpayee did not like me

Let me cite another instance of my tussle with politicians. Luckily in this case I succeeded in preventing misuse of government funds which the Minister wanted to pass on as grant to a semi-political outfit. In 1998, when the National Democratic Alliance (NDA) was in power and I was Secretary, Rural Development, my Minister from the Bharatiya Janata Party (BJP) was very keen to give a huge government grant to an RSS -based organization. In those days, the Minister was the Chairman of the Executive Committee of CAPART, a government parastatal under the Ministry, which had a substantial budget for giving grants to non-governmental organizations (NGOs). His note to Director General (DG) CAPART is produced as follows:

> "This is in continuation of the discussion that has taken place on 21.10.1998 in my Chamber in the presence of Secretary (RD), DG, CAPART and Smt. Rita Verma, MP and Convenor, Swadeshi Mela. After careful examination of the enclosed brief note received from the organisers of Swadeshi Mela, I am of the view that CAPART should be the Co-organiser of the proposed Swadeshi Mela. The objectives and highlights of the Mela are very relevant to our Ministry and also it will be in consonance with the objectives of CAPART. Since the matter is of sufficient importance and urgency, in exercise of the power under Rule 38(a)(i) of the Rules & Regulations of CAPART and in relaxation of conditions of grant to a voluntary organisation, I approve the proposal received for Swadeshi Mela and participation of CAPART as Co- organiser. Therefore, we may release ₹ 4 crores in phased manner as per the requirements and one DDG be nominated to coordinate and work out the modalities. The matter be placed before the next meeting of the Executive Committee. MOS [IC][RA&E[12]] and Chairman, CAPART)

This note was not endorsed to me, but to DG CAPART, who marked it to the DDG Ashok Thakur,[13] a very upright, bold and no-nonsense officer. He wrote a long note to DG why this order cannot be complied with. DG marked the file to me, and I sent DDG's note to the Minister on 5 November 1998 with the following advice:

> "MOS(IC) has already decided that this important matter should first be cleared by the Executive Committee. In the meantime we will ascertain from the Home Ministry whether Swadeshi Jagran Foundation can be dubbed

12. The name of the ministry then was Ministry for Rural Areas and Employment (RA&E). MOS(IC) stands for minister of state (incharge).
13. He retired as secretary, higher education, GOI, in 2015.

as a political organisation, and then from the Finance Ministry whether funds can be released to a political organisation.

The Minister overruled me as he did not want the matter to be referred to the Home or Finance Ministry. Somehow there was a news item about the whole controversy, and taking advantage of the newspaper coverage, I again sent the file to the Minister on 13 November 1998 with the following note:

> “MOS(IC), RA&E may like to see the newspaper cutting placed below, which alleges that Swadeshi Jagran Foundation is not a non-political organisation. The Government policy has, so far, been only to fund non-political organisations. If the facts stated in the newspaper cutting are correct, giving a grant of `4 crores to Swadeshi Jagran Foundation or to Centre for Bhartiya Marketing Development would mean a major departure from previous policies and will require approval of the Cabinet.
>
> “The main file, in which the application from the Centre for Bhartiya Marketing Development was processed, was submitted to Minister on 21.10.1998. The file has still not come back. I spoke to Shri Madan Gopal, PS to Minister, about the file and requested him to return the file so that further enquiries about the Centre for Bhartiya Marketing Development may be made.
>
> “I also spoke to Secretary (Expenditure), who advised that grants out of public funds to such organisations should be avoided.
>
> “MOS(IC), RA&E may like to re-consider his orders dated 5 November 1998, on pre-page.

Interestingly, within half an hour of my sending the file to the MOS, I got a call from the Cabinet Secretary Prabhat Kumar enquiring about the details. It was obvious that he had read my note, though his office was about a km away from mine! It appears that the Minister was in touch with him, and on more than one occasion had complained to him and to the Prime Minister Vajpayee about my rigid and uncompromising posture. I do not know how I survived in that job for another three months, but was finally shunted out in late February 1999 to the Planning Commission. Later I learnt that the Prime Minister was keen to punish me and revert me back to UP, but the Cabinet Secretary was able to persuade him to keep me in Delhi but dump me to an innocuous post. Any job which requires thinking and reflecting is considered a punishment post in the IAS, but I thoroughly enjoyed being in the moribund Planning Commission for the next three years. Thank you, Prabhat!

I faced Prime Minister's wrath again in September 2000, when I presented to him the mid-term Appraisal of the Ninth Plan (MTA 2000), of which I had myself written six or seven chapters. Cabinet Secretary Prabhat and Finance Secretary Mankad were also present. The practice was to present the Appraisal to a full meeting of the Planning Commission with the Prime Minister in the chair (and a few other Central Ministers) before it was put up to the larger National Development Council (NDC), in which all CMs are members. Many of my findings were extremely critical of the government. The Prime Minister just closed his eyes and said nothing as I went on making the PowerPoint presentation. Prime minister's secretary N. K. Singh[14] realized that the prime minister was upset. After a while, N. K. said: 'This meeting is over.'

In the afternoon N. K. rang and said: 'Yaar Naresh, the PM is very angry and unhappy about your report. He cannot approve such a critical report.'[15] My response was,'Okay, say so in the minutes. We will revise the report.' N. K. said: 'How can we do that? PM's disapproval will invite adverse publicity and the report would be all over the media headlines tomorrow.' So being the quintessential bureaucrat, I gave him the way out. I told him to write in the minutes that the Prime Minister was present but not to say whether he approved or disapproved. Say that the report would be presented before the NDC.

So we did not change a word in our report, and it was presented to the NDC, which approved it. No one reads these papers,[16] really.

14. My batchmate, and was Chairman 15th Finance Commission.
15. I also published a short article based on my findings in the *Economic and Political Weekly*, . epw.in/journal/2000/41/commentary/how-have-poor-done.html (accessed on 10 July 2019).
16. Raj Krishna once described the Fifth Five-Year Plan as the fifth edition of the First Five-Year Plan.

It was only the *Economist*[17] which wrote in its issue of 31 May 2001:

> The Planning Commission's account of various poverty alleviation schemes often reads like a criminal chargesheet. Writing of one rural development programme, the report cites 'leakages, misappropriation of funds, violation of programme guidelines, selection of the non-poor as a target group, absence of proper maintenance of accounts and poor quality of assets'.

Politicians have a knack of identifying officers by their caste. Once Vajpayee Ji told Mr Som Pal, ex-Minister of State, Agriculture, 'Kyasthas[18] are known for being sycophants and flatterers. This fellow Saxena is just the opposite!'

Many more stories of tussle as well as collaboration between bureaucracy and the politicians would be narrated in the next chapter.

Is Indian Politics Always Incompatible with Good Governance?

To conclude, despite perceptible decline in values, many IAS officers today consider maintaining a certain distance from politicians in their long-term self-interest. Administrative culture is not uniform throughout all the states, and has not remained stagnant overtime. In the past when some CMs such as Chandrababu Naidu and Digvijay Singh tried to improve governance in the 1990s–early 2000s, they eventually lost elections, giving an impression to other CMs that good governance is not compatible with political survival. Moreover, when the general expectation of a government lasting a full term of five years is low, politicians try to maximize their gains from office and minimize their accountability for performance (Sud 2010).

Happily, when a stable government comes to power, often a virtuous cycle of accountability is established. People expect better

17. A survey of India's economy: The rich get richer "http://www.economist.com/taxonomy/term/" (https://www.economist.com/taxonomy/term/106?page=52106) (accessed on 10 July 2019).
18. Referring to my caste.

performance from their political masters who, aiming to overcome anti-incumbency, reciprocate by delivering at least on some of the promises, be it public distributions system (PDS) in Chhattisgarh and Odisha, irrigation and crop production in Madhya Pradesh, roads in Bihar and power availability for agriculture in Gujarat. These success stories demand performance and leadership from the IAS too, keeping alive their faith in professionalism. Pressure from central government Ministries backed by strong civil society and judicial action also helps in improving governance and delivery. However, in the absence of political interest, state-level bureaucracy either does not perform well, as discussed in Chapter 4, or remains indifferent to policy initiatives taken by some maverick in GOI, examples of which are given in Chapter 11.

ANNEXURE

Political and Administrative Will in Land Reforms

A case study

This case study describes the efforts made by the Revenue Secretary, Naresh Chandra Saxena, towards land reforms in the State of UP during 1980–1981. Seventy-five per cent of the total population in UP was dependent on agriculture at that time. Fifty per cent of the rural population had either no land or owned less than one acre. Twenty per cent of the total arable land was held by one per cent of rural population in holdings of 30 acres and above. The State Government introduced ceiling legislation in 1972, which should have yielded a surplus of about 10 lakh acres; however, till 1982 only 2 lakh acres of land could be distributed to about 2 lakh families. Another 50,000 acres of land was involved in litigation. It was generally believed that the best quality land was either not declared surplus or possession could not be taken because of legal hurdles.

Tenancy laws

N. C. Saxena, Secretary of the Revenue Department, was convinced that other programmes to help the rural poor will not have much impact unless assets in the form of land are transferred to them. Although legislation against absentee landlordism was carried out successfully in the State in the 1950s, yet the Revenue Secretary had estimated that sharecropping was still being practised on about 5 per cent of the total cultivated land, which was about

40 million acres in the State. According to State laws, renting out of land was prohibited, but the legal position about sharecropping was not clear. If the sharecropping arrangement amounted to lease, it was unlawful, but if it amounted to a licence, whereby both the owner and the tenant were participating in crop production, it was not illegal. The general impression in the rural areas was that sharecropping was not permitted under law. Since the State laws did not admit of sub-tenancy, it was not considered necessary to record the names of sub-tenants and sharecroppers. If, however, in a court of law it was proved that a person had leased out his land he would immediately lose ownership, which would pass on either to the sub-tenant or to the State Government. Because of such stringent law, no cultivator would permit the sharecropper to cultivate the same piece of land over a considerable period of time.

The Revenue Secretary put up a proposal before the Cabinet suggesting that leasing out of land should be made lawful and names of the sub-tenants and sharecroppers should be recorded. He pleaded with the Cabinet that such recording could be feasible only if it was known to the landowners that they would not lose ownership and no rights would accrue to the sub-tenants or the sharecropper. During the discussions before the Cabinet, he was asked what useful purpose would be served by recording if no rights are to be given to the sub-tenants. He explained his scheme by stating that once 5 to 10 lakh people are recorded as sub- tenants, as in West Bengal, they would immediately be eligible for short-term credit from the Financial Institutions, and it was likely that after a period of 5 or 10 years, a pressure lobby would emerge of such identified sub-tenants and they would then ask the Government for occupancy rights for a longer duration, and may be, in due course of time, the State Government would not hesitate to grant them permanent rights, just as it was done by the British Government in stages between the period 1873 to 1936. The CM, V. P. Singh (who later became the prime minster in 1989), felt it was not proper for the Government to tell the landowners at the time of recording that no rights would accrue to the sharecroppers and then gradually give rights in a phased manner under pressure. It was obvious that the Cabinet Ministers did not wish to disturb the existing power equations in the village. The proposal was therefore not accepted by the Cabinet.

Saxena ignores the Cabinet

Despite such a decision, Saxena issued orders to all the Collectors (many of his colleagues thought this step to issue the circular was unethical and against the spirit of the Cabinet decision) to record the names of such landowners who owned more than 5 acres of land but were not living in the villages. Such lists were compiled, and it showed that roughly 10 lakh acres of land (8 per cent of the total in that category) was involved in such arrangements. He thought that perhaps some absentee landowners would get scared because of the Circular and sell out their lands to such people who were living in the villages. Although land would thus not pass on to the landless, but at least if ownership was transferred from absentee landowners to progressive cultivators living in the villages, production will go up. Later, informal enquiries from the field officers showed that there was hardly any sale of land. However, the scheme of recording absentee landowners did increase corruption at the lower levels as many clever revenue officials threatened rich landowners and extorted money from them for not recording them as absentee landowners.

Pro-poor circulars

Decision-making in the State of UP was, by and large, in the hands of bureaucrats. The Revenue Minister was highly sympathetic to the cause of weaker sections, and this helped the Secretary in issuing many orders for ensuring benefits to the rural poor. Some of the new Government orders initiated by him were as follows:

(i) In addition to ceiling land, the State Government had distributed wasteland or land meant for common utility to the rural poor. It was common knowledge that wherever land was of better quality, possession was still with the powerful people in the village. In order to ensure transfer of effective possession to the beneficiaries, the Secretary suggested to the Cabinet that such people who have illegally occupied common utility land should be prosecuted and a minimum punishment of six months imprisonment should be awarded to them. This suggestion was promptly accepted by the Cabinet and was in fact highly publicized by the CM as one of the achievements of his Government. The Secretary made it compulsory for senior officers such as Collectors and Commissioners to visit the villages personally and take action against subordinate officers for not reporting adverse possession by the landed elite over common lands.

(ii) Wages in the Agricultural sector were very low in many parts of the State. Implementation of the Minimum Wages Act was not the responsibility of the Revenue department, yet orders were issued making it compulsory for all revenue officials to prosecute landowners paying less than the wages prescribed in law. The entire procedure was explained, and a constant follow-up was attempted. As the Sub-Divisional Officers were themselves competent to impose fines and the recovery was up to 10 times the amounts not paid by landowners, it was thought that the implementation of this scheme would not cause much problem.

(iii) The Ceiling law provided that wherever irrigation facilities have been introduced because of State Government's efforts, such as canals, tube wells and so on, the ceiling limit would get reduced from 30 to 18 acres. No effort was made since 1972 to enforce this clause. Detailed instructions were issued on this point asking the Collectors to open up fresh ceiling files against those who had benefited by State irrigation works.

(iv) Legal provisions existed for realizing heavy fines against those who encroached upon public utility land. In the past, fines had been imposed, but no effort was made to realize the arrears. Attention of the field staff was drawn to this aspect also.

(v) The performance sheet on which the evaluation of revenue officials up to the Collectors was based was revised thoroughly so as to give greater importance to schemes which would benefit the rural poor.

However, most of the above reforms remained on paper. The field staff had no faith in the measures which the Revenue Department had been suggesting. Some of the Collectors agreed in principle to what was being suggested, but they had no time to go through the circulars or to monitor their implementation. They soon discovered that their superiors like the Divisional Commissioners or Members, Board of Revenue had themselves not read the circulars and never asked any question during their visit to the districts about the speedy implementation of the new measures which the Government had initiated. Short tenures in the field meant that officers did not wish to involve themselves in schemes which would upset the prevalent social power structure. The 'urgent' work was given priority over 'important' work. However, one or two Collectors took these instructions seriously and tried to enforce them despite indifference and hostility from the lower staff. There is no evidence to show that such Collectors were summarily transferred from the districts. On the other hand, their work was appreciated by the CM.

Take land away from 'Rich' non-residents

Saxena was convinced that any effort to lower the ceiling limit would not either be politically accepted or yield much land for the landless. He was also aware of the enterprising nature of the rich farmers who were controlling the village institutions and the political apparatus of the countryside. Therefore, he thought that the best way to get more land for the poor would be to attack such urban -based people who have got a good source of income from non-agricultural sources but are still holding land in rural areas. He issued a circular in September 1980 asking the Collectors to examine a proposal to debar such people from holding agricultural land whose income from non-agricultural sources was more than ₹10,000 a year.[19] As was his habit, he did not consult anyone before issuing the circular, neither his Minister nor the Chief Secretary. News about this circular got leaked to the press in due course of time, and Kuldip Nayar commented upon it adversely in the Indian Express in its issue dated 7 December 1980 under the heading 'UP Government plans to take land away from the "rich". One of his points of criticism was that identifying such landowners would lead to corruption. He wrote, 'Since village level functionaries are to provide the information, it is feared that information would

19. The median per capita income in rural UP in 1980 was about `1,500 a year, and the class IV government employee earned about `6,000 a year.

be fudged and many of those who fall in the ₹10,000 and above category may go undetected because of pressures or bribe.'

On that particular day of the newspaper story, a large number of Congress MPs from the State had gathered at the national capital for a meeting called by Rajiv Gandhi, the then Secretary of the Congress Party, to discuss the threat of agitation given by the rich farmers against low price of commercial crops like sugarcane, potato, onions and so on. They, most of them landlords themselves, were shocked at the steps which the Revenue department was planning to take, and they agitatedly asked the Government to withdraw the circular. The Chief Secretary of the State was present in the meeting, and he was also horrified at the cheeky and totally unwarranted circular from Saxena. It is learnt that Rajiv Gandhi reprimanded the Chief Secretary at this 'socialistic' but impractical initiative. Chief Secretary promptly asked Saxena from Delhi itself over the telephone to withdraw the circular. Saxena, however, refused to budge and wrote a long note justifying the circular and pleaded with the Government not to act in haste.

However, he was overruled in writing on the file and ultimately the controversial circular was withdrawn.

The orders of the Chief Secretary on the file on the note of Saxena were as follows:

> I had communicated the orders of the Chief Minister to the Revenue Secretary. It is unfortunate that these orders have not been complied with. It is rather strange that a circular hinting at the intention of the Government has been issued without obtaining orders of the Cabinet. In such important matters, before collecting information from the field the proposal should have been referred to the Cabinet. Order of the Chief Minister to withdraw the circular must be complied with immediately.

In retrospect Saxena thought that if he had kept the income limit as ₹100,000 per annum instead of ₹10,000 there would have been a greater chance of the acceptance of the Scheme. Although very little land would have been available through a higher income level, yet at a later stage this could have been reduced by a more progressive Government.

Tribal land alienation

In the tarai of district Nainital of the State, most of the cultivated land was until 1950 in possession of the tribals, Bhoksas and Tharus. The area was full of health hazards until 1960. The Government started an ambitious colonization programme by improving health and communication in that area and encouraged people from other areas to settle down. Gradually, people from the Punjab, who are known for their enterprising qualities, settled in that area. They were allotted farms of 100 to 5,000 acres by the Government. Gradually, they also occupied land which was till then being cultivated by the tribals. In 1969, the GOI issued guidelines to the State Governments for preventing alienation of the land from the tribals to the non-tribals. In pursuance of these guidelines, the State Government passed a law declaring further transfer of land from tribals to non-tribals as unlawful. However, all transfers to the enterprising immigrants until 1969 were regularized in stages.

Illegal transfer of land from the tribals to the non-tribals continued even after 1969. In many cases, the tribals were evicted by force and in many other cases they were paid paltry sum of ₹500 per acre, for handing over possession to the non-tribals, most of whom were from the Punjab. Market value of land in that area was ₹40,000 to ₹100,000 per acre in 1980. However, in all such cases of transfer of land the revenue records still showed the tribals as owners of land because of the restriction imposed under law in 1969. According to the estimates available, about 15,000 acres of land was in possession of about 500 non-tribals taken from about 5,000 tribals.

Since the problem was confined by and large to one district only, and the number of people concerned was not high, Saxena thought that it could be possible to restore possession to the tribals without hitting at the power structure of the ruling elite. He studied the laws made by other State governments and analysed the reasons for non-implementation of this programme. According to his analysis, a large number of loopholes existed in the law itself which resulted in delay. Since detailed drafting of such laws is done at the officer level, he was optimistic in getting sanction of the Cabinet on an amendment which eliminated the loopholes in the laws of other State Governments. The new law, that he suggested, read as follows:

'211. (1) Where any land held by a tenure-holder belonging to a Scheduled Tribe is in occupation of any person other than such tenure-holder, the Assistant Collector may, SUO MOTU or on the application of such tenure-holder put him in possession of such land after evicting the occupant and may, for that purpose use or cause to be used such force as may be considered necessary, anything to the contrary contained in this Act notwithstanding.

(2) Where any person, after being evicted from any land under sub-section (1), re-occupies the land or any part thereof without any lawful authority, he shall be punishable with imprisonment for a term which may extend to three years <u>but which shall not be less than six months</u> and also with a fine which may extend to three thousand rupees but which shall not be less than one thousand rupees.

(3) Any court convicting a person under sub-section (2) may make an order to put the tenure-holder in possession of such land or any part thereof and such person shall be liable to eviction without prejudice to any other action that may be taken against him under any other law for the time being in force.

(4) Every offence punishable under sub-section (2) shall be cognizable and non- bailable.

Is Saxena promoting 'Class War'?

Thus, unlike other state laws, the above draft empowered administration to physically throw out the encroacher and restore possession without waiting for any court order. This was hesitatingly approved by the State Cabinet (although one of the Ministers warned that it would lead to a bloody class war) and an ordinance was issued in June 1981, which was subsequently ratified by the Assembly and become part of the Zamindari Abolition Act in August 1981.

The district administration was not very keen to implement such an ordinance. Many officers at the district level thought that tribals would not cultivate land intensively and therefore production would suffer. Saxena himself visited the district a number of times and tried to convince the officers about the need to restore at least some of the alienated land to the tribals.

Before any action could be taken, representatives from the non-tribals met powerful ministers of the GOI and gave a number of representations. N. D. Tiwari, who was an MP from the Nainital terai, and thus depended upon the support of powerful non-tribal rich farmers, was then an important Minister at the Centre. Saxena had worked under him as District Magistrate (DM) Aligarh when Tiwari was the CM. He called Saxena to Delhi and strongly pleaded with him to withdraw the Ordinance. He even advised Saxena to take leave from the IAS and do research on land alienation so that concrete facts could be brought to surface.

Zail Singh, who knew many immigrants personally, was the Home Minister, and also incharge of tribal welfare, as this subject in 1981 was with the Home Ministry. He asked the Chief Secretary to withdraw the ordinance, who in turn asked Saxena to put up a letter to the Central Government explaining the position of the State Government. Since restoration of land to the tribals was one of the important policy directions of the Central government itself, and since the ordinance was approved by the State Cabinet, Saxena was in a strong position this time and he put up a strongly worded draft in justification of the ordinance. He quoted figures stating that about 1.50 lakh acres of land had already passed on from tribals to the non-tribals which was not being restored. The operation was going to be a limited one and confined only to about 15,000 acres which has been alienated recently. In his draft, Saxena included one para, which read as follows:

> 'The District Administration has been instructed to carry out the eviction operation in stages after careful verification of revenue records. The State Government has taken all possible precautions to avoid violence, but in view of the high prices of land and the economic and political muscle which the non-tribals have acquired in that area, a situation of confrontation between non-tribals and district administration cannot be ruled out. The Government is committed to protecting the interests of the tribals and weaker sections and, if need be, force shall be used to evict the unauthorised occupants over the tribal land.

The above paragraph was, however, not included by the Chief Secretary in his letter to the Home Minister.

Against the opposition of the Chief Secretary to use police force in that area to restore possession, Saxena appealed to the CM and got orders from him for posting six companies of police force in that area. Despite the presence of force, practically nothing was happening in the district. Saxena was in touch with the Collector practically every day. He was informed by the Collector that although the force had been posted, yet the inspector general had instructed his subordinates not to use force. Once he was told by the Collector that the CM had himself stayed the entire operation. He contacted the inspector general and the CM's Secretariat and was informed that no such orders were issued by them. It was obvious that the Collector was not very keen to implement the provisions of law.

Saxena was summoned to Delhi a number of times. He explained his viewpoint to the Central Ministers and officers and drew their attention to a large number of circulars issued by the Central Government in favour of the tribals. The GOI officials appeared to be sympathetic but they did not want confrontation with the powerful non-tribals. Saxena felt as if the GOI authorities were saying, 'We issue guidelines in favour of tribals with the understanding that these will not be taken seriously by the implementation agencies. Please do not embarrass us by acting upon our policy prescriptions. Let these remain on paper only.'

In the meantime, the non-tribals obtained a stay order from the High Court, thus saving the Central and UP Ministers from further embarrassment. Saxena continued as Revenue Secretary for a few more months. In October 1981, Saxena was transferred to a more important job as Food Secretary. Was his transfer linked with the efforts made by him to implement land reforms in the State? No one knows. In fact, transfer was seen as a 'promotion' by his peer group.

The High Court issued a notice to the state government to file a counteraffidavit while maintaining the stay order. However, the state government took no interest in the case and ultimately the Court passed an ex parte order sometime in 2011 repealing the law. Not an inch of land was restored to the poor tribals.

3 Chapter

IAS OFFICERS IN THE HEADLINES

IAS Officers are in the news for a variety of reasons. Some of them are because they have joined politics. Others who fought the system and landed in trouble. A few whose misdeeds are exposed by the media. In a rare case, the do-gooders are able to attract media attention. Highlighting their achievements creates a good impression about the IAS, as also about the regime in power.

Durga Shakti Nagpal: The She-*Dabangg*

India has produced not only male *Dabangg*[1] civil servants, but also many gutsy female officers the country can be proud of. While posted as Sub-Divisional Magistrate (SDM) in Gautam Budh Nagar, Durga Shakti Nagpal, keeping in line with her first name, took strong action against the 'sand-mafia' in Greater Noida. According to environmentalists and engineers, the massive amount of mining is responsible for soil erosion and change of the natural flow of the Hindon and Yamuna, which shifted its course by about 500 metres towards east and posed a threat to flood embankments in six sectors of Noida. However, the UP government rewarded her with suspension for confiscating 24 dumper trucks and 300 trolleys involved in illegal mining, just because people close to the ruling party were involved in sand mining! According to newspaper reports, Durga was suspended because she was not allowing Samajwadi Party (SP) bigwigs to run mining business on riverbeds.

Sharat Pradhan wrote in the 19 August 2013 issue of *Outlook*[2],

1. Bold and fearless.
2. Sharat Pradhan (19 August 2013) Speck of Sand in the Eye. *Outlook* (available at https://www.outlook india.com/magazine/story/speck-of-sand-in-the-eye/287328).

> And the suspension of the 2010 batch IAS officer, who has displayed extraordinary mettle on her first posting as SDM in taking on the all-powerful sand mining mafia, has become one more chapter in UP's continuing saga of infamy. Especially as SP leader and cabinet minister Narendra Bhati, who is also the party's declared candidate from GB Nagar for the 2014 Lok Sabha election, went about bragging, 'It took me just 41 minutes to get Durga Shakti Nagpal suspended.'

More damaging was the statement from Ramgopal Yadav, a Rajya Sabha member of the Samajwadi Party, who asserted that UP did not need IAS officers. 'We will manage with our state service officers', as they would never dare take action against the ruling mafia. UP ruling politicians have been notorious in trying to humble the IAS through frequent transfers; upright officers are known to live out of suitcases, often facing near permanent separation from their spouses. Many of them are able to withstand political pressures in the hope that they would be bailed out by GOI, but in case the state bureaucracy is manned only by state service officers, it would have no choice but to lick the politicians' boots all the time.

According to Pragya Singh (Outlook, 19 August 2013), Mrs Sonia Gandhi, the ruling Congress party president, wrote a letter to the Prime Minister Manmohan Singh, raising the issue and asking him to ensure that the civil servant was not treated unfairly. 'There is widespread concern because the officer, in the course of her public duty, was seen to be standing up to vested interests engaging in illegal activity.' Mrs Gandhi also said there was a need to 'assess whether there are adequate safeguards in place to protect executive functionaries working beyond the average call of duty to uphold the law'. Because of growing demand from various political parties, associations and social media, the UP government revoked her suspension in September 2013. Soon after that GOI transferred her to the Centre to work in the Ministry of Agriculture.

I attended a talk by Prabhat Kumar,[3] ex-Cabinet Secretary, who not only praised Durga Shakti Nagpal and other such officers who,

3. He resigned as Governor, Jharkhand, in 2002 following newspaper reports of his association with a businessman.

out of their internal conviction were emerging as public heroes, but also asserted that such ethical initiatives were on the increase lately:

> Unilateral ethical conduct of a significant mass of civil servants seems to have the potential of regenerating dormant energy in the bureaucracy. Of late, we are witnessing growing examples of such conduct especially among the younger ones. The collector of Kozhikode needed the endorsement of the people of his district, not political endorsement, for initiating Operation Suleimani to ensure that no one in the district goes to bed on empty stomach. The sub-divisional officer of Manipur did not require political approval for building a difficult hill road by people's participation. A headmistress of a village school in Budaun did not need any approvals for spending money for building state of art lavatories and sanitary napkin incinerator in her school from her own salary.
>
> These and many other civil servants like them are dismissed as exceptions by cynics and as aberrations by sociologists. Our studies indicate that the number of such 'aberrations' is increasing by the day. They have a demonstration effect too. It is our hypothesis that the cumulative impact of these ingenious initiatives would compel the people and the media to view the civil services differently, and help in humanizing governance. (Kumar 2018)

I leave it to the readers to judge whether such incidents of defiance against the political mafia are on the increase or decline. There are too many disheartening stories floating around, such as the one cited below.

H. C. Gupta: A Bona Fide Officer

H. C. Gupta, along with two other IAS officers, was convicted by a CBI Court in 2017 and 2018, although it was known to everyone that they were all officers of unimpeachable integrity, and at worst it was an error of judgement with no mala fide intention.

Gupta was the Coal Secretary, GOI, from 31 December 2005 to 30 November 2008. Since 1992, coal was being allotted to public and private sector companies on the basis of their applications; there was no open bidding. In 2004, Coal Secretary P. C. Parakh submitted a note to PM Manmohan Singh, who was the Coal Minister throughout 2004–2009, to change the process as there was potential of fraud inherent in the discretionary allocation of the captive coalfields, but his suggestion was not accepted. According to the CAG, the Government had the authority to allocate coal blocks by a process of competitive bidding, but chose not to do so, which led to 'windfall gain' to the allocatees to the tune of ₹1.86 lakh crore over the years. The issue received massive media reaction and public outrage, leading to a CBI enquiry as well as a change in the procedure to allot on the basis of open bidding. Later, all the allocations were cancelled.

H. C. Gupta chaired a committee that made recommendations for coal allocation, which were accepted at the Ministerial level. However, some of the documents that were put up before the committee provided incorrect information. These errors were not apparent on the face of the documents presented to him. In administration, it is not practical to verify all the facts that come before the Secretary; administration would come to a grinding halt if all committees of the government start verifying the facts that come before them. According to CBI, this lapse led to windfall gains for some of the applicants. CBI invoked Section 13(1)(d)(iii) of the Prevention of Corruption Act, 1988, according to which a public servant is said to commit criminal misconduct if he, while holding office as a public servant, obtains for any person any valuable thing or pecuniary advantage without any public interest. The loosely worded provision, with no universally agreed upon definition of 'public interest', sought to implicate officers even when there is no malafide intention, or knowledge of wrong doing. Simply the fact that a wrongdoing was committed was enough to implicate an officer even in the absence of any mala fide.

Gupta's conviction has been one of the most unfortunate incidents in the history of the IAS. Everyone who has interacted with him would easily certify his integrity. No less than three former cabinet secretaries, Naresh Chandra, T. S. R. Subramanian and B. K. Chaturvedi, through newspaper articles, have put on record their appreciation of Gupta's high integrity. It is rare for former cabinet secretaries to defend an officer in writing. If officers of exceptional courage and integrity are punished with criminal conviction who would dare to take fast decisions? Playing safe had been the hallmark of some bureaucrats. Many more will join them. This is An extremely unfortunate development.

The law was subsequently amended to prevent such 'injustice', but Gupta even in the absence of any mens rea has been put behind bars. We must distinguish between wrong administrative decisions and corrupt ones which have a quid pro quo. The Country needs officers who would take bold decisions and not keep shuffling files.

I recall my own days as Food Secretary, UP, during 1981–1983, when UP traders used to import coal from Bihar and Madhya Pradesh, but they had to take permission from the District Supply Officer before selling it in retail. This kind of control obviously bred corruption, as the file in each district pertaining to sale of coal would not move from desk to desk without speed money. The normal course for any Food Secretary wanting to simplify procedures and remove price controls would be to ask his head of the department or the Collectors to send proposals for deregulation, and then take up the matter to the Cabinet. However, I felt that following such a procedure would mean that the traders would come to know about such a proposal and then their Association would be informally asked by the Babus at every desk for bribes, especially at the office of the Minister. Therefore, one fine morning I just dictated an order removing all controls from the movement and sale of coal, and issued it. The file neither went to the Cabinet, nor to the Minister, and not even to the Chief Secretary. There was also no noting from my juniors in the file. Later, I learnt that the traders were very surprised at this order, which was also gazetted, so available to the general public. They were wondering how come a deregulation order favouring their interests was issued when they did not bribe anyone! Today no Secretary would dare to flout the established procedures and issue such an order, as without any office noting or approval from the Minister/Cabinet, he would be hard put to justify his bona fides.

But 'those' days were different. Breaking rules by senior officers was tolerated if their integrity was not in doubt. One could challenge even the Prime Minister as described in the story below.

P. S. Appu: A Folk Hero

In the world of the IAS, Appu would always remain a folk hero (Sarma 2012). He tried to foster the values of professional competence, political neutrality, total integrity and service to the poor. He never minced words in support of these values. Appu joined the IAS in 1951 and left the service in 1982. He was awarded the Padma Bhushan by the GOI in 2006. He became Chief Secretary of Bihar in 1977 but left after a year for a lower paid job in the GOI when he found that the conditions he had stipulated for functioning effectively were not being observed by the political executive. His brickbats with the Bihar government are described in Chapter 8.

As Director of the IAS Academy in 1981 when Appu found a young IAS trainee guilty of misconduct, he recommended to the government that the officer's services should be terminated forthwith. However, when the government dragged its feet in following his advice, presumably because the trainee had political backing, Appu promptly submitted his papers for voluntary retirement from the IAS. That led to such an uproar in Parliament that Prime Minister Indira Gandhi had to overrule Home Minister Giani Zail Singh and announce dismissal of the guilty trainee officer from the IAS, though Appu himself stuck to his decision to quit. He explained his decision in a letter to the Prime Minister, quoted as follows (Appu 2007):

> Dear Madam Prime Minister,
>
> It is unusual for a Civil Servant, however senior he be, to write directly to the Prime Minister. I am resorting to this unconventional step because I see no other way to bring to the Prime Minister's notice a case of grave misconduct on the part of an Indian Administrative Service probationer and the cavalier manner in which the Ministry of Home Affairs disposed of the matter. Since I was leaving the Indian Administrative Service on this issue, I thought I would be failing in my duty if I did not bring the relevant facts to the Prime Minister's notice. In the course of a trek in the Himalayas an IAS probationer committed several culpable offence while under the influence of alcohol. An enquiry conducted by a Deputy Director of the National

Academy of Administration revealed that at Badrinath the probationer had whipped out a loaded revolver and threatened two women probationers by pointing the weapon at their heads. He had also threatened some men probationers by brandishing the same weapon. Later on he harassed the frightened woman probationers who had taken refuge for the night in a Dharamshala room by banging at the door and shouting abuses. When all those facts were established in the enquiry I came to the only possible conclusion that the probationer lacked in the qualities of mind and character needed for the Indian Administrative Service. Accordingly, while forwarding a copy of the enquiry report to the Secretary, Department of Personnel I suggested as early as October 28, 1981 that the probationer be discharged from probation in accordance with the provisions of Rule 12 of the IAS Probation Rules.[4] In the past, probationers had been discharged for less serious offences. I may also add that subsequently it came to light that the probationer had been a cadet at the National Defence Academy, Khadakvasla, a decade ago and that he had to be withdrawn from there on disciplinary grounds. This was also brought to Government's notice. When I found that the undue delay in passing orders was having adverse effect on discipline and morale at the Academy, I wrote to the Secretary, Department of Personnel and the cabinet Secretary on 28.12.81 pressing for early orders. I also made it clear in that letter that if my recommendation was not accepted

4. Appu's stand needs to be contrasted with the decision that one of his illustrious predecessor, A. N. Jha, ICS, took as director of the academy in the early 1960s. When two probationers got drunk and fought in Kulri market with bottles and chairs and tables causing ₹12,000 damages, a shopkeeper called on Jha demanding reparation; to his surprise, Jha said 'there was no question of any action being taken against the boys as they were like children to him'; as for money, Jha claimed that only dogs and probationers were in Mussoorie at that time of the year (winter), so whatever profit the shopkeepers were making was only from his probationers—hence there was 'no question of payment' (Potter 1986).

I would not like to continue as Director. I took that stand because I was convinced that if a probationer who had indulged in such gross misbehaviours was let off lightly, it would become impossible to maintain the desired level of discipline at the Academy and that the Director and faculty would lose all credibility. The Secretary, Deptt. of Personnel, sent me a confidential letter on 4.2.82 saying that Government had decided to let off the probationer with a warning. Thereupon, I sought premature retirement from the Service. I proceeded on leave preparatory to retirement with effect from March 1, 1982. I am enclosing with this letter copies of the enquiry report and the correspondence with the Cabinet Secretary and the Secretary, Department of Personnel and Administrative Reforms. My letters of October 28, 1981 and December 28, 1981 speak for themselves. Further comment will be superfluous.

I grew up in the closing years of the freedom struggle and joined the Indian Administrative Service soon after Independence. To me the Service provided something more than a career. It gave me an opportunity to make some worthwhile contribution to the building up of an India of our dreams and also for self-actualization. The three decades I spent in the Service have, indeed, been rewarding. I have had the good fortune to hold several important posts under the State and Central Governments. My last assignment as Director of National Academy gave me the welcome opportunity to try to mould the new entrants to the different branches of the superior civil service on what I considered to be the inculcating in them values of professional competence, political neutrality, social commitment, fearlessness, impartiality and integrity. The endeavours of my colleagues and myself to shape the new entrants on these lines had begun to look rather futile and even ludicrous, in the context of the sagging morale of the civil service and the general environment in the country. As is well known, the services have been under great strain for some time. Preferment does not always go by merit or objective consideration—Lobbying for what are considered plum postings has become the order of the day. Upright and dedicated men are occasionally punished for refusing to budge from the right path. In such a context the new entrants naturally give in to despair and cynicism despite our efforts. Some new developments have accelerated this process. In the 1979 IAS batch a few probationers succeeded in getting their cadres changed as a result of successful lobbying. It has always been the practice to post IAS officers immediately after their training to hold charge of sub-divisions. A few officers of 1979 batch in the States of Haryana and Odisha were not, however, posted to subdivisions for extraneous reasons. And on top of all these has come the Home Ministry's decision to let off lightly a probationer who had indulged in grave misconduct. The only conclusion the probationers will draw is that with influence in the right quarters one can commit even heinous crimes with impunity. This decision will have a disastrous effect on discipline and morale in the service in general and at the National Academy in particular. In the circumstances I thought that NO useful purpose would be served by my continuing in the post of Director. As a senior officer if I had failed to take this step I would, in effect, be acquiescing in the action of the Home Ministry. I also felt that if a high standard of discipline and morale cannot be preserved at the National Academy it must be even more difficult to do so at other places. Hence, I decided to leave the Service rather than seek another posting.

With kind regards,Yours sincerely,
P. S. APPU

Shrimati Indira Gandhi
Prime Minister Government of India
New Delhi

Persons like Appu will always remind us that the civil services can justify their existence only when they are fully attuned to addressing the concerns of the vast mass of the population. Their accountability should be to the people, not to the self-serving political and bureaucratic elite.

S. R. Sankaran: Real 'Public Servant'

Another model IAS officer was S. R. Sankaran of the 1957 batch. It was my privilege to work with him as Supreme Court Commissioners on food and hunger from 2002 to 2006. He lived a very simple unostentatious life and donated a considerable part of his salary to the poor dalit/adivasi students. As Secretary for Social Welfare in Andhra Pradesh, he extensively toured the villages to enforce the 1976 Abolition of Bonded Labour Act and inspired the villagers to break free from bondage. Sankaran's efforts were not appreciated by the CM and he was asked to proceed on leave. Nripen Chakraborty, who was the CM of Tripura during that time, invited him to join Tripura as the Chief Secretary, a post he held for six years. He arrived at Agartala with a small suitcase as his only piece of luggage and, instead of waiting for his official receivers, hailed a rickshaw to proceed to the Circuit House. Sankaran once narrated to me how Nripen Chakraborty preferred to spend a night sleeping on an uncovered wooden bench in the verandah of a ramshackle single-room rest house in a remote part of the state, so as not to disturb Sankaran who had already gone to sleep by then.

When Sankaran in 1987 was selected to head the IAS Academy at Mussoorie, I advised him to get a new suit stitched, as there are many formal functions at the Academy, but very soon he was held hostage by the naxalites. This led to cancellation of his posting, as the government feared that he would propagate his socialist ideals at the institution. He was awarded the third highest civilian honour, of the Padma Bhushan in 2005, but he declined the honour. The state government appointed him as the chief negotiator for negotiations with the militants in 2004. He mediated two rounds of talks between the government and the militants, but the talks were not fruitful as the government insisted on total disarmament; however, this was the first instance the Maoists agreed to talks with the government. After the failure of talks with Naxal groups, he was involved with the activities of the *Safai Karmachari Andolan*, founded by Bezwada Wilson, and served as a mentor to the organization. Under his guidance, the initiative worked to free a majority of the manual labourers in the State handling human excreta until their number dwindled from 1.3 million to 300,000.

His personal example of simplicity and dedication to the poor inspired a large number of IAS officers of Andhra Pradesh cadre, such as Yugandhar, E. A. S. Sarma, K. Raju and so on. Prompted by him, Sarma as Collector of Guntur organized a 'camp' for agricultural workers to make them aware of their rights and responsibilities under the various laws, so as to enable them to resist bonded labour, untouchability, usurious moneylending and other such practices. Sarma (2012) writes,

> I still remember Sankaran, who was then Secretary (social welfare) in the government of Andhra Pradesh, unostentatiously mixing with the agricultural workers, sharing food with them and sleeping on the floor along with them, so as to be able to listen to their concerns and share their experiences first hand, more as a friend than as a senior officer of the state government. The example he set to all of us at the camp transformed each one of us into a 'Sankaran'.

Armstrong Pame: People's Officer

Retired bureaucrats have a tendency to talk disparagingly of the present, and indulge in lavish praise of the 'glories' of the past. The present generation IAS officers admittedly do face a more adverse political environment than their predecessors did, but still one can easily locate idealists in each cadre who have done immensely good work in the field.

Pame is the first IAS officer from Zeme Tribe of the Naga people. Originally from Tamenglong district of Manipur, Armstrong Pame of the 2009 batch of the IAS was posted as SDM of Tousem in 2012. He visited many villages and saw how people were walking for hours, carrying sacks of rice on their backs, as well as patients being taken on improvised bamboo stretchers because there were no motorable roads. When he asked villagers what they wanted him to do for them, they only wished for a road.

He asked the government for funds to construct the road, but there was no positive response. So he decided to raise the funds on his own through social media. He also contributed his own salary for this cause. He mobilized grownups, elderly and children alike to build a 100-km road connecting the most backward areas in Manipur to Nagaland and Assam. The toughest part about his achievement is that he built the 'Peoples' Road' without any financial help from the government. He is a true hero and an embodiment of quote 'where there is a will, there is a way'. The 28-year -old IAS officer from the Northeast has brought happiness to the people of Tousem by giving them what they wanted the most—a motorable road which connects them to the world. The opening of the People's Road has earned him the nickname 'The Miracle Man'. He is an epitome of selfless intentions and deeds.

Since then, Armstrong has kept busy with his many initiatives, a recent one being when he decided to invite 10 students from the fifth to tenth standards for dinner every week to give them a glimpse in the life of an IAS officer. The students are selected from a number of schools in the district.

He received India's 'Most Eminent IAS Officer Award' in 2015. He was declared in 2018 as a 'Young Global Leader' by the World Economic Forum. Pame was also invited to the talk show Aaj Ki Raat Hai Zindagi *Aaj Ki Raat Hai Zindagi* by the host Amitabh Bachchan Amitabh Bachchan in 2015 as the 'hero' of the ninth episode, where he performed the noted song 'Give Me Some Sunshine' along with the Bollywood actor Boman Irani Boman Irani.

Ashok Khemka: Undeterred by Multiple Transfers

A 1991 batch of the Haryana Cadre, Khemka is best known for cancelling the mutation of land deal worth ₹57 crore between the real- estate giant DLF group and Sonia Gandhi's son-in-law Robert Vadra in Gurgaon (Vaishnav and Khosla 2016). Prior to this, he had also unearthed a scam in the Haryana Seed Development Corporation, where the corporation was selling seeds at inflated prices. For his crusade against corruption, Khemka has been transferred 51 times in 24 years by the Haryana government. When he tried hard to address corruption and bring reforms in the Transport Department despite severe limitations and entrenched interests, he was moved to the Archaeology and Museums Department by the Khattar government.[5] In 2017, within three months of his posting as Principal Secretary, Social Justice and Empowerment, he was transferred as he had asked his boss and Minister to return the official vehicle of a junior officer. The Minister was using a vehicle belonging to a district social welfare officer in Ambala.[6] 'So much work planned. News of another transfer. Crash landing again. Vested interests win. Deja vu. But this is temporary. Will continue with renewed vigour and energy,' Ashok Khemka tweeted soon after news of his 51st transfer landed.

Arun Bhatia: Quintessential Whistle-blower

Known to be a no-nonsense bureaucrat who strictly followed the law and came down hard on squatters and corrupt politicians, Bhatia served in several important posts, including Commissioner of the Pune Municipal Corporation. For fighting against corruption, Arun Bhatia paid a heavy price in terms of denial of promotion, frequent transfers (26 transfers in as many years of service in India), numerous charges and enquiries, bad assessment reports, ridicule by peers, seniors and subordinates, lack of support when giant offenders like Glaxo or senior officers and politicians were prosecuted by him, ugly threats from the Bombay land mafia and so on.

He prosecuted the sitting Chief Secretary (the head bureaucrat in the state) for corruption in awarding road contracts. This predictably resulted in a premature transfer, but citizens approached the Bombay High Court in a public interest litigation defeating the government and reversing the government order. The Chief Justice, on 13 April 1999, in Writ Petition 1395 of 1999, observed:

> [T]he decision to transfer Bhatia, in the facts of the present case, is so outrageous that it defies all logic and any moral standard. No reasonable person could have arrived at such a decision. We wish to emphasise that

5. https://economictimes.indiatimes.com/news/politics-and-nation/moment-truly-painful-ias-officer-ashok-khemka-on-transfer-haryanas-health-minister-anil-vij-supports-him/articleshow/46781672.cms (accessed on 10 July 2019).
6. https://www.scoopwhoop.com/punished-for-honesty-again-haryana-ias-officer-ashok-khemka-transferred-for-51st-time/#.qbtuik7pj

during the present days when, unfortunately, corruption and dishonesty are at their peak, honesty and action as per law deserve a pat, rather than punishment. The transfer of Bhatia, in our view, is in the nature of punishment.

After retirement, he joined the campaign against corruption, and as part of the drive to cleanse the system, he took to politics but lost by a large margin to Mr Suresh Kalmadi, of all politicians, in the Lok Sabha election in Pune in 2009. But that was a year before Mr Kalmadi gained notoriety for corruption in the Commonwealth Games. Bhatia had also lost to him in the 2004 general elections. Bhatia fought the 2014 elections too, but ended up with a paltry 7,222 votes, as against more than 60,000 that he received in 2004.

As an insider, I find that there are very few within the IAS who admire the likes of Ashok Khemka and Arun Bhatia. The viewpoint of the majority about them is best expressed by Anil Swarup, who has an impeccable record in performance, whether in promoting health insurance for the poor or in streamlining coal distribution. He writes,[7]

> Honesty is a necessity, but not a sufficient condition for the welfare of the people. Such officers forget the fact that they are paid not merely to remain honest, but to perform as well. They evaluate their own performance in terms of punitive actions that they have taken against the others, the number of people or institutions they have exposed (becoming a quintessential whistle-blower that brings 'name' and 'fame'), the number of disciplinary proceedings they get initiated, and the number of FIRs they get lodged. Fortunately, there are indeed a number of bureaucrats who are honest and efficient. They may not be as visible as those that are going hammer and tongs against the 'dishonest'. They are not crusaders. They are the 'doers'. The Swachh Bharat Abhiyan led by the redoubtable Parameswaran Iyer is creating an impact. Fortunately, it is becoming visible as well.

7. https://www.financialexpress.com/opinion/is-just-being-honest-enough-for-bureaucrats/1432842/

There are, of course, exceptions, like Harsh Mander, who are both crusaders and doers.

Harsh Mander: an Icon of Courage and Hope

If any officer in the IAS ever deserved a Bharat Ratna or Nobel Prize, it would be Harsh. While there are many examples of IAS officers who have suffered because of their commitment to fight corruption, Harsh single-handedly has not only fought the system, but it is his contribution to bring joy and succour in the lives of thousands of victims of hate, hunger and homelessness that puts him at the top of the list of those who need to be admired and revered.

Harsh shot into prominence with his article on Gujarat riots that appeared in the Times of India on 20 March 2002. It was about the unprecedented killings of Muslims that were woefully brutal, about loot and rapine, and unimaginably cruel and inhumane treatment meted out to the women of all ages by the Hindu crowds. His article began as, 'Numbed with disgust and horror, I return from Gujarat 10 days after the terror and massacre that convulsed the state. My heart is sickened, my soul wearied, my shoulders aching with the burdens of guilt and shame.' He ended the article by writing, 'There is much that the murdering mobs in Gujarat have robbed from me. One of them is a song I often sang with pride and conviction. The words of the song are Sare jahan se achha Hindustan hamara.... It is a song I will never be able to sing again.' This outburst caused many people to cry.

Harsh then resigned from the IAS, and started working full-time for the survivors of mass violence, hunger and homeless street children. As Member of India's NAC from June 2010–2012, he convened the working groups on the Food Security Bill, Land Acquisition and Rehabilitation Bill, Child Labour Abolition, Manual Scavenging Abolition, Urban Poverty and Homelessness, Disability Rights, Bonded Labour, Street Vendors and Urban Slums, and co-convened the groups on the Communal and Targeted Violence Bill, Dalits and Minorities, Tribal Rights, amongst others. He virtually drafted most of these Bills, some of which were not to the liking of the Prime Minister, and he did not renew Harsh's term in the NAC after 2012. Mrs Gandhi would have liked him to continue, but could not overrule the Prime Minister. This story is described in chapter 10.

While in service, Harsh worked in the predominantly tribal districts of Madhya Pradesh and Chhattisgarh for almost two decades, and became extremely popular with the masses. It was his conviction that led him to defy his political masters again and again. Whether it was being quick to control the riots in Indore in 1984, even though the larger political climate did not quite insist on it, or his refusal to suppress the peaceful agitation of Medha Patkar and Baba Amte during the Narmada Bachao Andolan in 1989, or going ahead and distributing 2,000 acres of ceiling surplus land belonging to a powerful BJP leader in Raigarh in Madhya Pradesh in 1990, Mander listened more to the dictates of his conscience than to the diktats of his superiors.[8]

He is currently the Director of the Centre for Equity Studies, an autonomous institution engaged in research and advocacy on issues of social and economic justice and equity. He is also the founder of the campaigns 'Aman Biradari', for secularism, peace and justice; 'Nyayagrah', for legal justice and reconciliation for the survivors of communal violence; 'Dil Se', for street children; and 'Hausla' for urban homeless people. He worked with me as the Special Commissioner to the Supreme Court of India for the purpose of monitoring the implementation of all orders relating to the right to food (PUCL *v* Union of India and others, Writ Petition 196 of 2001).

Currently, he is engaged in spreading love and solidarity to families hit by hate and violence in the last four years through Karwan-e-Mohabbat. He writes,

> "We have by now made some 24 journeys to 13 states, and encountered levels of hate that continue to stun and shame me every time. My colleagues have in response tried modestly to build a legal support system for the victims, and also started a communication initiative for kindness and harmony. All of this has been possible because of the kind of support that many including the

8. https://www.telegraphindia.com/7-days/for-a-public-servant-disobedience-is-equally-important/cid/396987

members of this group[9] quietly continue to offer to the Karwan.

It was my good fortune to have him as a colleague at the IAS Academy in the mid-1990s. At that time, hand-pulled rickshaws were still the main mode of public transport in Mussoorie. Harsh found it intolerable that a town that had been sending out the country's senior civil servants every year for decades should still be scarred with this execrable symbol of human slavery, of thin malnourished tubercular men pulling other human beings. With his trainee probationers, he worked hard to bring an end to hand-pulled rickshaws for all time, and was successful in replacing these with cycle rickshaws that were specially designed for the hills for free, thanks to liberal funding from the Rajiv Gandhi Foundation.

Suresh, a serving IPS officer who was trained under Mander in IAS Academy, recalls, 'his impeccable integrity, remarkable humility and simplicity, indomitable courage when it came to defending the oppressed and weaker sections of the society and missionary zeal in rendering service to the needy will ever remain etched in my mind'.

He is the right role model for all future IAS officers as he leads by example. One would love to see more Harsh Manders in government service.

IAS officers in politics

K. J. Alphons: The Demolition Man

The Indian middle class does not consider politics as an ethical occupation. Politicians are seen as corrupt and heavily dependent on criminals and businessmen for their survival. Hence, those over-ambitious IAS officials who join politics, no matter how much they justify it in the name of 'desire to serve the people', are always suspect and lack credibility. However, they defend their decision as it is everyone's right to realize one's potential no matter in what field, so long as no law is breached. For joining the private sector within a year of their retirement, IAS officers need government

9. A group of about 150 retired civil servants who have come together to express themselves on issues of governance and public policy that have a bearing on constitutional principles, conduct and ethics.

permission, but no such permission is needed for joining a political party.

K. J. Alphons belongs to the 1979 batch of the IAS, and did excellent work as the district collector of Kottayam, Kerala where he drove the literacy movement and helped to make Kottayam as the first 100 per cent literate town in India in 1989. His national profile rose as the Commissioner of the Delhi Development Authority, he demolished illegal buildings and reclaimed land worth more than ₹10,000 crore.[10] These actions earned him the title '*The Demolition* Man'.The action also listed him in *Time* magazine's 100 young global leaders in 1994 (cover story, 5 December 1994).

He voluntarily retired from the service in 2006. He was later elected a Member of the Legislative Assembly, from Kottayam, with the support of the Communist Party of India (Marxist)-led Left Democratic Front (LDF). CPI(M) Central Committee member M. A. Baby said it was only logical that his party decided to field Alphons. 'He was always pro-poor in his approach. That's perfectly in line with our thinking too,' he said.

He resigned from his assembly seat in 2011 and joined the BJP in the presence of erstwhile party president Nitin Gadkari. For some time since September 2017, he served as the Union Minister of State for Electronics and information technology, culture and tourism. About his role in demolitions in Delhi, Alphons wrote[11]:

> No politician or bureaucrat has ever told me to do something or not to do something. All the politicians who get in touch with me are overflowing with courtesy. Even most of those whose buildings I have demolished have become friends of mine. After all I have not done something which was irrational or arbitrary. I have only enforced the law of the land. Even they realise that. I have survived for three-and-a-half years in this job. I have a year-and-a-half to go. I have disproved the myth that anybody who does his job is bound to get kicked out within days or maybe a month. There was a surprise on 20 September 1995. The vice-chairman, DDA, Anil

10. https://en.wikipedia.org/wiki/Alphons_Kannanthanam#cite_note-5 (accessed on 10 July 2019).
11. Taken from his book, at (accessed on 10 July 2019).

> Kumar, a 1965 batch IAS officer, issued orders shifting me out of my job as commissioner (land management) to the post of commissioner (systems & training). My responsibility as commissioner (S&T) would be to switch on the computer in the morning and switch it off in the evening. Great job of national importance! Hell broke loose in the media over the next one week. They attacked the government, the LG and the vice-chairman ruthlessly. The public was shocked. Almost every newspaper wrote an editorial condemning the transfer. There was story after story on television, commenting on the immorality of the transfer. I was surprised by such overwhelming support from the public. The Times of India conducted a poll which showed that 89 per cent of the people of Delhi supported me. I never knew that I enjoyed so much support in the capital According to the poll, 60 per cent of the people also believed that the land mafia was behind my transfer.

His observations on bureaucracy are also worth quoting (1996):

> Many of these bureaucrats are honest. But they have no guts; they have no guts to say no to an irregular decision. This is the tragedy of the Indian bureaucracy. This is the tragedy of Indian administration at its worst. Honest officers who do not make money and are well intentioned, totally falling in line and obeying commands which are totally irregular. I believe that over fifty per cent of officers in the IAS are honest, but less than one per cent have guts. It is not only that they pass on directions from the top, they are also pretty happy to advise the politicians on how to make a quick buck. Not all of them, only some.

P. L. Punia: Born of Political Creed

A 1970-batch IAS officer of the UP cadre and a native of Haryana, Punia shot into prominence in 1993, when he worked as personal Secretary to both Mulayam Singh Yadav and Mayawati, who were CMs of the SP–BSP alliance government in UP. Since then, Punia served two more stints with Mayawati when she became the CM in 1997 and 2002. Though there were IAS officers who wielded influence in state politics, none could match the clout of Punia, who had support from politicians cutting across caste and creed.

But bitterness set in after the ₹175-crore Taj Heritage Corridor scam broke out in 2003. Punia turned approver against Mayawati, against whom the CBI was preparing a charge sheet. Though Mayawati got a reprieve after Governor T. V. Rajeshwar refused to grant sanction for prosecution, she never forgave Punia for betraying her.

Punia, who retired in 2005, contested the 2007 Assembly election from Barabanki district, but lost to the BSP. Punia fought in 2009 from the same district for Lok Sabha. As in the 2007 polls, Mayawati had campaigned against Punia this time too. But Punia won by a margin of 1.67 lakh votes. The BSP candidate was a distant third.

According to Punia[12],

> I joined the Congress about 5–6 months after retirement in 2005. I wanted to join politics. What is the harm if someone wants to serve people after retirement? I did not get any favour in politics. In fact, I was among the people till 2009 when I contested and won the Lok Sabha election.

He also feels that there should be no cooling-off period for bureaucrats to join politics.

In July 2012, Punia appeared in the popular TV show *Satyamev Jayate*, hosted by Bollywood star Aamir Khan, to raise awareness of discrimination against Scheduled Castes (SCs). He was chairperson of the National Commission for Scheduled Castes between 2013

12. "http://www.hindustantimes.com/lucknow/there-should-be-no-cooling-off-period-for-bureaucrats-"https://www.hindustantimes.com/lucknow/therHYPERLINK "http://www.hindustantimes.com/lucknow/there-should-be-no-cooling-off-period-for-bureaucrats-"e-should-be-no-cooling-off-period-for-burHYPERLINK "http://www.hindustantimes.com/lucknow/there-should-be-no-cooling-off-period-for-bureaucrats-"eaucrats-to-join-politics-punia/story-bCPFdHywa71XdeUg2Ji1OI.html (accessed on 08 July 2019).

and 2016 and as such sat *ex officio* on the National Human Rights Commission (NHRC). He was appointed as Chhattisgarh incharge of the All-India Congress Committee (AICC) in July, 2017.

Others in the news

Aparajita Sarangi, a 1994-batch IAS officer of the Odisha cadre, was serving as the Joint Secretary for MGNREGA under the Ministry of Rural Development (GOI), before she sought voluntary retirement and within a few months she joined the BJP in December 2018. Party president Amit Shah was present at the BJP office to welcome the officer, where she said 'I want to work for people on a very large scale. Politics is the only platform which provides this kind of opportunity for me. The party's motto and leader made me choose BJP, which not only assures development but ensures speed in development.' Elections in Odisha are due in 2019, alongside the general elections. She had a very successful innings as Bhubaneswar municipal commissioner from May 2006 to July 2009, and is likely to contest the Lok Sabha elections from Bhubaneswar constituency on a BJP ticket.

It is generally believed that most of such retirements occur just before elections. 'And since there are no free lunches in politics, these officers would have thoroughly compromised themselves during this period in order to curry favour with the party of their choice.'[13] Another prime example was the 2005 batch IAS officer O.P. Choudhary, who resigned as Collector of Raipur (Chhattisgarh) in August 2018, and joined the BJP two days later. Within a few months of joining politics to 'serve the people', he received a ticket from the Kharsia constituency in Chhattisgarh, but lost the assembly polls to the sitting Congress MLA, though he did manage to secure 43 per cent votes. The fact that several retired bureaucrats are serving as Ministers in the Modi regime must have prompted these IAS officers to take the plunge and seek greener pastures in politics.

Of course, there are some, like Praveen Pardesi, who while still in service wielded more powers than many Cabinet Ministers. As Additional Chief Secretary in Maharashtra he was the CM's most

13. http://avayshukla.blogspot.com/2018/10/following-ones-conscience-or-gravy-train.html?m=1

trusted civil servant. As collector, the 1985 batch IAS officer helped rehabilitate victims of the 1993 earthquake in Latur, in which 52 villages were destroyed, 30,000 persons injured and 10,000 people killed. Pardesi's outstanding work was praised in a book by Sharad Pawar, who was then CM. He played a crucial role in providing logistic support for relief and rehabilitation plan for flood-hit Kerala in early 2018 and ensured medicines, clothes and material reach specific destinations in time. As Principal Secretary, Forest Department, Pardesi did excellent work in promoting Community Forest Rights (CFR) for tribals, pushing Maharashtra to the top amongst all states in granting maximum area for management to village communities. Under CFR, more than 500 villages of Maharashtra are drawing from ₹50 lakh to ₹1.5 crore a year from the sale of bamboo.

Politicians in India, unfortunately, do not have a good public image. Hence, those who are close to them are viewed with scepticism. However, there have been civil servants who have used their clout with the CM for public good. Centralization of power helps in coordination, improves collective performance of the bureaucracy, and focuses attention on outcomes, the lack of which leads to poor social development, as discussed in the next chapters. This, however, cannot be a sustainable model, as systemic changes matter more than individual excellence or rustic loyalties. We pick up this thread in chapter 11.

4 Chapter

BUREAUCRACY RESPONSIBLE FOR SEDIMENTARY DEVELOPMENT IN INDIA?

There are two prominent but conflicting trends in India: impressive economic growth and at the same time slow improvement in key social indicators, particularly amongst the disadvantaged populations (by region, social groups and gender). India is one of the fastest growing economies of the World, and has achieved compound annual growth rate of more than 7 per cent in Gross Domestic Product (GDP) in the last 25 years. However, high growth achieved through private enterprise has not been translated into satisfactory progress on the social front, suggesting failure of governance and delivery mechanisms (Chaturvedi 2014). There is broad political support in India in favour of inclusive development and social protection programmes, but the country's administrative system has not been able to convert political aspirations into reality. India failed to achieve its MDGs with respect to hunger, health, gender and sanitation. Though India has done well where contractors are involved, such as road transport, it does poorly in all programmes that require active involvement of grassroots bureaucracy without contractors, whether it is quality of education, immunization, medical care, maintenance of land records, supplementary nutrition through Anganwadi centres, groundwater management, crime control and so on. In addition, a large number of marginalized and disadvantaged people either have not gained from development (discussed in Chapter 7) or in many cases have actually been harmed by the process. Many programmes need correct selection of beneficiaries, without errors of inclusion and exclusion. However, according to the Planning Commission (2012), incorrect selection of beneficiaries led to 55 per cent of the subsidized food grain reaching wrong hands in 2004–2005. It is a matter of concern that India's pace of improvement on social indicators is much slower than that in poorer countries such as Bangladesh and Vietnam.

It is not the size of allocations on pro-poor services alone that matters. GOI transfers[1] close to ₹13.5 lakh crore every year to the States. If even half of it were to be sent to the 6 crore poor households[2] directly to their accounts, they would each receive more than ₹350 a day, which is more than ₹250 needed for lifting the household of five units above the poverty line! It proves that public expenditure needs to be effectively translated into public goods and services that reach the poor for it to have an impact on poverty and social outcomes. Unfortunately, different kinds of distortions can come in the way of resource allocations reaching the intended beneficiaries. Weak governance, manifesting itself in poor service delivery, excessive regulation and uncoordinated and wasteful public expenditure, is one of the key factors impinging on development and social indicators.

An efficient public service is necessary (though not sufficient) for benefits to reach the socially and economically weaker sections (EWS) of the society who have fewer alternatives to services provided by the government. Mere allocation of funds for programmes that do not work effectively would be a waste of public money unless extra efforts are made on improving government efficiency, and also to ensure that the poor are able to participate and put pressure on public administration to deliver so that they receive the intended benefits.

The argument that the Indian state has become indifferent to the poor after liberalization appears weak in the face of vast

1. About 9 lakh crore Rs from the Finance Commission, and the rest from Ministries
2. There are approximately 24 crore households in India, of which 22 per cent (or 5.3 crore) households were considered poor in 2011-12.

increases in central sector allocations by the GOI in the last decade through several flagship programmes in the social sector, as shown in Table 4.1.

Table 4.1 Central Plan Outlay in crore Rs		
	1999–2000	2021-22
Rural Development	8,552	1,61,643
Elementary Education	2,852	80,352
Health and Family Welfare	4,182	84,470
Women and Child Development	1,250	21,784
Water and Sanitation	1,310	88,517
Total of these sectors	18,146	4,36,766

Source: Various Budget documents of GOI

Thus, the allocation for the social sector assigned for the States has gone up by more than 24 times, although the price index increased only by four times during the period 1999–2000 to 2020–21. The increased interest of the centre in subjects which are constitutionally in the States' domain has presented a unique opportunity to accelerate social development and to cover the gap in the future between the desired SDGs and their present levels. However, unless bottlenecks impeding programme delivery at the State and cutting-edge level are identified and remedial action taken, attaining the SDGs by 2030 is unlikely.

How is Bureaucracy Doing on Social Sector Programmes?

The IAS is primarily responsible for India's failure to achieve MDG in hunger, health, malnutrition, sanitation and gender, as many IAS officers neither can design effective programmes (discussed in chapter 6) nor can implement them with accountability. Some decades back, one used to compare India with China and Sri Lanka, but these countries have left India far behind in development goals. On social indicators, India unfortunately does worse than countries poorer than India, like Bangladesh and Vietnam, as shown in Table 4.2.

Table 4.2 India and other developing countries on MDGs				
Indicators		**India**	**Bangladesh**	**Vietnam**
Infant Mortality Rate	1990	89	100	37
	2019	35	26	16
Malnourished stunted children under 5 years in 2020		35	30	22
Rural population with adequate sanitation 2016		70	92	89
Attendance ratio of girls to boys in secondary school (net) (%)		83	116	93
Total Fertility Rate (TFR)		2.0	1.9	1.8

Source: UNICEF (2021)

Despite some gains on the poverty front, India continues to lag behind the world—and in some instances regional—averages on human development outcomes. India ranks 132 out of 191 on the United Nations' 2022 Human Development Index (HDI), much below when compared to Sri Lanka (73), China (79), Bangladesh (129), and Vietnam (116)[3]. India's child malnutrition rates are the highest in South Asia: 35 per cent of children (under five) in 2019-21 were stunted and 19 per cent were wasted (NFHS 5). India accounts for one-third (nearly 300 million people) of the globe's illiterate people. India's principal social indicators have only now reached the levels that China achieved quite early in its take-off phase. Thus, India's literacy rate in 2019 (78 per cent) remains short of China's 75 per cent in 1993; similarly, life expectancy in India in 2020 is 70 years, and yet to reach China's 72 years achieved in 1993. India's investment rate as a share of GDP, at about 32 per cent, is significantly lower than the 40-plus per cent that China has enjoyed for well over a decade. Decline in poverty too has been much faster in China than in India (Figure 4.1).

Hunger

Although the number of people below poverty line has slowly declined from 50 to 16 per cent during 1990-2017 (or about one percentage point per annum), not a single state has succeeded in

3. http://hdr.undp.org/en/composite/trends

Figure 4.1: per cent living below $1.90 a day in India and China over the years

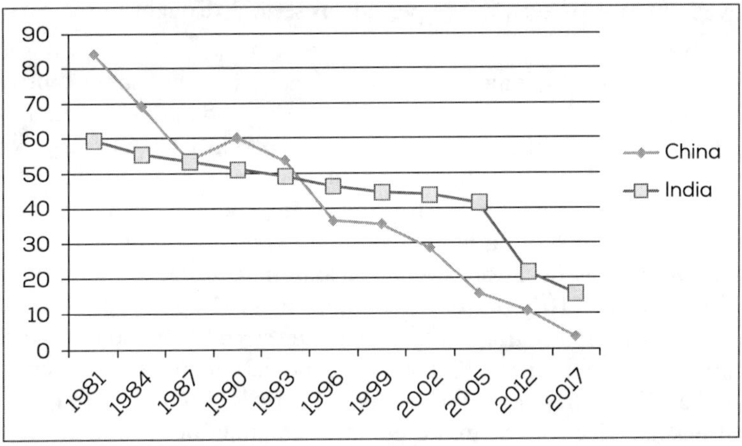

Source: https://data.worldbank.org/indicator/SI.POV.DDAY?view=chart

reducing the incidence of underweight children by half since 1990, which was the mandate under MDG to be achieved by 2015. India is home to one-quarter of the world's undernourished population and nearly half of the world's underweight children, in addition to nearly one-third of the world's food-insecure people.

India's age-old habit of defecating in the open—which distinguishes it from many other developing countries—makes matters worse. The proportion of Indians who do this has certainly fallen rapidly in the last four years, but unsafe disposal of human faeces spreads diseases and worms, and nullifies the progress made to control open defecation. Poor public hygiene may account for much of India's failure to make faster improvements in nutrition.

Cereal intake of the bottom 20 per cent in rural India was in 2011– 2012 only 10 kg per month as against 12 kg for the top decile of the rural population, though the poor need more cereals as they do harder manual work and their access to more expensive fruits, vegetables, poultry, and milk is limited (Gupta 2012). From their meagre resources the poor are forced to spend more on health, children's education, transport and fuel than before. Food is still needed, but is not demanded from the market for lack of resources (Sen 2005). In the process they get undernourished. Endemic hunger continues to afflict a large proportion of the Indian population.

Extreme distress and rising capital intensity in agriculture are leading hundreds of farmers to commit suicide, a phenomenon that was unheard of even in the periods of serious drought in the early 1970s.

There are also issues at the macro-level. According to the central government's Economic Surveys, foodgrain production in India has gone down from 207 kg per annum per capita in 1990-91 to 201 kg in 2015-16. Despite reduction in the per capita production, India almost doubled its stocks in government godowns in the period 1992-2016, and in addition has been exporting on an average 7 million tonnes (MT) of cereals per annum, causing availability to decline from 510 g per day per capita in 1991 to 465 g in 2015. This has adversely affected the open market price, as also the cereal intake of the bottom 30 per cent, and has increased hunger in India. The policy regarding export of cereals should be re-visited. If basmati rice is to be exported, an equal amount of ordinary rice must be imported. It is highly unethical to export foodgrains when India's own people are suffering from starvation.

The International Food Policy Research Institute shows India suffering from alarming hunger, ranked 107 out of the 121 developing countries studied, much below Vietnam and Nepal, countries poorer than India, as shown in Table 4.3 (IFPRI 2022).

Table 4.3 Country Global Hunger Index Scores by rank

Rank	Country	1990	1995	2000	2005	2021
5	China	25.1	23.2	15.9	13.2	<5
55	Vietnam	44.6	38.8	30.3	24.6	11.9
56	Thailand	28.4	22.3	17.6	13.6	12.0
64	Sri Lanka	31.3	29.7	27.0	25.9	13.6
81	Nepal	44.5	40.3	36.9	31.6	14.1
84	Bangladesh	52.2	50.3	38.5	31.0	19.6
107	India	48.1	42.3	38.2	38.5	29.1

Source: IFPRI 2022.

Education

Thanks to massive investment by the central government, the number of teachers, classrooms and toilets has greatly improved in

India. Access has been universalized with more than 98 per cent of habitations having access to a primary school and nearly 90 per cent with access to an upper primary school. Pupil–teacher ratios have improved significantly. Against a norm of one teacher for 30 pupils, the average for all states has improved from 31 in 2010–2011 to 24 in 2014–2015 (Report of the 22nd Joint Review Mission of Sarva Shiksha Abhiyan, GOI 2016).

However, there is no corresponding improvement in the quality of learning, a task for which teachers and their supervisors need to be held accountable. According to the 71st National Sample Survey Office (NSSO) Round, about 16 per cent children in the age group 6–14 still remained out of school in 2014 and failed to complete primary education. According to the UN Human Development Report 2022 there has been considerable slowdown in the progress on 'expected years of schooling' in India, as it has grown only from 4.4 years in 2000 to 6.4 years in 2020 as against a goal of 11.7 years. High proportions of children are not completing primary schooling, and drop out because the quality of education imparted in government schools is poor and deteriorating (ASER 2022). Percentage of children in class V in government schools who can read class II level text has declined from 53 to 44 per cent between 2008 and 2018. The situation with regard to arithmetic is equally abysmal—less than 10 per cent of class III children in government schools in UP and Madhya Pradesh could do a two-digit subtraction. Just 44 per cent of class VIII students can do simple division. This strike rate in 2017 is 4 percentage points less when compared with 2012 (ASER 2018). Giving up of examinations at the elementary level has diluted attention to improving outcomes. At the same time, the proportion of children enrolled in private schools in rural India has gone up from 22 per cent in 2008 to 35 per cent in 2021. India has failed miserably in translating schooling into learning.

Health

Despite notable gains in improving life expectancy, reducing fertility, maternal and child mortality, and addressing other health priorities, the rates of improvement have been insufficient, falling short on several national and global targets. Furthermore, there are wide variations across States in their health outcomes and systems performance (NITI 2018). Poor state of health care in India is one of the reasons why economic growth has delivered much less poverty reduction in India than it has in China.

In India, the infant mortality rate (IMR) was estimated at 80 per 1,000 live births in 1990. It reached 37 by 2015, against the MDG target of 27 infant deaths per 1,000 live births. Similarly, the under five Mortality Rate has declined from 125 in 1990 to 47 in 2015 but missed the MDG target of 42. As regards Maternal Mortality Ratio, India reached the level of 140 maternal deaths by 2015, but could not achieve the target of 109 per 100,000 live births. Fewer than two-thirds of children age 12–23 months were fully immunized by 2016 (NFHS 2017). However, with the sharp decline in the recent years, the gap between the achievement and the target is narrow.

As regards vacancies, Health workforce in primary health centres (PHCs) and community health centres (CHCs)[4] presents a grim picture. For instance, in Chhattisgarh, as against 793 medical doctors sanctioned for PHCs, only 359 are in position. In CHCs, the non-availability of general physicians is an acute problem, with only 13 physicians in position, as against the 163 sanctioned (NITI 2018).

Why does India continue to have poor health indicators? There are several reasons. Rural health care in most states is marked by unfilled staff vacancies, absenteeism of doctors/health providers (see Figure 11.1 in Chapter 11), low levels of skills, shortage of medicines,[5] poor management, inadequate supervision/ monitoring and a callous attitude. There are neither rewards for service providers nor punishments for defaulters.

Inequality

Had development during 1991-2021 been inclusive, the poor and disadvantaged would have gained equally if not more from

4. A Primary Health Centre (PHC) should cover a population of 20,000 in hilly, tribal, or difficult areas and 30,000 in plain areas with 4-6 indoor/observation beds. It acts as a referral unit for 6 sub-centres and refer out cases to a Community Health Centre (CHC), which should be a 30 bedded hospital at the sub-district level. However actual facilities are much less and vary from state to state.
5. MP spends 87 per cent of its health budget on salaries leaving little for drugs, equipment, and maintenance of infrastructure (Chand 2006).

economic growth, and inequality, both regional and between social groups, would have declined. Unfortunately, government data show just the reverse trend. Rising income inequality, therefore, is because of inequality in non-income dimensions such as education, health, nutrition and sanitation (Oxfam 2018).

High growth in consumption expenditure has not been shared equally amongst all sections of the society and has been accompanied by increasing inequality. Figure 4.2 gives the Gini coefficients of monthly per capita expenditure (MPCE) in rural and urban areas.

Figure 4.2: Gini Coefficients of monthly per capita expenditure (MPCE)

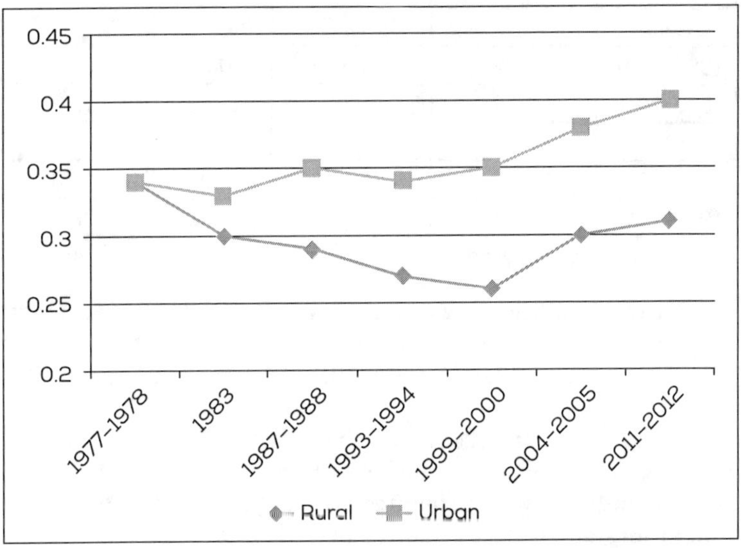

Source: Himanshu (2018)

As is clear from the chart in Figure 4.2, up to 1999–2000, rural inequality has been showing a declining trend, but urban inequality remained almost stable. However, in the last decade both have increased. Urban Gini rose from 0.35 in 1999–2000 to 0.40 in 2011–2012, whereas rural gini increased sharply from 0.26 to 0.31. Compared with the same Gini ratio of 0.34, for both rural and urban areas in 1977–1978, the gap between them rose to as high as 0.09 points in 2011–2012. Due to rising inequality, the share of poorest quintile in national consumption in India declined from 9.1 per cent in 1993–1994 to 8.5 per cent in 2009–2010. The Gini coefficient of income inequality further rose by 15 percentage points from 0.48 to 0.63 during 2013–2016.[6]

Table 4.4 confirms the above finding as the monthly per capita consumption of the top 30 per cent has been rising faster than that of the bottom 30 per cent for both rural and urban groups except for the rural group during 1983–1997, which resulted in the decline in gini coefficient for the rural population during that period.

Table 4.4 Annual growth rates of monthly per capita consumption

Period	Bottom 30%	Middle 40%	Top 30%	All Classes
Rural				
1983–1997	1.22	0.93	0.96	0.99
1993–2010	1.32	1.32	1.92	1.62
Urban				
1983–1997	1.36	1.41	2.00	1.73
1993–2010	1.71	2.25	3.32	2.77

Source: Radhakrishna (2015)

There is sufficient evidence to show that India's economic growth has accentuated the already existing interstate disparities (Dev 2016). India Today, in its issue dated 4 August 2017, compared the changes in per capita income of major states in 1960 and 2014, which showed that in 1960, the richest state Maharashtra was only twice as rich as Bihar, but in 2014, Kerala was almost five times richer than Bihar, which continued to be the poorest.[7] The inter se ranking of states had also changed in the last 54 years. West Bengal, which was a rich, industrialized state in the 1960s had slid down the ranks. Though poverty declined quite satisfactorily in West Bengal due to land reforms and spread of surface irrigation, de-industrialization between 1998–1999 and 2004–2005 reduced the number of people employed in the industrial sector. On the other hand, Kerala, which was only slightly better off than UP in terms

6. https://www.hindustantimes.com/india-news/the-proof-behind-india-s-rising-income-inequality/story-Khh2jqPaTHOFGCzuGoIc2L.html
7. http://www.indialivetoday.com/bihar-described-bimar-squalor-states-india/185133.html

of per-capita income in the 1960s, recorded impressive growth and became almost three times richer than UP by 2015.

Atul Kohli (2010) holds that the quality of state-level bureaucracy in the South has generally been superior. While this needs to be documented by further scholarly research, he adds, 'over years of field work I was repeatedly struck by a sharper sense of professionalism among state level bureaucrats, especially in Tamil Nadu, more akin to the IAS than to prevailing practices in the Hindi-heartland.'

Interstate inequality leads to social tensions, violence against immigrants, and even political instability, and this hampers the growth process. Rumblings of discontent across the tribal region in India discussed in chapter 7 suggest that the Indian government cannot afford to ignore regional and ethnic inequities.

5 Chapter

WHY IS BUREAUCRACY FAILING TO DELIVER?

Defunct legislatures

Holding bureaucracy to account for results through informed debates in the assemblies should be the main task of the State legislative assemblies. Unfortunately, in practice they rarely meet. Today, many legislative assemblies meet only for 20 to 30 days in a year. The Haryana Legislative Assembly, for example, held only 10 sessions from 2009 until March 2014, meeting for a total of 54 days—an average of 11 days per year. The assemblies for UP, Gujarat, Punjab and Uttarakhand sat for an average of 22, 31, 19 and 19 days, respectively, each year.

In the 12th Gujarat Assembly (2007–2012), over 90 per cent of all bills were passed on the same day that they were introduced. In the Budget Session of 2011, 31 bills were passed, of which 21 were introduced and passed within three sitting days. In 2012, the West Bengal Legislative Assembly passed a total of 39 bills, including appropriation bills. Most bills were passed on the same day they were introduced in the Assembly. In 2011, a total of 23 bills were passed. On average, five members participated in the discussions on each bill. Judging from the manner state assemblies function, one could conclude that India is not at all a 'deliberative democracy'. In practice, legislatures only rubber-stamp executive decisions.

Most legislators at the state level are not interested in their legislative responsibilities, but rather seek a share in the executive. Many use their back-door access to influence decisions relating to contracts and licences, as well as transfers and posting of officials, and such backseat driving affords legislators informal control over the bureaucracy, but in a way that promotes irresponsible decision-making and encourages corruption. The constitutional separation between the executive and the legislature has disappeared in India. This has resulted in erosion of internal discipline amongst civil servants.

Though the Lok Sabha (lower house of Parliament) sits for far more days than state assemblies, but on many days in the past 10 years no worthwhile discussion took place, as it had to be adjourned because of the tactics adopted by the opposition.

Let us look at some of the factors that are hindering bureaucracy to do its best on social sector programmes.

Low tax base impinges on social spending

The overall expenditure on the social sector is constrained by the low tax collection, as the Tax-to-GDP ratio in India is just about 17 per cent, as opposed to 31 per cent in South Africa, 32 per cent in Russia and 34 per cent in Brazil. This is the main factor why investment in health, education and social protection in India does not reach the level of other middle-income countries. The total expenditure (counting both plan and non-plan) by the Centre and the state governments combined as a percentage of GDP on education and health has been only around 3 and 1.2 per cent, respectively, as against the global norm of 6 and 3 per cent, respectively. Poor revenues and evasion of taxes do not permit the government to substantially enhance financial allocations for the social sector. Let us hope that the introduction of GST would result in more funds in the future for the social sector. The Government should also remove corporate loan waivers and tax exemptions, and introduce wealth and inheritance taxes.

Archaic laws and procedures

While going through the stories about Mr Naronah and Mr Ghosh in the last chapter, readers must have wondered why the stalwarts did not make any efforts to simplify government rules and only stopped at permitting their juniors to flout the rules in order to achieve the desired goal. Despite some relief due to online system of governance, the plight of average Indian citizens continues to be pathetic. They face enormous challenges in simple matters such as an electricity connection, a caste certificate, or a driving permit. These tasks can require repeated visits to unresponsive government offices, payment of bribes, connections in the government to unblock obstacles, or a combination of all of these. Average Indian citizens have many avenues for recourse in theory, but they know well the futility of trying to use them. The problems are magnified even more for the poor and the weaker sections of the society (Sud 2010).

The maze of laws, organizations and practices that confront the ordinary citizen in his or her dealings with government makes it very difficult to pin responsibility on the individual government servant or blame him when things go wrong. Deregulation has made almost no impact at the state level. The systems of buying and selling land, getting a ration card or your security back, and Rent Control Acts, all need a thorough revision. Unfortunately, the state-level bureaucracy has made no effort to simplify these laws and procedures. One can set up an industry worth billions of Rupees in India without any licence today, but a farmer can neither set up a brick kiln unit, nor a rice shelling plant, and not even cut a tree standing on his own private field without bribing several officials. Women were prosecuted in Odisha in 1995 for keeping brooms in their homes! This story is described in detail in Chapter 9 on corruption.

Delhi has about 0.6 million rickshaw pullers, but the city government has put a limit of 99,000 on licences to pull rickshaws. Thus, about half a million rickshaws operate illegally in Delhi. Ironically, there is no limit to the number of polluting motor cars, whereas the non-polluting, eco-friendly and cost-efficient transport providing livelihood to the poor has a ridiculously low ceiling! Many rickshaw pullers sleep at their stands and public spaces because they cannot afford to rent a shared room even in the slums.

According to the Ministry of Housing and Urban Poverty Alleviation, there are 10 million street vendors in India, with Mumbai accounting for 250,000, Delhi has 450,000, Kolkata, more than 150,000, and Ahmedabad, 100,000. Most of them are immigrants or laid-off workers, work for an average 10 to 12 hours a day and remain impoverished. Though the prevalent licence-permit raj in Indian bureaucracy ended for most retailing in the 1990s, it continues in this trade. Inappropriate licence ceiling in most cities, such as Mumbai, which has a ceiling of 14,000 licences, means more vendors hawk their goods illegally, which also makes them prone to the bribery and extortion culture under local police and municipal authorities, besides harassment, heavy fines and sudden evictions.

GOI has formulated a National Policy on Urban Street Vendors in 2009 that clearly recognizes that street vendors form a very important segment of the unorganized sector in the country. This was followed by the Street Vendors (Protection of Livelihood and Regulation of Street Vending) Act, 2014, in March 2014. However, in most cities the Policy or the Act is yet to be implemented.

As Food Secretary of UP in 1982, I had taken a proposal to the Cabinet to do away with Rent Control Act on shops and commercial establishments, and allow the rent to be determined by market forces. However, it was rejected, and I recall a Minister openly saying in the Cabinet meeting that such proposals hit at their patronage and hold over businessmen and, therefore, cannot be accepted.

However, I did remove price control on coal in UP (see chapter 3), as it did not involve seeking approval from the politicians. Within a week of my taking over as Food Secretary in UP in 1981, I removed price control on wheat products, such as maida and suji, giving considerable relief to the Roller flourmills. The economic philosophy that I followed throughout my career was 'socialism for the poor and free market for the rich'. The political and administrative system in India, on the other hand, seems to be believing in 'indifference to the poor, and controls over the rich to facilitate rent seeking!'

The controls and restrictions, imposed under the Essential Commodities Act, are disincentives to the production and distribution of essential commodities. These have led to a situation where the trading class has to operate at very high margins so as to provide the maximum benefits being reaped by the inspectors. With the increased agricultural production in essential commodities, it is recommended that all agricultural produce and its products should be deleted from the definition of 'essential commodities' of Section 2(a) of the Essential Commodities Act, and all Control Orders relating to or affecting agricultural produce/products should be rescinded. This would reduce the influence of various inspectors and their discretionary activities.

The non-farm sector in India has immense potential to generate new jobs with relatively low direct investments. However its expansion depends upon a number of factors, which are influenced by government policies—directly or indirectly. Unfortunately, deregulation introduced after 1991 has not touched the rural or the small informal sector, and has largely been confined to the modern manufacturing sector. For instance, marketing of agricultural products is hampered by various regulations passed under the Essential Commodities Act and the Mandi Acts. All perishable agricultural produce should be removed from the aegis of the APMC Acts. Famers must be given freedom to sell directly to food processing companies, aggregators and retailers in addition to selling in mandis. The controls and restrictions, imposed under these laws, are disincentives to the production and distribution of essential commodities. Such controls should be re-examined so as to promote the growth of small and cottage industries.

It is a sad commentary on our laws that the informal sector, which provides maximum employment, is mostly declared as illegal and subject to the whims of law enforcing agencies. A Committee should be set up to identify specific laws and rules which hamper entrepreneurship. A systematic review needs to be undertaken to review the areas in which government must withdraw, albeit in a phased manner, and departments which need to be wound up.

Outdated 19th century land laws

Transactions in agricultural land are subject to several cumbersome and antiquated laws. Changing such laws needs initiatives from IAS officers working as Revenue Secretaries in the states. In almost all states except Punjab, Haryana, Assam, Andhra Pradesh (but not Telangana) and Tamil Nadu, there are tenancy laws that do not permit land being leased to tenants for agriculture. Maharashtra goes a step further and bans sale of agricultural land to a non-agriculturist. One recalls some years back when Amitabh

Bachchan wanted to buy agricultural land in Maharashtra, he could not do so. He had to say that he is a landowner in Barabanki in UP, because according to the laws in Maharashtra, only agriculturists can buy agricultural land. This means if the industry wants to buy agricultural land, it is not possible. Such restrictions retard industrialization, encourage speed money, and therefore must be changed.

There are restrictions that agricultural land cannot be used for industrial purposes, unless written permission is taken from a designated authority, which is time-consuming and promotes corruption. Often, politicians and land mafia operate as middlemen to facilitate getting the required permission from the government for the change in landuse. Both these laws need to go. We have liberalized the capital markets, but not the land and labour markets.

A ban on leasing was imposed after Independence in many states to encourage owner cultivation and to give security of tenure to sharecroppers and tenants. Although such laws should continue in tribal areas where agricultural markets are not well developed, in other states where the mode of production has become capitalist, there is a need to liberalize and free leasing-in of land from all government controls.

Studies show that the lease market facilitates a shift of control of land to smallholders and tenants. Big owners are found to lease out and the resultant distribution of operational area is less uneven than the ownership pattern. Thus, the lease market enables the landless to gain access to land that, in turn, enhances employment opportunities since poor farmers tend to saturate their land with inputs of labour. In areas experiencing technological change and high growth, marginal farmers may also gain by leasing out their area and taking up non-farm employment, while still retaining ownership and the right to resume their control over the land after the lease period. Nearly 20 years back, as Rural Development Secretary, GOI, I requested the states to repeal such laws and permit leasing of land. The experience of Punjab and Haryana shows that free leasing has not brought back landlordism in a new garb, as was the fear that led to stricter control on tenancy. The states, however, did not heed to my advice. Recently, the NITI Aayog has also come out with similar suggestions.

The second issue of freeing from all controls conversion of land-use for industrial purposes should also be addressed. Industry serves a social purpose since employment generation per unit of land is higher in non-agricultural uses than in agriculture, and therefore change of landuse should be free from all hassles. For instance, a 4,000 MW thermal plant may displace about 250 households but would create tens of thousands of new jobs by providing power to small industry, and to tubewells that would increase both gross cropped area and productivity. At present, the share of urban dwellers in the total population of India is 36 per cent, but they occupy only 6 per cent of the total area of the country. Growth through industrialization and urbanization would not only increase labour productivity but will reduce pressure on farm land by pulling people away from land to non-farming occupations.

The argument that this would lead to food scarcity is bogus. During 2009–2014, 60 MT of food grain was rotting in government godowns or was being eaten by rats while another 10 MT of our grain that is exported is being fed to cattle in the United States and Europe. So we have more than enough food; if need be, exports can be reduced and internal offtake improved. Thus we can afford to change the landuse of our lands from farm to non-farm to meet the requirement of the industry. Of course, in handing over land to industry, priority should be given to wastelands and mono-cropped lands rather than fertile lands.

Besides, should not the farmer decide whether he should grow food or not? If he is getting a lifelong opportunity of earning from land in some other way, why should anyone prevent that? There is no scarcity of land in this country. What is contentious is the issue of passing over ownership of land, and who determines landuse.

Lastly, in many states such as UP and Delhi, a marginal farmer cannot sell his land even to agriculturists; he has to follow a number of subterfuges in order to benefit from growing prices of land. These cumbersome state laws on land stand in the way of faster industrialization and urbanization, and thus affect employment generation.

So even though the worst of the 'licence Raj' has been dismantled since the early 1990s, the 'Babu Raj' at the state level remains as oppressive as ever.

New land acquisition law 2013 not industry friendly!

The GOI law on land acquisition enacted in 2013 that I criticized in my article in the Indian Express (given in chapter 10) has some good features, such as high compensation and consent clause, but it has many negative clauses. As member of the NAC, I tried to convince Jairam Ramesh, Minister for Land Resources, to simplify the law, but he did not listen. Jairam's intention was not to simplify the law, but make it almost impossible for land to be acquired for industry through legislation. He wanted all private parties to buy land from farmers through open market, 'willing buyer, willing seller' transactions, not realizing that large corporations and big builders rarely get into the messy business of buying land. They leave that task to 'brokers', who are mostly low-level politicians and thugs good at bribing people and threatening landowners (Gupta 2017).

Interestingly, a Parliamentary Committee headed by Sumitra Mahajan of the BJP in 2012 also took a similar impractical stand and recommended[1] that no acquisition should be done for private companies, and they should be forced to buy the entire land directly from landowners in the open market. This recommendation may help farmers of the developed regions who are aware of the market conditions, but may result in large-scale cheating and deception in tribal and remote areas where antisocial elements will be hired by the land mafia, and tribals will be forced to sign land transfer deeds. In any case, in many central Indian states, tribal land cannot be sold to non-tribals through market transactions. To get possession over such lands, the industry would have to use extra-legal methods of showing sale in the name of some non-existent or compliant tribal. It may also legalize transfer of land that originally belonged to tribals, but is now alienated from them, and has not been restored back to them despite laws to the contrary. Moreover, land records are hopelessly out of date in many states, which will delay private transfer of land. Often, land is cultivated by the poor, especially tribals, but their possession and ownership has not been recorded in the official documents. Such people would be compelled to give up their possession without any compensation.

1. Mani Shankar Aiyar, a leftist Congressman is said to have drafted this report

Further, land purchased under 'lawful contract' will not carry the responsibilities of R&R, which will deprive benefits that are proposed under the new Act to the landless livelihood losers. Besides, even in developed areas where farmers are aware of markets, it is seen that small farmers are the first ones to sell to a buyer as they need immediate cash to meet other pressing exigencies, and large farmers who delay their sale are able to get a higher price, often several times what was paid to the small farmers. Pranab Bardhan, an eminent economist, has also supported (Bardhan 2015) the principle of eminent domain, as in many cases the state must get involved in acquiring land even for private parties, and rehabilitate those whose land is not acquired, such as tenants and landless workers.

Whenever land acquired by the government is transferred to an individual or a company for a consideration, a part of the appreciated value should be given to the original landowner. However, Section 102 of the Act completely defeats the intention behind the idea of sharing capital gains with the landowner, as payment would be made only when no development has taken place on such land. The builder can plant one tree on that land and get away by not paying any capital gains to the original landowner! Moreover, such benefit shall accrue only on the first sale, and not on subsequent transactions. It should have been made applicable for all transactions for at least twenty years.

In many ways, the new Central Land Acquisition Law has remained a non-starter and has forced many states to enact their own state-specific laws, which are not very sympathetic to the poor.

Dilatory Budgetary Procedures

GOI Ministries transfer more than six lakh crore Rupees every year to the states. Evidence suggests that many state governments, especially the poor ones, are neither able to draw their entitled funds from GOI, nor are able to release these to the districts/villages in time, with the result that GOI is often constrained to divert the unclaimed funds to better performing states. The reason for poor performance by Bihar, Orissa, UP and MP is often due to the widespread shortage of staff at all levels (discussed later) that adversely affects implementation and supervision of programmes.

Similarly, some ministries such as the Ministry of Human Resource Development, Women and Child Development, and Tribal Affairs, are unable to spend even the meagre funds that are allotted to them. For RMSA (Rashtriya Madhyamik Shiksha Abhiyan, a programme for secondary education, in (FY) 2015–16 only 39 per cent of the approved budget was spent. This decreased further to 36 per cent in FY 2016–17. There was a marginal improvement in FY 2017–18, with 46 per cent of the approved budget being spent (AI 2019a). Non-receipt of adequate number of complete proposals in accordance with the scheme guidelines from the State governments, non-receipt of utilization certificates, and lack of physical progress by State governments, non-filling of vacant posts, austerity measures, non- receipts of bills from the suppliers, etc. have been cited by the Tribal Affairs ministry as the reasons for the surrender of funds.

The Pradhan Mantri Matru Vandana Yojana (PMMVY), is a maternity benefit scheme providing conditional cash transfers to pregnant women and lactating mothers for the first live birth. On 31 December 2016, the Prime Minster announced the pan-India implementation of this programme. While the eligible population is estimated at 130.1 lakh, only 20 per cent of the beneficiaries could be enrolled in FY 2017–18 and 27 per cent in FY 2018–19 till 10 December 2018. The percentage of beneficiaries enrolled out of the estimated number of beneficiaries also differed significantly across states. While Himachal Pradesh, Madhya Pradesh and Kerala enrolled more than 45 per cent of the estimated number of beneficiaries, West Bengal, Assam, Tamil Nadu, Odisha, and Telangana enrolled less than 10 per cent (AI 2019b).

An evaluation of Integrated Child Development Services (ICDS) in Bihar in 2007 by Unicef showed that only fewer than 10 per cent of grassroot workers received honorarium regularly, most received it only twice in a year rather than monthly (UNICEF 2007). Although the overall picture of utilization of CSS funds in Bihar has considerably improved, it is still dismal in NREGA because of shortage of technical staff at the block and village level (see Figure 6.1 in Chapter 6).

Another study by UNICEF showed that only 18 per cent of officials in Jharkhand working at the grassroots level are paid their salaries in time. In FY 2014–15, Jharkhand spent only 40 per cent of its total approved budget of the National Health Mission (NHM), down from 61 per cent in FY 2013–14 (AI 2016). Similarly, in Sarva Shiksha Abhiyan (SSA), a programme for promoting elementary education, there are significant variations in the proportion of funds spent out of available funds by states (CPR 2018). In FY 2015–16, Tamil Nadu, Uttarakhand and Rajasthan spent 99 per cent, 96 per cent and 92 per cent of SSA funds available to them, respectively. The Utilization, however, was low in Odisha (59 per cent) and Jharkhand (53 per cent).

GOI's own studies show that even electronic transfer takes months with the result that in Mid Day Meals programme, ground staff such as cooks and helpers are not paid for months, the Food Corporation of India withholds supply of grain, and mid-day meals are served only for 60-70 per cent working days in some states. Similar delays take place in supply of text-books in SSA, filling up of vacancies, especially in the remote and tribal areas, capital works, funds for maintenance, etc.

The Aide Memoire to the Twenty-Second Joint Review Mission on SSA in 2015 had the following remarks on utilization of funds:

> "Delays often occur in release of funds for SSA at various levels. For example, in Arunachal Pradesh, payment of salary of teachers is made every two or three months instead of every month. In Maharashtra, payment for textbooks has not been made for over five months and district offices are borrowing funds from local bodies to pay teachers' salaries. The delay in flow of funds is primarily due to two main causes: (a) documentation required for releases by the GOI; and (b) ways and means position of States. The existing manual accounting system at sub-district level (particularly in schools) with only a cashbook, cannot provide annual accounts in prescribed format in time. This leads to delay by the States in submitting prescribed documents to MHRD for releases.
>
> "There is also delay in release of State share. The delay may be seen in the perspective of thin State resources,

> with grants released in September being 50 per cent of the annual grant. Some States may find it difficult to release their share of six months in one instalment. This situation is particularly serious for the North-East States, which receive 90 per cent grants for SSA, as their own budget largely depends on devolution of resources from the GOI. (GOI 2015)

Funds allocated to the departments in the State budgets are not released during the year in an orderly manner and that far too many references have to be made to the Finance Department (FD) for prior approval for release of funds on ways and means considerations. The same is found to be true in respect of release of funds to zila panchayats. Large funds are released at the end of the financial year, resulting in many irregularities in booking the expenditure.

It is also observed that the contractual staff in centrally sponsored schemes, such as SSA, ICDS and NHM do not receive their emoluments regularly. For instance, 39 per cent of contract teachers received their monthly salaries with a delay of three months and more (Table 5.1).

Table 5.1 Delay in transferring monthly salaries for contract teachers (2015-16)

Type	Mean Salary	Delay in months				
		No Delay (%)	1 (%)	2 (%)	3 (%)	4 or more (%)
Head Master	43,034	94	3	2	1	1
Regular	35,797	96	2	1	0	0
Contract and Others	12,590	23	13	21	39	4

Source: AI 2015

Empirical studies are needed to suggest what changes are needed in financial procedures at the state level so that utilization of funds improves, timely payments are made to the staff and utilization reports are sent to GOI in time without delay. In addition, there are several schemes implemented by the states themselves using their own funds for different development related purposes. As evidence suggest, these schemes also face the same challenges of poor and weak implementation due to capacity constraints and delays in fund transfers from state to district and lower levels of implementation.

Release of budget is neither certain nor timely. The budget cycle is too short for full utilization of funds for capital works. Expenditure budget should be valid for two to five years, so that capital expenditure can be completed without surrender of funds. Similarly, for centrally sponsored schemes, approval of the State legislature should not be necessary every year for using central funds that are transferred to the State consolidated fund for continuing schemes. In Singapore, expenditure budget is valid for five years, and departments are free to exceed or delay their annual allocation without any reference to Parliament. The need to reform financial procedures is more urgent now because of the changes in the pattern of fund flow from GOI since March 2014, as central funds are no longer passed on to state societies and agencies as before.

The Poor States lack Manpower for Better Delivery

Insufficient revenues with the poorer states result not only in weak infrastructure, such as schools without buildings and deficient power generation, but also in an inadequate number of government staff. This, in turn, affects these states' capacity to draw tied plan funds from GOI Ministries or submit utilization certificates in time. Thus, shortage of staff results in weak governance that further limits their access to GOI resources, each factor being the cause as well as the effect of the other, resulting in a vicious cycle.

Several facts about the structure of government employment in India need to be noted. First, the total number of government staff, including central and state governments, public sector undertakings (PSUs) and local bodies, is about 1.2 per cent of the population, as against the global average of more than 3 per cent. On a per capita basis, India's total civilian employment is less than half the average for Asia and less than one-sixth the average for Organisation for Economic Co-operation and Development (OECD) countries. Figures for some of the countries are shown in Table 5.2.

Table 5.2 Civil service staffing per 100 population in selected countries	
India	1.2
Sri Lanka	4.5
China	2.8
Malaysia	4.5
United Kingdom	7.0
United States	7.1

Source: World Bank (2003)[2]

Second, the number has been going down over the years as Table 5.3 shows.[3]

Table 5.3 Total government employment ('000)

Year	Central Govt	State Govt	Quasi-Govt		Local Bodies	Grand total
			Central	State		
2000–2001	3,261	7,425	3,291	2,901	2,261	19,138
2011–2012	2,520	7,184	3,449	2,349	2,107	17,609

Third, there are too many government servants in the support positions, such as clerks, orderlies and drivers, who are now not needed, and too few people in the line positions, such as teachers, nurses and policemen, who can deliver public services. To some extent, CSS have tried to make amends for such shortage by permitting states to appoint contractual staff at lower salaries. Their number, not shown in Table 5.3, is not readily available, though it could be almost a quarter of the total number of regular state government employees. A World Bank report (Beschel 2003) described the situation as follows:

2. According to another study (Sukhtankar and Vaishnav 2015), this number is 1.4 for India, 5.4 for China and 7.3 for the United States and Germany. Yet, even with this low base, a quarter of police vacancies across the country are unfilled. For certain states, the vacancy rate veers on the alarming: UP, for example, which faces serious law and order difficulties, has nearly 60 per cent of its police posts unfilled.
3. Data in Tables 5.3, 5.6, 5.7 and Figure 5.1 are taken from mospi.nic.in/sites/default/files/statistical_year_ book_india_2015/Table-32.1.XLS.

> A given section officer (the lowest working level officer in the secretariat) can have from 5 to 10 assistants, consisting of upper division clerks, lower division clerks, and peons. Many are being made redundant through advances in information technology, yet continue to draw their salaries. Ironically, this excessive logistical tail often exists alongside significant shortages of staff with skills in information technology, financial management, and policy analysis. In many states, there is also often a dearth of staff in critical front-line positions such as primary school teachers, police, and rural health workers—yet differing cadre rules and the tradition of a 'job for life' can make it very difficult to let go of staff or to transfer them from surplus areas into those where there is more demand.

Singapore also had 67 per cent Group C&D staff in 1970, but by 2008 it was reduced to just 20 per cent, whereas the share of Group A staff increased from 5 to 52 per cent (see Table 5.4; Saxena 2011a).

Efforts should, therefore, be made to identify surplus support staff set up an effective re-deployment plan, and devise a liberal system for exit. There should be incentives for clerks and class IV staff to become teachers and constables.

Fourth, salaries of regular government staff as a multiple of per capita income is highest in India when compared with other countries, as shown in Table 5.5.

Table 5.4 Civil service strength by divisional status 1970–2008 (as a percentage of the total)

Group	Singapore		India (Central Government Only)
	1970	2008	
A	5.3	52.1	3
B	27.3	28.2	8
C	29.7	14.1	63
D	37.7	5.6	26
Total	**54,195**	**67,814**	**2.5 million**

Source: Saxena (2011a)

Table 5.5 Average government wage as multiple of per capita GDP	
Region	**Multiple**
Africa	5.7
Asia	3.0
Eastern Europe and Central Asia	1.3
Latin American Countries	2.5
Middle East and North Africa	3.4
OECD[4]	**1.6**
India	7.2
Overall	**3.0**

Source: World Bank (2003)

On a visit to Vietnam in May 2015, I learnt that a teacher for elementary schools gets about $100 per month (₹6,300 per month), whereas in India the gross salary for a regular teacher is more than ₹30,000. Pay increases in India are not intended to serve as a reward for increased productivity, but are given instead to gain support from the unions and to eliminate the threat of labour unrest. Moreover, government servants manage election booths, and no political party can afford its collective anger.

Lastly, it is instructive to look at the interstate availability of regular government employees. Table 5.6 compares the situation in Bihar with undivided Andhra Pradesh, two states with comparable population.

Table 5.6 Number of government servants ('000)		
	Andhra Pradesh	**Bihar**
Central government	185	95
State government	396	200
Quasi-government (central/State PSUs)	176	47
Local Bodies	281	37
Total	1,038	379

4. The Organisation for Economic Co-operation and Development, 34 richest countries are members of this group.

Table 5.7 Number of state government employees

	Tamil Nadu	Bihar
Population 2011 (crore)	7.2	10.4
Total number of state government servants (lakh)	10.41	2.84
Number of government servants per 1,000 population	14.4	2.7

Table 5.7 compares the number of state government employees (including state PSUs and local bodies) in Bihar with Tamil Nadu.

Table 5.7 Number of state government employees

	Tamil Nadu	Bihar
Population 2011 (crores)	7.2	10.4
Total number of state Govt. servants (lakhs)	10.41	2.84
No of govt servants per 1000 population	14.4	2.7

Thus, as compared with the global average of more than 30, Bihar has only 2.4 employees per thousand population. No wonder all schemes are in disarray there! State-wise position is given in Figure 5.1.

With limited revenues it is just not possible to increase staff in social sector programmes on a regular basis, and therefore there is no escape from hiring ill-paid contractual employees, leading to a bizarre situation that a para teacher gets far less than a regular peon or driver. The control over social sector flagship programmes in the coming years is likely to be transferred to the states, where politicians would find demand from contractual employees to be regularized difficult to resist. The extra fiscal burden due to regularization would mean that further expansion of line staff would be halted at the cost of satisfactory delivery of social sector programmes. Budget cuts on non-wage component (medicines, textbooks, repair of buildings) have already reduced efficiency in delivery for many programmes.

Figure 5.1 Number of state government employees per 1,000 population

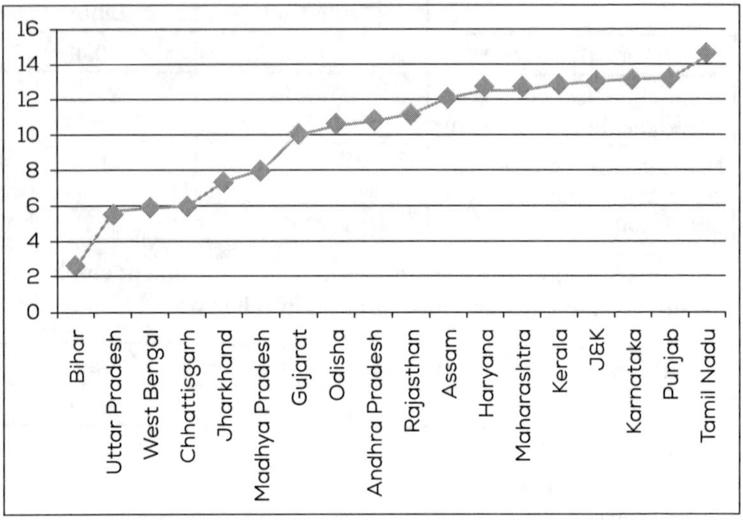

To sum up, India is awfully short of government servants when compared with the world average—it is 1.2 per cent of the population in India, whereas in East Europe it is 6 per cent, and in Asia it is 3 per cent. The skill mix is also wrong in our country. We have too many orderlies, clerks, drivers and peons, who are not needed now, but we are very short of doctors, nurses, teachers and even policemen. So, people who are needed in the line positions are missing while people who are not needed in support positions are too many. Therefore, support functionaries need to be reduced and line functionaries need to be increased.

Recent Political Initiatives in Some States[5]

There has been a growing realization amongst some CMs on the need to improve governance, and some have been able to translate this into concrete action. Their calculation is that improving programme delivery may overcome anti-incumbency and lead to electoral victories, as in Gujarat, Bihar, Chhattisgarh, Odisha and Madhya Pradesh. This would necessarily involve keeping the

5. This section is based on the author's previous papers such as Saxena (2010, 2016a).

MLAs and Ministers under check, which is difficult when the state is under a coalition regime, or the ruling party is constrained by a thin margin in the Assembly, or is divided into factions. The reformist CM is often at odds within his own party officials who hate getting sidelined in the process of establishing rule-based policy procedures. In some other states, even CMs seem to be averse to professionalizing administration. But some CMs (and their number is increasing) are able to drive policies that are much more coherent and cohesive than typically what has been seen in the past. In order to improve delivery they seem to be centralizing power within the CM's office.[6] Having a clear majority in the legislative assembly has helped such CMs to focus on outcomes.

For instance, Bihar, which was lagging behind earlier, is improving at a tremendous pace. The share of per capita income in Bihar in the All -India average rose from 33 per cent in 2004–05 to 42 per cent in 2013–14. During the last 15 years, due to superlative growth in the road construction and power sector, the economy has grown at an annual rate of more than 10 per cent; but agriculture, the bedrock of Bihar's economy on which a large majority of households depend, has performed poorly. Bihar is discussed in detail in chapter 8. On the other hand, in Jharkhand, which is amongst the poorest performing states of India today, political instability and inability of the coalition to work together over a long period led to its poor performance.

Similarly, Madhya Pradesh concentrated on utilizing the irrigation potential already created in major, medium and minor irrigation projects through improving governance, whereas AP and Maharashtra made massive new irrigation investments, which created rent-seeking opportunities, but did not result in increasing the irrigated area. Production of wheat in Madhya Pradesh increased from 3.2 MT in 1990–91 to 22.4 MT in 2021-22. Percentage share of Madhya Pradesh in all-India wheat production increased from 6 per cent in 1990–1991 to 22 per cent in 2021-22, showing one of the best growth rates amongst all Indian states. Gross state domestic product growth in Madhya Pradesh during 2013 and 2017 was 8.1 per cent, as against the all-India average of 6.9 per cent.

6. Among bureaucrats, this is often referred to as the 'Gujarat model'.

Public Distribution System in Chhattisgarh

A survey of PDS in Chhattisgarh revealed that 88 per cent of the respondents were satisfied with the functioning of their ration shops and were getting their foodgrains regularly at the correct prices. Government has shifted the management of ration shops from private dealers to community-based organisations such as gram panchayats, self-help groups (SHGs) and cooperatives. To reduce leakages, the government decided to dispense with private players and directly deliver foodgrains to ration shops in government trucks painted yellow. Transition from a targeted to a 'quasi-universal' PDS, one that covers approximately 80 per cent of the state's rural population not only helped in improving the functioning of the PDS by giving a majority of the people in villages a stake in their local ration shop, but also reduced exclusion errors that occurred due to the faulty targeting system used by the central government. The other steps are: increasing the commission paid to ration shop owners from Rs 8 to Rs 30 per quintal of rice, procuring more foodgrains from farmers in the state to encourage them to raise outputs, making electronic weighing scales mandatory in all ration shops, and conducting verification drives to identify and cancel bogus ration cards (Puri 2012).

When I complimented the Chief Secretary on the grand success of PDS in his state, he said that departments in Chhattisgarh have been divided in two categories: 'vote kaa vibhag' and 'note kaa vibhag'. Whereas PDS and NREGA are in the first category, mineral development is in the second category, providing revenues for both, welfare programmes and 'under the table' resources to the ruling party!

Governance Issues

Addressing governance issues will need a shift in the way India prioritizes for social sector and focus on cross-cutting systemic issues such as monitoring and evaluation (M&E) of programmes, personnel and administrative reforms and accountability. Actions are needed along several critical areas, and these can be incentivized by GOI without expecting revolutionary changes in the nature of State-level politics to emerge and precede governance reforms. These issues are discussed in detail in Chapter 11.

6 Chapter

ARE BUREAUCRATS GOOD AT DESIGNING PROGRAMMES?

As pointed out in the previous chapter, India spends far too little on social sector programmes such as education and health, which improve people's livelihoods and capacity in the long run. On the other hand, expenditure on safety net programmes that provide immediate benefits, such as NREGA, PDS and supplementary nutrition, is quite significant, presumably because of perceived political benefits. The distinction between the two sets of programmes is like the proverbial saying 'training someone how to catch a fish versus handing him over the fish to eat'. While the objectives of the welfare programmes are commendable, as addressing extreme poverty needs both instant help and long -term improvement in their capacity, the end results of these programmes are not satisfactory, leading to a lot of criticism that the government is wasting scarce public resources for political ends. On the other hand, the left believes that these safety net policies are good and helpful to the poor, but its implementation is weak, and hence all that is needed is to improve governance at the state and district levels so that the intention of these policies is fully realized.

We take a somewhat different position between the two schools of thought. If programmes such as ICDS, NREGA and PDS are not doing well, it is not only because of the weak capacity of the delivery machinery, especially in poorer states, but often the design of these schemes is flawed and needs to be amended if benefits are to reach the poor. When a scheme is badly designed (in addition to ICDS, NREGA, PDS, even housing for urban poor and rural sanitation have design flaws), it fails to achieve results even in those states that are considered to be relatively well governed. On the other hand, when a programme is well designed, adequately funded and frequently evaluated (such as the Pradhan Mantri Gram Sadak Yojana [PMGSY], NHM and MDM), it does well even in the so-called BIMAROU or backward states. Even when programmes such as ICDS and NREGA are not doing well, the GOI cannot (and should not) reduce outlays for such programmes, it should improve outcomes by making improvements in the design of such programmes (where the role of concerned Ministries and Niti Aayog is vital) by comparing programmes of similar nature, such as MDM versus supplementary nutrition in ICDS, PMGSY versus NREGA and rural housing versus urban housing, and study why one does well and the other does not.

We discuss below how the design flaws in some of the important programmes can be corrected to achieve better results. The primary responsibility of initiating correction in the design of such faltering programmes is that of the IAS Joint Secretaries posted in the central Government Ministries and Niti Aayog.

ICDS

Discourage the distribution of manufactured 'ready-to-eat' food - The ICDS has not yet succeeded in making a significant dent in reducing child malnutrition, as the programme has placed priority on food supplementation rather than on nutrition and health education interventions, and targets children mostly after the age of three when malnutrition has already set in. Very little of the ICDS resources, in terms of funds and staff time, are spent on the under-three child, and this low priority must be reversed.

The focus of the ICDS programme should be on components that directly address the most important causes of under-nutrition in India, specifically improving mothers' feeding and caring behaviour, improving household water and sanitation, strengthening referrals to the health system and providing micronutrients. The basic nature of the programme should be changed from centre-based to outreach-based, as the child under three cannot walk to the centre and has to be reached at his/her home. Another advantage of visiting homes is that the entire family, not just the mothers, are sensitized and counselled. As the Anganwadi worker is too busy with pre-school teaching of theolder age group of children who are three to six years old, she has no time to visit homes.

Ready-to-eat food (RTF) prepared in industrial establishments under the supplementary nutrition programme of the ICDS does not reach the intended beneficiaries (six months to two-yearold children) even in the better governed states such as Gujarat, Maharashtra and Karnataka, whereas the MDM programme is able to provide hot cooked meals every working day to at least 80 per cent children even in states such as UP, Jharkhand and Odisha, where administrative capacity for delivery is considered constrained.

There are large-scale irregularities in the supply of Supplementary Nutrition by the engagement of contractors in ICDS in many states, such as Maharashtra, Karnataka, UP and Gujarat. Eighty-eight per cent of children under three years of age in Maharashtra were not consuming THR (Take Home Ration), 78 per cent opted to feed it to cattle and other domestic animals (Shukla and Marathe 2017). Despite Supreme Court orders, THR packets continue to be manufactured and distributed across Maharashtra by selected companies operating under the guise of 'women's organizations'. A study by the National Human Rights Commission showed that despite Supreme Court orders to provide hot cooked meals, all centres in UP supplied packaged RTF (ready-to-eat food), containing only 100 calories, as against a norm of 500 calories, and 63 per cent of food and funds were misappropriated.[1] Food being unpalatable ends up as cattle feed (LANSA 2017). People have started calling it 'Pashu Ahaar' rather than 'Paushtik Ahaar'.

Interestingly, when I sent this study to the concerned officer in UP to take action, he rang back to say that he was helpless because of high-level corruption at the political level in the centralized procurement system.

In addition to Ministerial-level corruption, even the AWWs are deeply involved in malpractices and share ₹2,000 per centre

1. http://nhrc.nic.in/Reports/misc/SKTiwari_Gorakhpur.pdf

every month with their supervisors routinely. The RTF is produced in poor hygiene conditions. Some of the ingredients shown on the bags containing the finished product were not found in stock at the time of visit and the stock of maize was only enough to meet 25 per cent of the daily requirement. A comprehensive evaluation of ICDS (Planning Commission 2011) concluded that despite the fact that the outlay for ICDS was increased from ₹121 billion in the Tenth Plan (2002–2007) to ₹444 billion in the Eleventh Plan (2007–2012), the outcomes were most disappointing. Only 19 per cent of the mothers reported that the AWC provides nutrition counselling to parents. More than 40 per cent of the funds meant for supplementary nutrition (SN) are siphoned off; for FY 2008–2009 the amount of SN allocation diverted is estimated at ₹29 billion. Although 81 per cent of children below six years of age were living in an area covered by the Anganwadi centres, only 31 per cent children received SN and only 12 per cent children received it regularly. Only 38 per cent of pregnant women and lactating mothers and 10 per cent of adolescent girls received supplementary nutrition.

Comptroller and Auditor General of India's (CAG) performance audit[2] in 2013 revealed how ICDS was failing to help infants and young children. The audit, covering the period 2006–2007 to 2010–2011, found that 52 per cent of anganwadis surveyed lack toilets, and 32 per cent do not have drinking water. Around 61 per cent anganwadis did not have their own buildings and 25 per cent were functioning from semi-pucca or open or partially covered spaces. Medicine kits are not available in 33 to 49 per cent of anganwadis. The audit also revealed 33 to 45 per cent gap between eligible beneficiaries and actual recipients of SN. CAG noted distribution of substandard food by the AWCs as 'ready to cook mixes' were unpalatable. The Audit found that some of these items had sticky texture, which became inedible within minutes of preparation. The Audit further found that there was no system of watching the expiry of food items.

Therefore, even for this younger age group, hot cooked meals appropriate to their age prepared at the Anganwadi centre

2. http://articles.timesofindia.indiatimes.com/2013-03-06/india/37499356_1_cag-audit-icds-malnourished-children and http://zeenews.india.com/news/nation/substandard-food-being-distributed-by-anganwadis_834305.html(accessed on 7 July 2014)

should be given. If there is no such arrangement (for lack of space or infrastructure), it is better to give cash to the mother till the time infrastructure is created, rather than involve contractors in supplying packaged meal or RTF, which leads to huge corruption at the state level.

Non-functional child care system in urban India: ICDS runs very poorly in urban slum areas because of the lack of space for the setting up of Centres. In urban slums, the problems of appallingly low rent allocations (₹1,000 per month for Delhi, for instance) for hiring spaces and non-availability of government buildings need to be addressed urgently to fill the gap in universalizing services for slum populations. In the short term, temporary structures can be put up to provide toilets in those slums where due to either legal issues or space constraints, it is not possible to put up permanent structures.

NREGA

Pre-fixing state-wise allocations is more equitable: NREGA follows a 'free-for-all' strategy in the interstate allocation of funds with the result that better -governed states corner most of the funds irrespective of a low incidence of poverty in those states. On the other hand, PMGSY fixes state-wise allocations based on predetermined gaps in infrastructure, and funds are released accordingly, thus benefit- ting states with poorer infrastructure more. For instance, in 2017–2018, the government spent `12,312 under NREGA on each rural poor in Kerala—the least poor state in India—as against a paltry `918 in Bihar and 943 in UP! The number of rural poor in Bihar is six times similar number in Tamil Nadu, but expenditure on NREGA in Tamil Nadu in 2017–2018 was three times that in Bihar (see Figure 6.1). The combined share of Bihar, Jharkhand, Odisha, Madhya Pradesh and UP in the total expenditure in NREGA was only 25 per cent in 2015–2016, but it was 60 per cent in PMGSY.

The Ministry needs to earmark NREGA funds for states, on the basis of poverty, just as PMGSY allocations are in proportion to the state-wise shortage of rural roads. The 'Free-for-all' approach punishes poorer states as they are not able to compete with better -governed states in attracting funds from the GOI (Saxena 2016a).

Figure 6.1: Wage Expenditure in Rupees per rural poor in NREGA 2017-18

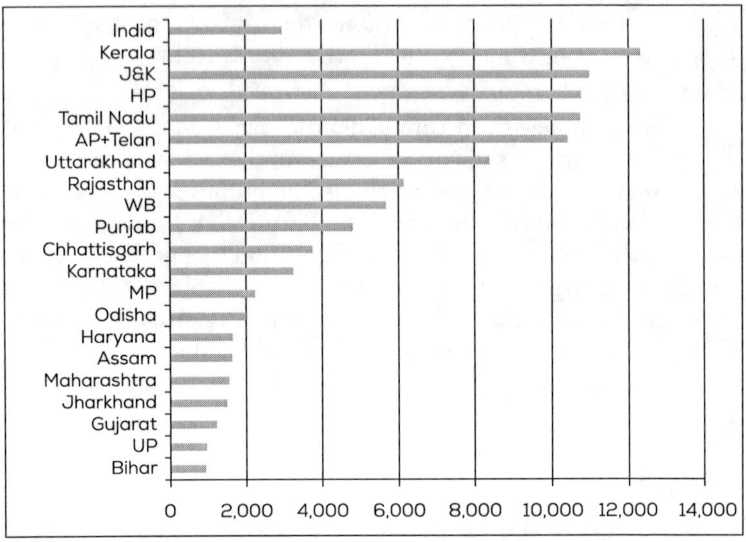

Source: Calculated by author based on data given in the official web site of NREGA

This design flaw can easily be fixed by allocating resources to the states in NREGA proportionate to the number of rural poor in that state.

There could be many possible explanations of high expenditure in the richer states. First, a large number of women from non-poor households are supplementing their incomes through NREGA, whereas their husbands find more remunerative jobs elsewhere. Second, a large number of households though above the poverty line are still not able to meet their desired financial aspirations and therefore are willing to do wage employment. Third, in some states such as Himachal Pradesh and the north-east, work is being done by migrants who are below the poverty line (BPL), but have been left out of the poverty census because they are not able to exert pressure on the local administration for inclusion in the BPL list. And lastly, this could also indicate bogus and inflated reporting in the muster roll.

Thus, the participation rate in public works is uncorrelated with the poverty rate across states. Some of the poorest states

(Bihar, Jharkhand and Orissa) have low participation rates and high levels of unmet demand. This is in contrast to other states such as Chhattisgarh, Rajasthan and West Bengal that perform better in providing employment under the scheme.

The government auditor (CAG) has highlighted gross irregularities in the scheme in many states, apart from an overall decline in the rural employment (per household) from 54 days in 2009–2010 to 43 days in 2011–2012. The report also questioned the crucial linkage between NREGA implementation and poverty alleviation. 'It was also seen that Bihar, Maharashtra and UP, which together account for 46 percent of the rural poor, utilised only about 20 percent of the Central funds,' it stated.

The reasons for poor performance by Bihar, Odisha, UP and Assam are well known. Their weak capacity is often due to the widespread shortage of staff at all levels, which adversely affects the implementation of the scheme (see Figure 5.1 in chapter 5). Second, poorer states tend to have a weaker capacity for administering schemes, draw funds from GOI and ensure that these reach the villages in time. Third, poorer states will be less able to afford the share of the costs that are to be borne by the state and local governments. And lastly, the poor may well be less empowered in poorer states.

As the number of job seekers who succeed in getting work is far less than the number of poor households in many states, not all those who seek MGNREGS employment receive work, despite the legal right to work. MGNREGS jobs are then often allocated on the basis of social status, personal connections, nepotism, political or religious affiliations, or corruption, thereby undercutting the programme's self-targeting design and its capacity to reduce poverty[3] (Liu and Barrett 2013).

Richer states are doing better than poorer states in creating jobs. It makes no sense to run the programme in the labour-scarce districts of Kerala, Punjab, Haryana, Himachal Pradesh and the north-east. On the other hand, the upper limit of work guarantee of 100 days should be enhanced to 150 days per household in the

3. Yanyan Liu, and Christopher B Barrett (2013): Heterogeneous Pro-Poor Targeting in the National Rural Employment Guarantee Scheme, Economic & Political Weekly, March 9, vol xlviii no 46.

poorest 200 districts, with assets such as ponds, bunds, check dams and planted saplings being monitored for at least five years.

Unemployment allowance is not paid in most cases: In a Rajya Sabha Unstarred Question No.1011 due for 3 August 2010, asked by Mani Shankar Aiyar, it was revealed that the total number of cases where unemployment allowance was paid by the States under NREGA over the years was much less than 5,000, although crores of job card holders have either not been provided any employment or it is much less than 100 days. In another question, number 763, answered on 20 March 2012, the government informed the House that unemployment allowance during 2010–2011 was paid only in 514 cases in the entire country. As per unstarred question no. 1614, answered on 28 December 2017 in the Lok Sabha, not a single rupee was paid as unemployment allowance in UP and Bihar in the years 2014 to 2017. Thus, law is being flouted openly by the state government administration.

Monitoring assets should be part of the programme design: Although the stated objective of NREGA is to accomplish drought proofing and increase agricultural production on marginal holdings, especially in semi-arid regions and uplands, but the sustainability and productivity of assets created is never monitored with the result that the programme is reduced to creating short-term unproductive employment with no focus on asset creation or soil and water conservation. Its impact on agriculture may even be negative, as alleged by the Ministry of Agriculture. At present, community upkeep of public assets is limited, possibly due to ambiguity over ownership and usage rights.

Moreover, a large number of studies on NREGA point out to the following weaknesses in the programme:

- High percentage of incomplete works
- The objective of drought proofing is not being achieved
- Delay in wage payment
- Inadequate monitoring and third-party assessments.

Summing up: The Sameeksha review[4] of the Ministry of Rural Development acknowledges that the labourers under NREGA programme learn no new skill and that the ponds, roads, drains, dams

---

4. http://nrega.nic.in/circular_archive/archive/mgnrega_sameeksha2_english.pdf

and other assets built with manual labour are often of wretched quality. The idea behind the MGNREGA programme is to create as many jobs as possible for unskilled workers. In practice, say critics, it means no one learns new skills, and the poor stay poor—dependent on government cheques.

The Twelfth Five-Year Plan document says that there are problems in the NREGA primarily because it is a dole that involves a huge expenditure that could have been spent more productively. It does not create permanent assets or a sustained increase in incomes. Employment guarantee should be linked to the idea of human development with a focus on growth through enhanced labour productivity—that is, growth through a combination of physical capital formation and human capability. One should evaluate the success of the scheme from the perspective of an increase in the productivity of small and marginal landholdings in low rainfall regions, and the quality and contribution of productive assets.

It is difficult to escape the conclusion that the NREGA has not performed well. The solution lies in a drastic overhaul of this scheme as suggested above with greater transparency and accountability through social audits.

Design issues in other development programmes

Housing for the urban poor: Similarly, due to flawed design, many other programmes are not doing well. For instance, 99 per cent of the urban housing shortage is from the EWS and the low-income group (LIG) households, but most new houses that are coming up in the cities are meant for the HIG (high -income group) category. At today's prices, even a modest tenement of 300 square feet would cost close to two to three million rupees, well beyond the reach of poor residents. These are then allocated to ineligible households, or worse they stand vacant, and gradually fall into disuse, as monuments of official waste, because in the classic mode of bureaucratic failures, those for whom they are intended cannot afford them, and those who can afford them, do not want them.

Promote rental housing and Night shelters: The Government is promoting owned housing under the assumption that the poor would be able to access a home loan from a bank, which presents a host of problems for those living and working outside the formal sector. It is not realistic to expect that the poor would be able to muster funds for a privately owned house. But there has still been no spurt in the construction of low-income housing for rentals. Public rental was the social solution to housing during inter-war and post-war periods in Europe and elsewhere, and very large housing estates were built in several countries. India will do well by emulating their example, and promote rental housing to target towards low-income earners, such as rickshaw pullers and auto drivers. The poorest such as beggars, rag-pickers and unskilled wage earners cannot afford even houses on a rental scheme. For them the scheme of night shelters should be revived as a centrally sponsored scheme. Such shelters should be built close to place of employment, as the poorest cannot afford even travelling by public transport.

Reduce leakages through technology in PDS: All is not well with the PDS in India. Weaknesses in the distribution system include ration cards[5] being mortgaged to ration shop owners, large errors of exclusion of BPL families, prevalence of ghost cards, with weaknesses in the delivery mechanism leading to largescale leakages and diversion of subsidized grains to markets and unintended beneficiaries. These problems arise because grain is given to the shopkeeper at the subsidized rate which leads to leakages.

It may, however, be added that large-scale substitution of PDS by direct cash transfers (DCT) is not feasible, as foodgrains purchased from the farmers through MSP mechanism need an outlet for distribution. Introducing DCT nationally would mean that GOI would have to end the state procurement regime. That is neither politically feasible, nor can it be in the realm of consideration by any government in India, given that more than half of the population is still dependent on agriculture. At best, DCT could be tried on a pilot basis in a few poor localities of metropolitan cities, as is being done in Delhi.

Direct Benefit Transfer (DBT) is, however, different. Under this programme, the entitlement holders would still buy their food rations from Fair Price Shops (FPS) as they do now, with the difference that they would submit their biometric details to the

5. Niehaus et al. (2013) surveyed 14,074 households in rural Karnataka to learn about the process for obtaining BPL cards. They found that bribery is widespread: 75 per cent of households reported paying bribes to obtain the cards.

FPS owner through a point-of-sale device that is connected either through a GSM network or through other means to an integrated stock management system.

The Government should abolish the dual pricing system in PDS and sell stocks to the fair price shop dealer at the market price, say ₹24 for wheat. The consumer would go to him with only two rupees in cash as before and her/his UID card to buy a kg of wheat but the rest ₹22 would get transferred to the shopkeeper through the card. This will vastly reduce leakages and subsidy as well as improve the dealer's attitude towards the buyer. As of now the dealer avoids the consumer as his main interest is in selling the grain in the open market. Once he is given grain at the market price he would be forced to welcome the cardholder and persuade her/him to come to his shop at the earliest so that the transfer of subsidy could take place.

This would not only ensure that the right person gets their rations, but would also free entitlement holders to buy their rations from any FPS and not be tied to a single vendor. In other words, it would ensure 'entitlement portability' that will allow PDS entitlements to be accessed anywhere in the country and greatly help the poor migrant workers, who are unable to access their entitlements now. This would revolutionize the PDS by providing genuine choices to entitlement holders. It would also cut down significantly on corruption.

Modify Right to Education Act: Entry of more and more private schools charging low fees into the educational landscape across the country has been a reality in recent years. Absenteeism of teachers and poor quality of outcomes in government schools is the main factor behind the popularity of private schools with poor infrastructure that cater to the needs of the underprivileged. The management pays pittance to the teachers, but such schools are still attracting students because of better teacher attendance, personal attention to each student and testing of their homework by the teachers, faster scholastic learning and in some places greater emphasis on English. Often they run under a banyan tree or in a dilapidated building. However, the Right to Education Act (RTE) insists that such schools would be closed down if they do not have an all-weather building consisting of at least one classroom for every teacher and an office-cum-store-cum-head teacher's room, barrier-free access, separate toilets for boys and girls, safe and adequate water facility to all children, kitchen for MDM, playground, library and qualified teachers.

Shutting down private schools that do not meet the required norms and standards will place an additional burden on SSA funds at a time when the overall demand for primary education is still greater than supply. This is particularly so in urban areas that cater to migrants and slum dwellers. At the very least, the answer lies in improving the quality of outcomes in government schools and not in shutting down the private schools, thereby denying access to education to the deprived sections. The Government should discourage mushroom growth of private schools through competition by improving quality of teaching in public schools, and not eliminate private schools through coercion. This would require making amendments in the Right to Education Act.

However, as chairman of the 16th Joint Review Mission, when I suggested in 2012 not to burden private budget schools with unrealistic financial expenses on barrier-free access and so on, the Ministry refused to make any change in the RTE Act. Interestingly, Anil Swarup, who remained Secretary in GOI from 2016 to 2019 in the Department of School Education and Literacy, was convinced that the Act had proved counterproductive. After his retirement he wrote (2019), 'The legislation made the task of delivering quality education complex and difficult. The focus of the Act is primarily on inputs (like infrastructure) rather than outcomes.... The RTE Act has done more damage to the delivery of education'.

To sum up, most IAS officers, as commented frequently in this book, are status quoists and resist reforms (Mathur 2014). They do not encourage comprehensive evaluation of programmes that are not doing well. Had they done so, they would have been under pressure to make the necessary changes in the design of the programmes. It should be incumbent upon the IAS Secretaries working in the states to suggest such changes to their colleagues at the Centre. They unfortunately hide the pathetic performance of development programmes by sending inflated or bogus reports to the Centre, an issue that we have discussed in Chapter 11.

7 Chapter

IS BUREAUCRACY FAIR TO MARGINALIZED GROUPS?

Another major weakness in the governance structure is that the growth is not sufficiently inclusive for many groups, especially SCs, STs, urban poor, migrants, single women (widowed, divorced, or just abandoned), the disabled and Muslims. Their economic deprivation derives from the lack of productive assets, such as land and water, and access to credit. These chronically poor tend to remain in poverty for much of their lives, passing on the tragic legacy of deprivation and exclusion to their children. The brutal expulsion of those who most need it, from support and succour, from care and rights—often by their own families (as in the case of women), by local communities (as in the case of dalits and Muslims) but most importantly by the State—is one of the most profound public crimes of our time. It is important, therefore, to identify those classes, social categories and local communities, who are destitute and socially expelled, and sensitize bureaucracy to ensure that development benefits reach them, otherwise economic inequalities would keep on increasing (Saxena and Farrington 2003). However, as of now, even their proper identification leaves much to be desired.

Poorest of the poor excluded from benefits

There are serious problems in the identification of the poor. For instance, despite three surveys (1992, 1997 and 2002), the errors of exclusion and inclusion in the list of the poor remained above acceptable limits.[1] Errors of exclusion are those that misclassify the poor in the non-poor category, while errors of inclusion include the non-poor in the poor category. According to the Eleventh Plan (Vol. 2, chapter 4), there are huge exclusion and inclusion errors in identifying the poor. More than half of the poor in 2004–2005 either had no card or were given APL cards, and were thus excluded from the BPL benefits. These must be presumably the most poor tribal groups, Muslims,[2] women-headed households and people living in remote hamlets where administration does not reach. Thus, the people most deserving of government help are deprived of such assistance. On the other hand, almost 60 per cent of the BPL cards had been given to households belonging to the non-poor category.

The Government conducted a massive Socio-Economic Caste Census (SECC) in 2013 to prepare a village-wise list of the deprived. The primary purpose of conducting village-wise census of poor households by contacting each household was to identify the deprived households that could be assisted under various government programmes. Such a survey is necessary if there are programmes and benefits exclusively targeted to the poor. However, some studies show that even this survey suffers from misclassification, and a large number of poor seem to have been left out (Saxena 2015). For instance, the total number of the poorest households, such as homeless, destitute households, 'Primitive' Tribal Groups, households with disabled persons as bread-earners, and bonded labour, who were to be automatically included for all government benefits was only 16.5 lakh out of a total number of 18 crore rural families according to the SECC survey.

Thus, their total number is shown as less than 1 per cent of all rural households in India, whereas Antyodaya card holders themselves are 2.5 crore. This gross underestimation of the poorest of the poor does not tally with other government figures.

1. In Karnataka, 48 per cent of households are misclassified (Niehaus et al. 2013).
2. While inspecting several slums of Firozabad city (UP) in 2003 where polio outbreak had particularly affected Muslims, I was appalled to see filth and pollution around Muslim habitations. When questioned, a municipality official remarked,'this is Pakistan, we don't visit these areas!'

For instance, the overall number of 16.50 lakh is far less than the number of houseless alone as estimated by the Ministry of Rural Development. The Ministry's target in the next four years to provide Indira AwasYojana house for all rural homeless is 2 crore families! SECC is also not compatible with census, as according to Census 2011, 4.3 per cent households (74 lakh) in rural India are homeless.

A survey done by the Ministry of Labour in 2014 shows that in about 5 per cent of the households, there are no earning members aged 15 years and above. These 9 million households should have been automatically included in the category of the poorest. This number is shown in the SECC as only 6.9 million, or 3.8 per cent, as opposed to 5 per cent estimated by the Labour Ministry. Coming to the number of manual scavengers, according to a Lok Sabha report, 0.77 million manual scavengers and their dependents were identified by States/UTs during implementation of the National Scheme for Liberation and Manual Scavenging in India in 2007. SECC admits far less, only 0.18 million.

The inference is inescapable; the poorest have not been able to convince our bureaucracy to recognize them.

Categorizing the deprived

As is well documented, India's high rate of economic growth has not benefited four groups: Muslims, Dalits, women and tribals. Their problems are different, so is the social context of their subjugation. Of these, Muslims and Dalits face a great deal of bias and discrimination in their daily lives, such as dalit children being asked to sit separately at schools, being denied drinking water from the village well, or not being allowed to ride a horse in weddings. Police has generally been hostile to Muslims as described by various studies and Commission reports on Hashimpura, Bhagalpur, Bhiwandi and Gujarat riots. Their problems of discrimination, physical insecurity and loss of livelihoods have considerably increased in the last eight years. However, I do not know if government in the last 70 years has passed any law or adopted a policy which could be interpreted as discriminatory against Dalits and Muslims, though at the micro- and societal levels their problems are immense.

The other two groups—women and tribals—face not only cultural subordination, but also have been harmed by various iniquitous laws and declared policies. In that sense, they are worse off than Muslims and Dalits. For instance, laws relating to inheritance of agricultural land in UP still do not allow married daughters to claim their share in their father's inherited property. Section 46(1) of the Rajasthan Tenancy Act places women at par with lunatics and idiots. The Indian Penal Code section dealing with adultery is not gender neutral, as a married man having an affair with an unmarried woman is not violating any law. In the Narmada R&R policy every major son of 18+ was to be treated as a separate family, but unmarried major daughters, widows or deserted wives had no such rights. Therefore, in addition to fighting patriarchy at the social level, one needs to get rid of gender discriminatory laws and practices.

Of all the disadvantaged groups, tribals, especially in Central India, have been the worst sufferers, primarily because of anti-tribal forest policy, displacement laws and poor governance. Production of minor forest products (MFPs) from Government forests has gone down in the last 70 years, affecting tribal livelihoods. Living in mineral rich areas, they have often been displaced without proper rehabilitation. Thus, in addition to improving delivery, we need to address policy issues too, both for women and tribals.

It is generally believed that 'programmes for the poor (or socially excluded) are poorly run programmes', describing how it is the powerlessness of those experiencing social exclusion that results in the low quality of delivery of poverty targeted schemes. The root cause for their hopeless situation is their inability to access and retain rightful entitlements to public goods and services due to existing institutionalized structures and processes of exploitation.

The Twelfth Five-Year Plan, as expected, on paper gives high priority to inclusive growth and reducing inequality. But past trends are not very encouraging as inequality seems to have gone up, while the much needed policies and programmes for the disadvantaged have still to be implemented. The following paragraphs contain a brief description of each of these marginalized sections and provide suggestions for actions required to alleviate their situation.

Dalits: Victims of Prejudices

These excluded groups are disadvantaged in many ways. They are victims of prejudices, are ignored, and often treated as less than human beings by village elite and government officials. Living in remote hamlets they are geographically separated from centres of delivery. Since their hamlets are scattered, the cost of contacting them is higher. Finally, extreme poverty prevents them from taking advantage of government schemes, such as free schooling (their children are withdrawn from schools because their labour is needed at home or in some other work) and immunization (since the children migrate along with their parents, they are not present in the village when the health worker visits). The crux of such a hopeless situation for them lies in their inability to access and retain their rightful entitlements to public goods and services due to institutionalized structures and processes of exploitation.

Amongst the 20th-century social reformers, the contributions of Mahatma Gandhi and Dr Babasaheb Ambedkar in improving the social status of the 'untouchables' need to be emphasized, although they differed greatly in their approach. Mahatma Gandhi believed that untouchability was an aberration in the otherwise ideal Hindu religion and was capable of being resolved through understanding within the Hindu community. For him, the battle against untouchability was essentially a religious one. He, therefore, called for a change of heart amongst the upper -caste Hindus as an act of expiation and reparation for the centuries of oppression, and launched a movement for the entry of untouchables to temples.

Dr Ambedkar, on the other hand, viewed untouchability as an institutionalised expression of socio-economic oppression and exploitation and domination by a certain section of society. He viewed the 'awakening' of untouchables, as a precondition to the remedy of their woes. He, therefore, focused on educating the untouchables about the values of self-respect and the need to embark on a struggle for justice. He also considered legal measures as being powerful instruments for the upliftment of depressed classes and maintained that political power was the only effective method of advancing the interest of the entire class of deprived communities. As chairman of the drafting committee for the Indian Constitution, his opinion prevailed in ensuring several safeguards for SCs.

Various field studies show that untouchability is still practised in many forms throughout the country. Jagjivan Ram held several top constitutional posts, but at the social level he was always treated as an inferior notwithstanding his political heavyweight status. As the Defence Minister, he unveiled the statue of Sampoornanad in

Varanasi, the present constituency of Prime Minister Narendra Modi, in January 1978. But after his departure, the same statue got 'purified' by some Brahmins who poured Ganga jal on it, claiming 'unsolicited' touching by a Dalit.[3] On 25 June 2011, a Hindu temple at village Ranapada in Puri refused entry to P. L. Punia, a dalit, former IAS officer and the then chairman of the National Commission for SCs. Even President Kovind could not visit every part of the Jagannath temple, as a group of servitors had blocked the President's path near the sanctum sanctorum of the shrine and shoved the First Lady. The chief administrator of the temple, IAS officer Pradipta Kumar Mohapatra, admitted that the President and the First Lady were inconvenienced.[4]

Dalit women suffer the triple burden of caste, class and gender. They routinely suffer sexual abuse and rape by upper-caste landlords in many parts of the country. Dalit women are also raped as a form of retaliation. No one practises untouchability when it comes to sex. Far greater anonymity and occupational mobility in towns and cities enable blurring of caste identities. It is documented that dalits are impelled to migrate to urban areas not only due to economic compulsions, but also to escape the social degradation of untouchability.

Being poor and assetless, they are mainly employed in rural India as agricultural labourers. Their other forms of livelihood include scavenging, flaying, and tanning of leather. They are located on the outskirts, and they are secluded from the mainstream settlements, manifesting social segregation. Also, their dwellings remain devoid of basic minimum amenities such as, safe drinking water, health and sanitation, and roads, amongst others. Therefore, special packages of basic minimum services including safe drinking water, nutrition supplementation; primary health care; primary education and employment-cum-income-generation activities need to be designed and developed to cater to dalit clusters and bastis. To break this caste-based, occupational stereotyping, special efforts are needed to encourage them to make the best use of educational

3. https://www.news18.com/news/opinion/opinion-the-jagannath-temple-incident-shows-that-the-socially-ruling-class-can-nudge-even-the-president-1795125.html
4. https://timesofindia.indiatimes.com/city/bhubaneswar/at-puri-priests-block-president-ram-nath-kovinds-way-shove-first-lady/articleshow/64757587.cms

concessions and programmes extended by the government. Also, education needs to be vocationalized at the middle-school level to promote occupational mobility for these groups.

Despite increasing focus by the government and programmes such as the Swachh Bharat Mission, unsafe sanitation work, loosely captured under the catch-all phrase 'manual scavenging', still exists in India. Five million people are employed in sanitation work of some sort in India with about two million of them working in 'high risk' jobs such as septic tank cleaning, sewer cleaning, public toilet cleaning and drain cleaning, whereas three million workers primarily clean household toilets as domestic help.

This problem of 'manual scavenging', as it is commonly called, is not new and is deeply rooted in India's caste system, which assigns duties such as the cleaning of human faecal waste to people born in the lowest sub-castes of the Dalit community in urban India, where men and women physically get inside sewer networks and septic tanks to clean blockages despite extreme hazards and risks. There are deaths daily, reported and unreported. Most septic tanks are emptied manually in Indian cities. The lack of proper safeguards puts manual scavengers at risk of infections, which are occasionally fatal. Statistics show that 80 per cent of India's sewage cleaners die before they turn 60, after contracting various infectious diseases.

Despite these problems, the success rate for the SCs in reducing poverty has been better when compared with STs (see Table 7.1). Though ostracized, the SCs or the erstwhile untouchables had been integral to the dominant community whether in a village or town, the only difference being that the untouchables were unjustly segregated from the community and subjected to all forms of discrimination. The SCs have, therefore, had a greater exposure to the larger society as compared with the STs, who lived an isolated life, totally oblivious of the mainstream developments. Thus, in effect, opportunities made available to the larger societies or the higher castes in the form of knowledge, information, technology and employment were also in sight for the SCs, even though they were denied access to it. Once the element of discrimination was legally removed and affirmative policies introduced, the dalits took full advantage of the new opportunities. Such an environment was absent for the STs. Tribes thus suffered the disadvantage of isolation in this regard. The other difference is due to language; while SCs spoke the same language as the dominant group, the STs often speak a different dialect or even language, and their children have the handicap of being taught at schools in a language they do not understand, resulting in higher dropout rates. This is one of the most serious handicaps facing the tribes.

Scheduled Tribes: The Most Vulnerable Population

From the viewpoint of policy, it is important to understand that tribal communities are vulnerable not only because they are poor, assetless and illiterate compared with the general population, but, often, their distinct vulnerability arises from their inability to negotiate and cope with the consequences of their forced integration with the mainstream economy, society, cultural and political system, from which they were historically protected as a result of their relative isolation. Post-independence, the requirements of planned development brought with them the spectre of dams, mines, industries and roads being built on tribal lands. With this came the concomitant processes of displacement, both literal and metaphorical—as tribal institutions and practices were forced into an uneasy existence with, or gave way to, the market or formal state institutions (most significantly in the legal sphere). The tribals found themselves at a profound disadvantage with the influx of better-equipped outsiders into tribal areas. The repercussions on the already fragile, socio-economic livelihood base of the tribals were devastating—ranging from loss of livelihoods, land alienation on a vast scale, to hereditary bondage.

The central region of India, despite being resource rich in terms of minerals and forests, inhabits the poorest people who have not benefited from social and economic development to the same extent as others. Persistent problems faced by Adivasis—land alienation, indebtedness, vanishing MFPs from government forests and displacement from their ancestral lands are some of the causes for their impoverishment. In addition, Adivasis have suffered because of the poor quality of governance, as government servants are reluctant to work in remote tribal areas and are often absent from their official duties. Poor implementation of existing schemes in the tribal regions has meant that not only poverty continues at an exceptionally high levels for Adivasis, but the decline in poverty has been much slower for them than for other social groups, as shown in Table 7.1.

Table 7.1: Percentage of people below poverty line and its rate of decline

Category	1993–94	2011–12	Rate of annual decline
Scheduled Tribe (ST)	62.6	43	1.7
Scheduled Caste (SC)	60.1	29.4	2.8
Other Backward Class (OBC)	39	20.7	2.6
Others (General)	39	12.5	3
All	45.1	21.9	2.9

According to the 2011 Census, about half of the ST households in many central Indian districts possessed neither a mobile phone nor a bicycle nor radio. As per the latest Annual Health Survey, 44 per cent of women in the age group of 18 to 59 years in Koraput, a tribal district of Odisha, had body mass index below 18.5 kg/m2, and 80 per cent of them were anaemic. Widespread poverty, illiteracy, absence of safe drinking water and sanitary conditions, and ineffective coverage of national health and nutritional programmes are the major contributing factors for dismal malnutrition indicators of tribal communities.

According to the India Human Development Survey, in 2011–2012, the annual per capita income of the STs in Chhattisgarh represented 51 per cent of the per capita income of the non-STs, a significant climb down from 2004 to 2005, when this proportion was 68 per cent. In Madhya Pradesh, this proportion has fallen from 65 to 55 per cent. In Gujarat, STs' annual per capita income represents only 35 per cent of the annual per capita income of the others (Jaffrelot and Kalaiyarasan 2018).

Land records: The official land records in central India are in a bad shape and have often ignored tribal occupation. For instance, in Odisha, cashew plantations were raised by the Soil Conservation Department on 120,000 hectares of 'Government Wastelands' in Schedule V areas. In many cases, such lands in the past were under cultivation by tribals but their rights were not recorded. When settlement took place, tribals because of their ignorance were not in a position to get their possessions recorded, and thus land under their possession got recorded as government land and the poor tribals were described as encroachers even on lands which were cultivated by their ancestors. These cashew plantations, raised on land that was supporting livelihood needs of tribals, were handed over to the Orissa State Cashew Development Corporation for management. As the Corporation could not run profitably, it started giving annual leases for harvesting of cashew crops to private parties through open auctions. This is land reforms in reverse! It is ironical that these plantations that deprived the tribals of their possession were funded by a scheme called,'Economic Rehabilitation of the Rural Poor' (Planning Commission 2000).

Displacement: Adivasis have generally been harmed by displacement due to industrialization. Nearly 0.85 million tribals had been displaced until 1990 on account of some mega project or the other, reservation of forests as National Parks and so on. Tribals constitute 8 per cent of the population but are 55 per cent of the total displaced people in the country (Planning Commission 2008). Cash payment does not really compensate them for the difficulties they experience in their living style and ethos.

The clause in the new 2013 law requiring consent at least 70 per cent of the project affected people is highly welcome. It is unfortunate that Gujarat in 2016 diluted the Land Acquisition Act and has done away with social impact assessment and consent clauses for acquisition of land for public purposes, industrial corridors and Public –Private Partnership projects.

Often, land values go up after acquisition, and the original owners feel cheated when they find that their land after a few years is being sold for 10 times the price that was paid to them. Therefore, whenever land acquired by the government is transferred to an individual or a company for a consideration, 20 per cent of the appreciated value should be given to the original landowner. In addition, the Government must ensure that displaced tribal families have a standard of living superior to the one before their displacement and have a sustainable income above the poverty line. Gains to the displaced should be of the same scale as to the project beneficiaries.

Even under the new law of 2013, affected households are not compensated when forest or common lands and water bodies are resumed by the government and passed on to private bodies, on the plea that these are government lands and require no acquisition.

In the absence of any protection the poorest people as users of common lands and forests and slum dwellers are thus deprived of their livelihoods without any rehabilitation benefits. This is particularly relevant in view of the state governments' reluctance to implement the community clauses of the Forest Rights Act (FRA).

Forest Policy: There is much evidence to show that tribals' access to forests for meeting their basic subsistence needs has deteriorated in the last 70 years, and that this is fairly widespread. Some of the processes which have caused this are the anti-tribal policies, such as Forest Policy 1952, preference for man-made plantations in place of mixed forests, diversion of MFPs and forests to industries, nationalization of MFPs, and exploitation by government agencies and contractors in marketing of MFPs. Tribal women in Rayagada were once arrested in 1995 and jailed for keeping brooms in their homes! This case is described in detail in Chapter 9.

FRA was a landmark legislation enacted in 2006 to correct the 'historic injustice done to forest-dwelling communities', mostly tribals, who were cultivating/ occupying forest land and using forest produce since ages but had no tenurial security, as their rights of occupation and usage were not recorded during the settlement process. Although counting both individual and community rights, more than 1.8 million titles have been issued covering 5.5 million hectares, in many places the area settled with the forest-dwellers is much less than their occupation; boundaries of the settled area is not demarcated; and rejections are being done without assigning reasons. The picture is also dismal when it comes to recognizing community forest rights (CFR). Granting of titles cannot be considered the end of the story. If the objective is to strengthen livelihoods of the forest dwellers, state governments need to improve productivity of assigned land by linking it with soil conservation works with NREGA funds, and assist in marketing of harvested products.

Similarly, in addition to recognizing community rights, government should actively promote improving the livelihoods of the forest dwellers through higher production of gatherable biomass, and better opportunities for its collection and marketing. MFPs play an important role in the economic wellbeing of the forestdwelling communities. Unfortunately, the overall production of MFPs (except of tendu leaves) has fallen rapidly due to Forest

Department's preference for planting species, such as teak (in place of sal), which yield no recurrent products for gathering. Therefore, silvicultural practices should be radically changed to boost the production of gatherable biomass, and not merely timber. We need crown-based, and not trunk-based, forestry that mostly benefits contractors.

Moreover, the important MFPs continue to be 'nationalized', that is, these can be sold only to government agencies. Then many state governments have created new rights of industrialists through long-term agreements to supply forest products at a low price, bypassing local peoples' rights and privileges. Sale of MFPs is usually governed by a complex set of rules and regulations. A limited number of buyers thus operate under monopolistic conditions. For instance, in Tamil Nadu, an area of abundance of Prosopis juliflora (an excellent coppicing shrub with high calorific value), charcoal producers have to obtain a certificate of origin from Forest Officers. This results in constant harassment. Over-regulation and complex procedures hurt value addition. Licences have been done away for large industries in India, but not for tiny and cottage industries based on forest raw material (Saxena 2003a).

If farmers are free to sell their wheat and paddy in the open market, why restrict tribals from doing so for MFPs? States should attract tribals to their depots by paying them remunerative price support rather than coerce them to sell to government agencies.

Therefore, in addition to guaranteeing that FRA is implemented in letter and spirit, one would have to address three interrelated issues for ensuring that tribals' livelihoods are supported and enriched by MFPs:

1. how to increase MFP production, while sustaining the resource,
2. how to improve access of the poor to MFPs and
3. how to maximize their incomes through marketing.

Governance: It is unfortunate that the Ministry of Tribal Affairs (MOTA) does not give sufficient attention to the important problems of the tribals on the plea that many of these subjects such as land alienation, displacement and forest policy have not been allotted to it. Even then, the ministry should play a more activist role in addressing these issues by pursuing with the concerned ministries, where tribal concerns are often neglected. An effective monitoring mechanism should be set up to bring out the dismal picture of tribal areas that would put pressure on the sectoral ministries and the states to improve their programmes and implementation.

When MOTA was set up in 2001, it was expected that it would take a holistic view of tribal problems and coordinate the activities of all other ministries that deal with the subjects impinging on tribal livelihoods. The new ministry, however, took a minimalist view of its responsibility and reduced itself to dealing with only such schemes (such as distribution of scholarships and grants to NGOs) for which budget is provided to the ministry. Such an ostrich-like attitude defeats the purpose for which the ministry was created.

Even the Niti Aayog does not regularly monitor the impact of existing policies on the tribal population and pull up the concerned sectoral Ministries. There seems to be an obsession in GOI with financial budget and not with the impact that policies (or the lack of it) have on the marginalized peoples. Policies and budgetary provisions, despite the rhetoric, have not been integrated so far. Changes in policy or laws are not seen as an integral part of the development process because these have no direct financial implications. One lesser known reason for this isolation is that development and planning in India are associated with spending of money. That Planning means Expenditure, and this will lead to Development is the mindset behind such beliefs. The IAS officer unfortunately has still to understand the difference between planning and budgeting. This is where a systemic change is needed in India. In addition to spending budgets, we need to give equal importance to non-monetary issues such as institutions, laws and policies.

For instance, MOTA does not monitor whether the basic services in education, health or nutrition are reaching the tribal hamlets. The Ministry should develop meaningful partnerships with advocacy organizations that could produce credible and evidence-based reports with a view to engage with other ministries that oversee various programmes such as ICDS, NHM, PDS, etc in a way that such programmes reach the Adivasis. Even in areas where there is Naxalite presence in very remote and apparently inaccessible areas, civil society organizations can be funded to run mobile clinics and feeding centres. Clearly, it is a lack of will on the part of the administration that needs to be set right first.

Tribal leadership: One of the main factors behind the success of dalits in India has been excellent leadership provided by the SC community, which has, unfortunately not been the case for the STs. Whereas the SCs can boast of having produced leaders and administrators such as Ambedkar and Jagjivan Ram in the past and K R Narayanan, Buta Singh, Paswan, Kanshi Ram and Mayawati in more recent times, it is hard to find any of national stature from the ST category. A few civil servants, such as B. D. Sharma and S. R. Sankaran, tried to alleviate their conditions, but such efforts could not be sustained for the lack of institutional support.

The oppressed tribals, unlike other disadvantaged groups, generally suffer and endure their exploitation silently. In some areas, however, they have taken to armed insurgency. The middle path of agitational politics by organizing bundhs, taking out processions, and putting pressure on the politicians, so successfully adopted by other groups in India to articulate their grievances, is alien to the tribals and has historically been unknown to them. Civil society needs to play a big role here, and the government too should not brand all tribal activists as Maoists.

Adivasis are unable to put democratic pressure on the bureaucratic and political system, from which they were historically protected as the result of their relative isolation. A few respond occasionally with anger and assertion, go underground and get attracted to naxals. Unfortunately for them, Indian history of the last 150 years shows that terrorism and violent insurgency have never succeeded in achieving their aims (creation of Mizoram may be the only exception), but overground agitational strategies have been most successful, leading to creation of new states, and changes in government policy (such as declaration of emergency in 1975 due to the JP movement). Arvind Kejriwal is the latest example of success in agitational politics.

What about Naxals? Though in a few exceptional cases Naxals have been able to improve tribal livelihoods, such as adivasis getting minimum wages for the tendu leaf gatherers in Andhra Pradesh, naxals have, by and large, degenerated into a terrorist outfit with little impact on the day-to-day agony of the local population. In the 1970s and early 1980s, the naxalite movement may have had ideological base, today they are just brigands. The poor tribals are often subjected to physical violence by both Maoists and state forces; they even get deprived of educational and health facilities or access to PDS on the ground that the area has become unapproachable for normal 'development' efforts of administration.

Although there are some activist organizations who speak for the tribals openly through the social media and do advocacy to stop their exploitation, their number and effectiveness is limited. They have been able to neither reduce the lack of trust between the people and the State, nor improve governance in the tribal belts. We need more democratic, well -informed and overground grassroots organizations for effective advocacy in both policy and implementation. The poor adivasis are today trapped between the Maoists, on the one hand, and the armed forces on the other. Mere sympathy for the Naxals is self-defeating as the path of underground violence is not the answer for tribal problems and will not end tribal oppression.

Genuine grassroots organizations and tribals themselves must learn the strategy of agitational politics from the likes of Shiv Sena and Kejriwal.

Social Constraints of Patriarchy on Women

Despite India's remarkable economic growth over the past two decades, the progress in achieving gender equality and women's empowerment has been unsatisfactory so far. The ratio of females to males in 2011 for the age group 0–6 is 914 to 1,000, which is the lowest since 1947. This child sex ratio was 945 and 927 in 1991 and 2001, respectively. Thus, rather than showing improvement, it has been going down with every new census report. According to newspaper reports (Times of India, 28 January 2019), sex ratio has fallen even in southern states during 2007–2016.

The literacy rate amongst females ages 7 and above has certainly increased from 54 per cent in 2001 to 65 per cent in 2011, but it is still 17 points less than for men. In 2011, 273 million people in India were still illiterate, out of which two-thirds were women. Gender in- equalities are reflected in the country's human development ranking; India ranks 113 of 157 countries in the Gender-related Development Index. More than 90 per cent of women continue to struggle in the informal/unorganized sector with no legislative safeguards. According to the Global Wage Report (ILO 2018), of the 73 countries studied, India had the dubious distinction of having the highest gap between what men earn and what women do. It was 34.5 per cent for India in 2018 against a World average of 20 per cent.

The prevailing social constraints of patriarchy largely relegate women to the inside sphere. Added to this are the dual responsibilities of women tagged with heavy work responsibilities in agriculture, animal husbandry and other traditional sectors, which create a syndrome of gender stereo-types, marginalization, alienation and deprivation of women in the informal sector. Even when their hard work produces surplus they do not generally control its disposal, which has traditionally been and continues to be in men's domain.

Women's unrecognized workload: While women in India have always worked harder than men, their role as workers has not been fully recognized by the planners and policymakers. According to the 68th Round NSSO survey, for the age group 15–59 years, Work Participation Rate (WPR) at the all-India level in 2011–2012 was only 26 per cent for females and 84 per cent for males.[5] The reasons for the under-reporting of women as workers are many: women's work is often informal, unpaid and home-based; it is flexible, non-standard and an extension of domestic work and therefore frequently indistinguishable from it. Greater gender sensitivity is needed to correctly appreciate and record productive nature of women's work.

In addition to under-reporting, what is even more alarming is the fact that WPR for rural females has been consistently going down since 1983, and has remained as low as 14 per cent for urban females, as shown in Figure 7.1 (based on various NSSO reports).

The decline in the number of female workers is a matter of concern as it increases their dependency on men and thus strengthens patriarchal norms.

There could be many explanations for the fall in the number of women workers in the last 30 years. First, the number of women students in the age group 15–25 has increased, and therefore they are not in the labour market. Second, as prosperity increases, there is a tendency in Indian households to withdraw women from work outside their homes. In the Indian mindset, a household in which females do not perform manual work for others has a higher status than one in which females do so. Poor females work because they

5. Key Indicators of Employment and Unemployment in India, 2011-12, 68th Round NSSO

have no choice. But as the family incomes rise, they are withdrawn from paid work. The ratio of working women declines as we move up the caste hierarchy.

Figure 7.1: The percentage of 15-59 age women in workforce

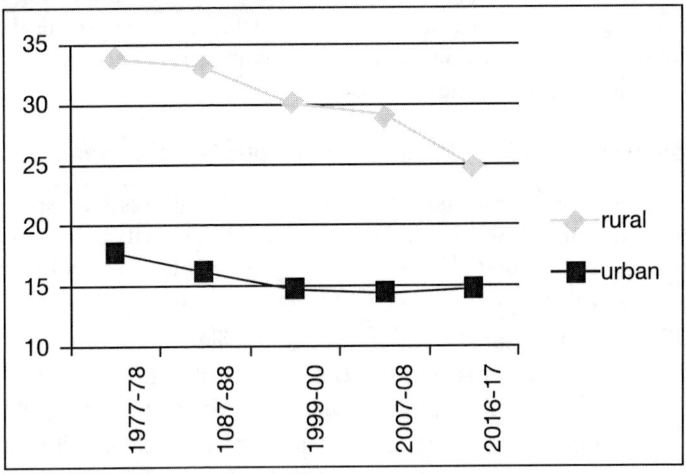

Source: based on various NSSO/NFHS reports

Third, rural women are being displaced by growing mechanization. Punjab farmers are switching to mechanical rice transplanters, and combine harvesters are spreading even in Bihar. Fourth, MFPs that women used to collect are disappearing, as the preferred forest policy is getting now more timber oriented. And lastly, non-farm jobs such as in construction, retail trade and hospitality sector are largely male oriented. These are generated some distance away from the village where men can go on a cycle, but most rural women do not know how to ride a bike.

Do women own agricultural land?

Before 1956, the devolution of both acquired and inherited property was governed by the personal laws of the community. Although equal rights were granted to women in acquired property through the Hindu Succession Act (HSA) of 1956, rights in inherited agricultural land were specifically exempted from the Act, and were made subject to tenancy and land reform laws of the states. For example, in the tenurial laws of Haryana, Himachal Pradesh, Jammu and Kashmir, Punjab, Delhi and UP, the specified rules of devolution show a strong preference for agnatic succession, with a priority for agnatic males.

Section 46(1) of the Rajasthan Tenancy Act, 1955, holds, 'the restrictions imposed by Section 45 on letting by a holder of Khudkasht and on sub-letting by a tenant shall not apply to (a) a minor, or (b) a lunatic, or (c) an idiot, or (d) a woman (other than married).' This is discriminatory, and women have been placed at par with minors, lunatics and idiots.

How I persisted in getting the iniquitous law changed

In my own home state UP, wives and daughters had no right to inherit agricultural land. As Revenue Secretary UP, I went to my Minister and requested him to agree to change the law and permit them too to share inheritance rights. His reply was,

> "Saxena Sahab, you reduce the ceiling limit from 18 to 10 acres and distribute the entire surplus to the poor, and I will sign the file, but I will never agree to give rights to women, as it would lead to intra-household bitterness and destroy harmonious family life.

I decided not to pursue the proposal, as I did not want to lose his trust, which I needed for my battles that I was fighting as Revenue Secretary, some of which are described in Chapter 2.

I received another opportunity to look at this discriminatory law as Secretary Land Resources, GOI in the late 1990s. This time I decided to directly approach the then CM of UP, Kalyan Singh. He hailed from Aligarh, where I was DM, and fortunately had a good opinion about me. I told him, 'Sir, I will sit in dharna here and will not leave your office unless you agree to change this law.' He got samosas and jalebis for me and we talked. With great difficulty he agreed to include only wives, but not daughters. The amended section 171 of the UP Zamindari Abolition and Land Reforms Act read as follows: 'After a landowner's death, his land will devolve to the widow and male issues in equal shares.'[6]

I did not give up and thought of a new strategy, of amending the central law, the HSA, so that no state then can discriminate at

6. By the time amendment was approved by the legislature, Mayawati had taken over as chief minister, who agreed with the changed law.

least against Hindu women. Before putting my ideas on the file, I tried to seek in principle approval of the then Prime Minister, Sri I. K. Gujral. He was shocked when I told him of my intention of making women landowners. He blurted,'But Jats are not going to like it!' Being an MP from Punjab, he did not want to annoy the patriarchal Jat community, and therefore shot down my proposal.

Amendments in 2005: Finally, as a member of the NAC (the controversial body set up in 2004 and discussed in detail in chapter 10), I convinced Mrs Sonia Gandhi, who sent my note to the Law Ministry, which amended the 1956 HSA and did away with these discriminatory laws by bringing agricultural land at par with acquired property and made Hindu women's inheritance rights in land legally equal to men's across States, overriding any inconsistent State laws. This can benefit millions of women dependent on agriculture for survival. However, neither the Department of Land Resources in GOI nor the Ministry of Women and Child Development has issued a single circular asking states to implement the law. States too have, by and large, ignored its implementation. The result is that anti-women laws and practices merrily continue in the states. For instance, UP added unmarried daughters in the category of those who inherit agricultural land in 2008, but married daughters are still not included. Let us hope someone would go to the Court and get this illegality removed.

When its non-implementation was brought by me to the notice of Syeda Hameed in 2011, who as member, Planning Commission, was chairing the Steering Committee on 'Women's Agency and Child Rights' for the Twelfth Five -Year Plan (2012–2017), she promptly set up a sub group under my chairmanship. I submitted the group's report, which is now gathering dust in the archives of the Niti Aayog.

Even though the legal framework has been amended in favour of women, women often forgo their claims in anticipation of support from their natal family in case of marital problems or their marriages breaking up, even though such support may not actually materialize. Women also face impediments in operationalizing the statutory codes and getting their names included in the records. Also, ownership does not always translate into control, as is the experience of matrilineal societies of Meghalaya where control is exercised by the maternal uncle. Decision making in cropping patterns, sale, mortgage and the purchase of land or the instruments of production remains in the hands of the men of the household.

Thus the issue is not only legal, it is also cultural. As women's control over loans, income and assets goes down, their access to social resources such as knowledge, power and prestige diminishes. Disparity in gender status gets intensified with the emergence and deepening of other forms of stratification. Subordination and seclusion of women is more noticed in communities where social differentiation and hierarchy based on ownership patterns or on prestige is more pronounced.

The Department of Land Resources in the Ministry of Rural Development should launch a campaign to correct revenue records and ensure that women's landownership rights are properly recorded by the states with intimation to women. Monitorable targets should be set for the district collectors to ensure timely implementation of law. It may be prudent to make these rights inalienable and non-transferable for the first 20 years on the pattern of pattas under the FRA. Further, the ministry of women and child development should prepare and circulate pamphlets to MPs that enable them raise concerns about women's rights to land and property in the Parliament.

It has to be understood that asset redistribution is superior to income redistribution. It provides a basis for overcoming distortions in the functioning of markets and for restructuring gender relations in the field of property rights, access to technology, healthcare, and governance. Asset ownership and control rights are preferable to numerous policy alternatives for women's empowerment. These are likely to bring in changes in public opinion about gender roles and deep-seated inequalities in prevailing sociocultural norms and inequalities practised against them. Government schemes unfortunately ignore intra-household inequities. Currently, the food security schemes do not address the needs of single women within the existing framework. Ration cards are usually in the name of the man and in cases where couples are separated, the wife does not have access to a card. The Food Security Act, 2013, mandates that the provision of ration cards

Lastly, equal pay for equal work is one of the cornerstones of the gender equality movement the world over. But Labour Bureau data show there has been little progress in terms of parity of salaries for men and women for equivalent work in India. Even more alarming is the fact that even though wage disparities have always existed in rural parts of the country, in some spheres of activity, the divide has widened. So while men were paid 70 per cent higher wages than women for ploughing work at the end of 2004–2005, the difference rose to 80.4 per cent in end-March 2012 and stood at 93.6 per cent at the start of 2013–2014.[7]

Bias Against Muslims

Even during the Congress regimes, Police had often shown strong bias against Muslims and sided with the Hindu mobs in cases of communal riots. Unfortunately, in the last eight years, mob lynching incidents of Muslims without any provocation have almost reduced Muslims into second-class citizens with no security of personal life and property. While delivering a judgement on a set of petitions against mob lynchings, the three-member bench of the Supreme Court headed by the Chief Justice observed that 'horrendous acts of mobocracy cannot be permitted to inundate the law of the land', adding that the recurring pattern of violence 'cannot be allowed to become the new normal' (Teltumbde 2018). What is worse is the dealing of the state in these open-and-shut crimes. Within a year, the six men Pehlu Khan named as his attackers before he died have all been absolved of any guilt by the police (Mander 2018).

While lynching needs to be strongly condemned and controlled, the unfortunate fact is that administration in the distant past, too, has been grossly unfair to Muslims. This has been amply discussed in various Commissions of Enquiry reports. For instance, the Madon Commission on Bhiwandi (Maharashtra) riots, 1970, observed:

- Discrimination was practised in making arrests, and while Muslim rioters were arrested in large numbers, the Police turned a blind eye to what the Hindu rioters were doing.
- Some innocent Muslims were arrested, knowing them to be innocent.
- Some Muslim prisoners were beaten both when arrested and while in police custody.

7. http://www.thehindubusinessline.com/economy/in-rural-india-gender-equality-in-wages-is-still-a-distant-dream/article4915110.ece

- There was almost no food or water for the prisoners on 7 and 8 May 1970.
- Muslim prisoners were made to stay in the compound of the taluka Police station, with the shade of trees for only a few of them, while Hindu prisoners were made to stay on the verandahs.
- There was discrimination in the distribution of food and water between Hindu prisoners and Muslim prisoners.

The Bhagalpur Inquiry Commission Report in 1995 remarked:

> We would hold Dwivedi, the then superintendent of police, Bhagalpur, wholly responsible for whatever happened before 24 October 1989, on 24th itself and after the 24th. His communal bias was fully demonstrated by his manner of arresting the Muslims and by not extending them adequate help to protect them. The manner in which the search was conducted was reminiscent of the searches in occupied Europe by the Nazis.'

It is unfortunate that Mr Dwivedi retired as the DGP of Bihar, incharge of law and order!

Rajat Sharma, who is considered close to the BJP wrote in *Onlooker* about the Meerut riots of 1982:

> 'Steel-helmeted, rifle-wielding jawans forcibly entered the Muslim houses, breaking down doors that were not opened. They refused to obey the order of the civil officers and commenced reckless ransacking of the houses. They overpowered everybody inside and beat them up with rifle butts. Then suddenly the jawans opened fire, their weapons aimed at the residents. At this point the civil officers fled from the scene. More than 100 bodies were removed by the PAC. It is said that 450 houses were raided by the PAC and each house had now at least one occupant who will live with a deformity for the rest of his life. A PWD Engineer was killed in Kotwali area and his 16 year old boy was shot dead at Bhumia Pul. His mother, a convent school teacher was assaulted. The trauma made her go insane. Ustad, a motor mechanic and his helper were shot dead in Shahghasa, their hut

> was set afire. Sakhawal, a rickshaw puller was killed in Purwa Faiyaz Ali.'

This riot was officially investigated by me as Joint Secretary, Minorities Commission, GOI in 1983. I quote from my report[8]:

> 'Inside the Feroze Building, I met Shabana, aged 11, who still bears many marks of knife injuries on her body. I visited the houses of Abdul Rasheed, Sheru, Anwar, Sherdin, Zafar Ali, Abdul Aziz, Irshad, Kalwa, Moin, Salim Iqbal, Abdul Zayyam and Wali Mohd., all deceased in the unfortunate police action on October 1. I was shown bullet marks on the walls, blood-stained clothes belonging to the deceased and many photographs of the houses which were taken soon after the incident which prove not only the fact of entry of force inside the houses, but also looting and wanton destruction of property. After detailed enquiries I was convinced that at least the killing of eighty innocent people by the PAC were not accounted for in the Police records.'

Unfortunately, GOI did not like the frankness of my report, and I received a written warning from the then Home Secretary, MMK Wali, a Kashmiri Brahmin of 1953 batch from Rajasthan cadre. I was verbally told that I could not continue in GOI (I had come to Delhi just six months back), either I opt to go back to UP or suffer kalapani (a punishment posting) to Afghanistan, which was then under Russian control. I chose the latter. I was very upset at being victimized for bringing to light unprovoked firing at innocent women and children, and I retaliated by getting my paper published,[9] though publication by a government servant without government permission is not permitted under the Service Rules. Luckily, senior IAS officers are not in the habit of reading serious stuff, so my publications went unnoticed and I escaped retribution.

---

8. Premature repatriation back to the state cadre is considered a punishment in the IAS
9. This paper has been included in two books, Shukla, K.S. ed. (1988). Collective Violence: Genesis and Response. Indian Institute of Public Administration, Delhi; and Iqbal A Ansari (ed), 1997: Communal Riots: The State and Law in India, Institute of Objective Studies, New Delhi

Had the government acted on my report and taken action against the culprits, perhaps similar but even more horrendous atrocity against Muslims in the same city five years later in 1987, so aptly described by the then SSP Ghaziabad, Vibhuti Narain Rai (2016), in his book *Hashimpura*, would not have happened. In this horrible massacre, Police picked up some 40 innocent Muslim youths from the Hashimpura neighbourhood of Meerut district that had seen no rioting, loaded them onto an official truck, drove them to a canal in the neighbouring Ghaziabad district, shot each to death one by one, threw them into the water, and then returned to the camp for a regular life as though they had executed a routine job. I quote below from the blurb of his book:

> Searching for survivors among the blood-soaked bodies strewn around the canal and between the ravines near Makanpur village, on the Delhi–Ghaziabad border, on the night of 22 May 1987, with just a dim torchlight—the memories are still fresh in Vibhuti Narain Rai's mind. On that fateful night, when Rai first heard about the killing, he could not believe the news was true until he, along with the district magistrate and a few other officials, went to Hindon canal. He quickly realized that all of them had become witnesses to secular India's most shameful and horrendous incident—personnel of the Provincial Armed Constabulary (PAC) had rounded up dozens of Muslims from riot-torn Meerut and had killed them in cold blood in Rai's area of jurisdiction. Offering a blow-by-blow account of the massacre and its aftermath, Hashimpura is a screaming narrative of the barbaric use of state force and the spineless politics in post-Independent India.

Twentyeight years later, on 21 March 2015, the verdict on the crime was pronounced and all the accused were released. Fortunately, the Delhi High Court has recently overturned the acquittal of police personnel involved. What has not emerged in the judgement is the role of V. N. Rai as SSP Ghaziabad and Kamalendu Prasad as Addl SP who are shining examples of integrity and impartiality expected from leaders. These cases need to be discussed in training academies so that young officers are aware of the pitfalls in following illegal directives by prejudiced superiors. A relevant portion of the High Court order reads[10]:

> 'How do we check the abuse of police power? Transparency of action and accountability perhaps are two possible safeguards which this Court must insist upon. Attention is also required to be paid to properly develop work culture, training and orientation of the police force consistent with basic human values. Training methodology of the police needs restructuring.

Finally, we quote below Home Ministry's own conclusion on the role of administration in an internal report:

> 'With few exceptions, it has been observed by almost all the commissions of enquiry that police were not sincere in meeting the important objective of protecting minorities, or the people who were in a weaker position and were either victim or target of killing in a communal disturbance. There were serious allegations that the police remained passive on many occasions. In many instances, police remained idle while looting, arson, and murders were committed in their very presence. In certain cases, police were an active participant in the violent mob.'

In all the cases described above, the Congress was in power at both the state and central levels. It is interesting that in the city of Moradabad (UP), where the two communities have equal share in population, educational institutions tend to be located in Hindu dominated areas but most of the police stations and Chowkies (outposts) are located in the Muslim dominated area. It would appear as if the Hindus need education and the Muslims need the police *Danda*.

Inter-community differences are both, irrational and rational

Prejudice is an attitude that predisposes a person to think, feel and act in an unfavourable way towards a group and its individual members. A prejudiced individual evaluates a person belonging

10. https://www.thehindu.com/news/national/1987-hashimpura-massacre-delhi-hc-sentences-16-ex-pac-personnel-to-life/article25377502.ece

to another group not as a person but on the basis of his group membership. When Sharma cheats Gupta, he thinks that Sharma is a cheat, but when Bashir cheats Gupta he thinks all Muslims are cheats. Certain negative traits are first associated with the members of the other group and all individuals are then presumed to have those objectionable qualities ascribed to that group. Prejudice results in five types of rejective behaviour: taking ill of the other group with friends, avoidance, discrimination, physical attack and in its extreme form it leads to wanting extermination of the other group.

An average Hindu's prejudice towards the Muslim community is because of his misconceived perception of, first, the implied attempts made by the Muslim rules in medieval times to destroy Hindu culture; second, the separatist role played by the Muslims in the freedom struggle; third, their supposed reluctance to modernize themselves and accept a uniform civil code and family planning and lastly, accusation of their having extraterritorial loyalties. Rise in Islamic radicalism across the globe has further alienated the two communities from each other. After the riots of Ahmedabad in 1969 in which 24 Hindus and 430 Muslims were killed, many educated Hindu rioters felt that they had avenged the plundering of the Somnath temple by Ghazni. An incident which had happened 10 centuries ago was still fresh in the minds of the Hindus, and in their perception, an attack on the present -day population of Muslims meant vindicating themselves against Ghazni, with whom India's Muslims have no relationship of descent or ethnicity except religion.

Rational conflict arises when two groups compete with each other for better share in scarce resources such as political power, government jobs and social status. Conflict may also arise if two groups follow mutually contradictory goals in matters of political and cultural policies. The Hindus would like to define an ideal society as one in which all citizens participate freely in all forms of social interaction with no concern for communal affiliation. In its view, the state should not be concerned with the problems of any group based on religion. It may allow for some degree of cultural diversity, but its basic premise is denial of any social obligation to preserve communal identities. On the other hand, most minority group leaders will view this lack of protection for their cultures as tyranny. They would like to believe in policies of political pluralism in which privileges are distributed according to their proportion in the population.

There are, thus, two broad kinds of policies to deal with groups' demands. One seeks assimilation of the entire population of the state into a common identity and recognizes only individual rights, privileges and duties. The erstwhile Soviet Union, China and Thailand have been pursuing this approach towards the Muslim segment of their population. The success of this method depends on the willingness of the minority groups to abandon their group demands and assimilate into the dominant society. The other approach recognizes the existence of differentiated groups in the population and concedes to such groups rights, privileges and obligations based on their proportion in the population. Lebanon and Malaysia have been following this approach where political and administrative reservations are built in the constitution for various religious and racial communities. No general guideline can be laid as to which approach is superior. Much would depend on the history, traditions and economic capabilities of the different communities as also on the nature of the state, whether it is authoritarian, democratic or elitist. From the experience of other communally divided societies perhaps it can be suggested that if the political leaders seek to bring about an identity between the state and the nation, the problem of conflict management becomes more complicated.

Official Policy: The Indian State lays down, and perhaps rightly so, a middle-of-the-road policy as far as Muslims are concerned. It frowns upon demands of a covertly political nature, like separate electorate, proportional representation, formation of religious parties and so on, and at the same time conceding cultural and educational demands like encouragement of Urdu, preservation of Muslim Personal Law, minority status to Aligarh Muslim University and so on. Thus, at least till 2014 the Central government's ideal seems to be political assimilation and cultural pluralism. This, however, leaves a certain amount of grey area, the most important being reservation of jobs, whether formal or informal. Purely from the interest of communal harmony, it will be better to take a once for all decision on such issues and not give an impression that these issues are negotiable on the eve of the elections. Keeping these problems open and alive would always result in an increase of communal agitations for and against such demands.

The community needs another Sir Syed Ahmed

Muslims in India have not done well in acquiring higher education, and hence their share in government jobs continues to be low, of which discrimination is a minor causative factor; other reasons are lack of preparedness and sufficient educational qualifications. This has further increased their sense of frustration. As against their share of roughly 14 per cent in the population, Muslim share in Class III and IV jobs varies between 5 and 9 per cent. However, for Class I and II posts, where recruitment is free from bias and made on the basis of written examinations followed by interview by Public Service Commissions, the figure is much lower, between 3 and 4 per cent (Saxena 1989).

In a survey (Sherwani 1983: 204)[11] of nine Inter-Colleges of the town of Rampur,[12] which has 72 per cent Muslims and 28 per cent non-Muslim population, the performance of students who appeared in the Intermediate (class XII) Examination, 1982 was as follows:

Table 7.2: Performance of Muslim Students in Rampur

	Muslims	Non-muslims	Percentage of share of Muslims in total
Population	72%	28%	72
Number of students appearing for Intermediate examination	197	534	27
Students who passed the examination	89	344	20
Students who got 1st Division	2	40	5

Source: Sherwani (1983)

11. A.R. Sherwani, Muslim India, May 1983: 204. The author also worked as Chairman Minorities Commission, GOI.
12. Rampur was princely state under a Muslim Nawab, and has remained singularly free from communal violence in the last 100 years, unlike its neighbour, Moradabad. It could be because of lack of political mobilisation of the two communities by both Congress and the Muslim League in the colonial period, as the state was not under British rule.

A.R. Sherwani, who had conducted this study, concludes as follows:

> And all this while, the Muslim leaders and the Hindu secular leaders have been telling the Muslims they are not getting jobs because of discrimination. I do not deny discrimination. We Indians are the most discriminating people on earth. The Agarwal Bania discriminates against a Gupta Bania, the Sarjupari Brahmin against a Kayakubja Brahmin and so on. But the position is that the Muslims are not even giving anyone a chance to discriminate against them in worthwhile services. Anyone can discriminate against the Muslims only when they qualify and compete. How many Muslims are competing? This no one tells, neither the Muslim 'leaders' nor the secular Hindu leaders who go about as the best friends of the Muslims.

Certain Urdu papers and Muslim political leaders such as Syed Shahabuddin (of the Indian Foreign Service), Azam Khan and Asaduddin Owaisi[13] from Muslim majority areas of Kishanganj (Bihar), Rampur and Hyderabad respectively have developed a vested interest in romanticizing and exaggerating Muslim grievances. In tandem with such politicians, the ulema too have been more concerned with the cultivation of Muslims' socio-religious particularism than with their economic uplifting (Jaffrelot and Gayer 2012). It suits them if the Muslim masses suffer from a sense of permanent injury, it will keep their leadership intact. Muslim leadership has been harbouring under the notion that the economic well being of the community is dependent on its achieving due share in political power. Unfortunately, the geographical dispersal of the Muslim population renders it impossible for them to convert their cultural identity into a political pressure group. An objective analysis will perhaps show that the Muslim problems (except violence) are not so much the cause of the disturbed Muslim mind

---

13. In March 2016, while addressing a public rally in Maharashtra, Owaisi said that he will never say the slogan *Bharat Mata Ki Jai* (Hail mother India). Such remarks deepen Hindu antagonism against all Muslims. Unfortunately, except for Javed Akhtar, no other Muslim leader condemned Owaisi.

as the consequence of that disturbance which is the result of lack of political participation on the terms of their liking.

In a competitive situation only confident and assertive communities can do well. Because the Muslims find themselves in a non Muslim and hostile environment, they like to imagine that they would be rejected in the employment market on grounds of religion and, therefore, do not concentrate on developing their talents. Thus, Muslims become victims of a self-fulfilling prophecy. They predict rejection first, and their withdrawal from competition proves their own prediction.

Mr Bahuguna, CM of UP, who was considered to be very close to the Muslim community, once in one-to-one chat with me in 1974 quipped, '*Hindustan ka musalman ek dedh taang ka admi hai, yeh kabhie seedha nahin chal sakta*' (Indian Muslim is a one and a half legged animal, he can never walk straight). In colonial India Muslims passionately supported two movements, Khilafat and partition; the former amounted to supporting Turkish imperialism over Arab nationalism while fighting British imperialism at home, and the latter resulted in losing whatever safeguards such as proportional representation they would have enjoyed in undivided India.

Post-Independence, Indian Muslim leadership has been asking for certain group rights such as preservation of Muslim Personal Law, reservation in jobs and so on, and at the same time it would like that individual Muslims be not subjected to discrimination. Gopal Krishna (1982) thinks that there is something of an incongruity between these two sets of demands: the desire that they be treated as a separate and distinct community cannot go hand in hand with the desire of individual Muslims to be treated like everyone else in matters of employment.

> 'It is a dilemma, community recognition and assertion is needed for certain purposes, and anonymity is desired for others. The gains from community assertion are far from obvious, though they seem to be of considerable psychological import, while the cost to individuals arising from lack of anonymity is tangible and immediate.'

M.R.A. Baig who was in the Indian Foreign Service in his book 'The Muslim Dilemma in India' traces the roots of their stagnation to general orthodoxy which is perpetuated upon the Muslim community because of the hold of religion over them. According to him, 'as a community we are imprisoned, mentally and morally, within a completely static religious system' (Baig 1974: 101). Islam preaches submission to authority rather than critical examination of ideas and institutions. Baig is, therefore, convinced that unless social reform takes place within the community, Muslims will continue to suffer from communal and social degeneration, economic stagnation and educational backwardness. He is optimistic that 'Islam not only should but can be reformed' (Baig 1974: vii).

Reformers such as Hamid Dalwai who had the 'potential to take their community out of a medievalist ghetto into a full engagement with the modern world' (Guha 2018) were unfortunately unpopular with the Muslim masses. Maxime Rodinson (1974), in his book Islam and Capitalism, argues that as an ideology for socio economic upliftment orthodoxy is impracticable. Therefore, if a Muslim society wishes to progress it will have to undergo a profound transformation where old interpretations of Islam will give way to a synthesis of religious and humanist values from which both economy and society will benefit.

These ideas have been challenged by several other perceptive scholars of Islam; nevertheless, it is common observation that Muslim children coming from similar socio-economic background do rather poorly in schools and colleges as compared to non-Muslims. The fact that they have remained behind other communities in almost all countries of the world also cannot be a matter of sheer coincidence. This includes even countries where they are in a majority, such as Malaysia,[14] Lebanon, Nigeria and Egypt. A perceptible and growing shift of the educated in South Asia from sufi Islam to salafi or wahabi Islam also makes them suspect.

To sum up, the primary responsibility of providing security and discrimination-free environment to Muslims as individuals lies with the administration, but Muslim leaders too should dispassionately analyse why the Hindus hate them, and therefore are easily swayed by the Hindu propaganda against them. Hindu parents aspire to send their kids to Christian convent schools, why not to Madarsas? If institutions controlled by Muslims—and this includes Aligarh

14. In a study of Malaysian society, Parkinson (1967) has argued that the Malays retardation is due to their resisting change and being fatalistic in their approach to life.

Muslim University and Jamia Milia—could become world class, image of Muslims would certainly improve. As of now, many wounds such as on Kashmiri Muslims, appear self-inflicted.

The Sachar Committee, 2006, has demonstrated that on most socio-economic indicators, the average condition of Muslims in India is comparable to the country's acknowledged, historically most-disadvantaged communities, the SCs and STs. Whether this is due to cumulative and comprehensive official discrimination and neglect, or due to the general educational backwardness of Muslims arising from their religious orthodoxy and cultural ethos, or due to their perception of their contemporary social situation in which they see themselves as being politically powerless, demoralized and insecure can be debated. This psychology of despair and insularity does not promote investment in higher education.

The community needs another Sir Syed, not only to increase Muslim share in quality education, but also to improve their image, which would happen if in 20 years the best doctors, teachers and software experts in the country are Muslims. Why should their excellence be confined to music and films only?

It may be worthwhile to recall what Allame Iqbal wrote in Jawab-e-Shikwa, 'God has not been unjust to the Muslims; they have been unjust to themselves'.

Extreme Inequality Detrimental to Economic Growth

The Indian Constitution prevents the government from recognizing Muslims as a category for affirmative action, but greater effort needs to be made to ensure granting of scholarships and opening of schools in minority -dominated districts. It may be noted that the poorer states, namely Bihar, Jharkhand, Madhya Pradesh, Odisha, Rajasthan, UP, Chhattisgarh and West Bengal, account for 56 per cent of the SC and 55 per cent of the ST population in the entire country. Further, 58 per cent of the Muslim population is concentrated in these states.[15] This highlights a two-way relationship. These states are poorer because large proportions of the excluded social groups live here; conversely, in the poorer

15. thttps://www.scribd.com/document/131728416/Human-Development-Report2011

states, development programmes do not reach the targeted population—especially the economically and socially deprived sections.

Overcoming corruption, theft, leakages, inefficiencies and cost constraints are imperative, but still not sufficient, in a highly unequal society like ours to overcome the barriers that powerless and expelled dispossessed people face in accessing food and livelihood with dignity. The strategy for inclusive growth should not be just a conventional strategy for growth to which some elements aimed at inclusion are added.

On the contrary, it should aim at achieving a particular type of growth process which will meet the objectives of inclusiveness and sustainability. This strategy must be based on sound macroeconomic policies which establish the macroeconomic preconditions for rapid growth and support key drivers of this growth. It must also include sector-specific policies which will ensure that the structure of growth that is generated, and the institutional environment in which it occurs, achieve the objective of inclusiveness in all its many dimensions. (GOI 2007)

In summary social exclusion frequently reflects the powerlessness of the most vulnerable and is a direct function of their weak political bargaining power as a collective entity in a democracy. Our inability to include them in State programmes in the last 60 years is a severe indictment of public policy and its implementation.

Wealth created by sustained high rates of growth in India remains unevenly distributed at macro-level as well as in terms of significant interstate and intrastate regional disparities. Low growth rates in poorer states have further widened the disparity in the provision of public services. The polarization has divided the country into two distinct groups of rich states and poor states (Hari and Hatti 2015). The goal of equitable economic development is to enable income levels of poorer states to reach the levels of the richer states. For this, the incomes of poorer states must grow faster than those of the rich for a long time. However, this has not quite happened in India, although some poor states have done well lately when compared with their own dismal past record (CRISIL 2018).

If growth increases inequality, gains to the poor would be limited. Other things being equal, one percentage point of growth leads to a smaller reduction in poverty in a very unequal country than in a less unequal one. And if inequality rises during the growth process, benefits to the poor become even fewer. The impact of the same amount of growth on poverty reduction is significantly greater when initial income inequality is lower. The higher the initial level of inequality in a country or the greater the increase in inequality during the growth spell, the higher the rate of growth that is needed to achieve any given rate of poverty reduction (WDR 2006).

Economic liberalization rewards those with better initial endowments such as resources, assets and skills that can be used in market exchange. It follows that inequality cannot be reduced effectively in an environment of laissez-faire, and therefore interventionist policies and market coordination are needed. Public policy matters, market driven policies aimed at economic freedom or economic growth may not help simply to reduce income or horizontal inequality. Successful policies aimed at correcting market failures, facilitating the accumulation of physical and human resources by the poor and backward groups, adequate allocation of central funds to the poorer states, and the provision of safety net programmes to all vulnerable sections of the population are essential pre-requisites for reducing inequality.

Extreme inequality is not only detrimental to poverty reduction, but also to economic growth. The issue of inequality is a concern of humanity and well-being, including the right of people to have a life of dignity and access to basic goods and services (Sekher and Chakraborty 2016). Inequality has a negative impact on social cohesion and on the quality of institutions. Given that in the long-run, efficiency and greater equity are complementary, governments should take appropriate measures to ensure that the reduction in inequality and disparities in life chances are accorded greater prominence in the design of development policies and strategies. Dealing with inequality while encouraging productivity growth and job creation, is now probably one of the biggest policy challenges facing India.

8 Chapter

THE STRANGE CASE OF BIHAR: FROM LALU YADAV TO NITISH KUMAR

We have chosen Bihar for a detailed study, not because it is the poorest state in India, but because in the entire history of Independent India it is the only state where the ruling political regime decided for a long period of 15 years during 1990 to 2005 to deliberately slow down economic development by weakening the state capacity and not spending development funds, as such expenditure was perceived to be helping only the upper caste, and not the lower castes who were the vote banks of the ruling party. As is well known, during this period Sri Lalu Prasad Yadav ruled Bihar, either directly as CM from 1990 to 1997, or indirectly as CM's husband from 1997 to 2005 following corruption charges against him relating to the Fodder Scam.[1] Whereas other states in India—both poor and non-poor—clamour for more financial devolution from the central government, Bihar opted for the reverse strategy and chose not to spend even the allocated funds, not to fill up the vacant posts, and allow law and order to deteriorate, as Lalu thought 'good' administration was not in the interest of 'his people'. One of his party slogans translates as 'We need dignity, not development.' His strategy seemed to work, as his party with the

1. The scam involved the embezzlement of about ₹10,000 crores from the government treasury by fabricating of 'vast herds of fictitious livestock' for which fodder, medicines and animal husbandry equipment were supposedly procured. Both, bureaucracy and senior politicians were involved in the scam.

help of Yadav–Muslim[2] votes won the state elections in 1995 and 2000.

Lalu, thus destabilized state institutions since they were perceived to be mainly serving the interests of upper -caste groups. Good governance was seen by Lalu as not compatible with 'good' politics. Finally, in 2005, people got sick of lawlessness and economic stagnation and threw Lalu's party out of power.

Bihar is India's third most populous state, with 104 million people (2011 census) and with 89 per cent living in rural areas, the largest rural population share amongst major Indian states with a heavy dependence on agriculture. The bifurcation of Bihar into two states in 2001 further deepened the development challenges facing the state. The new state of Bihar, minus the wealthier, more urbanized and industrialized southern districts that constitute Jharkhand, left Bihar with a much weaker revenue base, a larger share of the population in poor rural districts, and greater capacity challenges than before bifurcation.

Bihar was regarded as one of the better governed states in the 1950s, but administration started showing signs of deterioration from the mid-1960s onwards. Mr Appu (2005a), a legendary civil servant, recalls his years as Health Secretary, Bihar, from 1962 to 1967, when intense lobbying to secure plum postings was the order of the day. Ministers, legislators, senior officers and other influential people openly pleaded the cause of their protégés. Doctors succeeded in getting desired postings by resorting to bribery. He recalls:

> "On the eve of the 1967 elections, the minister sent down over 100 transfer orders from his camp office. They were in conflict with the guidelines and quite a few were confusing inasmuch as two doctors were posted to the same place, or one person was posted to more than one post. I did not carry out the orders. I submitted a note to chief minister Sahay through the chief secretary pointing out why the orders should not be implemented. The chief secretary supported me. The chief minister decided that the minister's orders should not be implemented. All the doctors who had paid money were disappointed. In several other departments also corruption became widespread.

2. Together, they constitute 31% of divided Bihar's population.

> In the works departments corruption had existed since a long time in the matter of awarding contracts. Now bribes were freely offered to secure transfer to particular posts, and even for getting promotions.

The nature of political power also started changing with mass mobilization, which began with the JP movement in the 1970s, and helped form the basis for caste politics that characterize Bihar politics even today. Though the backward castes constitute nearly 60 per cent of Bihar's electorate, till the early years of the 1970s, these castes were politically not significant. The year 1977 was the turning point in their political organization when reservation for backward castes in government service was introduced (Verma 1991), and a backward caste leader, Karpoori Thakur (a barber by caste), became CM in 1977.

Mr Thakur was keen to appoint Appu as Chief Secretary, but he (Appu) wrote to the CM why the CM should reconsider his decision. When the CM still insisted, he laid down several conditions, including that he should have a free hand in restructuring administration, making appointments, with no interference in delegated spheres. Ruthless action should be taken against corrupt and incompetent officials. He explained (Appu 2005b),

> I did not lay down the above conditions because of my arrogance or any feeling that I was indispensable. I did so because I felt that the situation in Bihar was so bad that there was no hope of effecting the necessary improvement unless those conditions were fulfilled.

Seven months later, when he felt that the CM had failed to stand by his commitments, he refused to continue as Chief Secretary. Appu writes in his memoirs:

> When the atrocious behaviour of some legislators came to my notice I asked the additional inspector general of police (intelligence) to make a confidential enquiry. After a few days he reported that there were 44 legislators with criminal records, equally shared by the Janata and the Congress. I discussed the matter with the chief minister. I asked him why he could not throw out the criminals from his party. He frankly confessed his inability to do anything

because the criminals enjoyed the support of some of the top leaders of his party. When I realised that there was absolutely no possibility of revamping the administration, I left Bihar in April 1978. While quitting as Chief Secretary, he outlined the government's failure to stem the rot in the political system, the growing criminalization and declining morale of the bureaucracy and the ensuing uncontrollable chaos as reasons for opting out.

Political gains at the cost of good governance

Class and caste mobilization in Bihar increased further during the 1980s, culminating in the election of Lalu PrasadYadav as CM in 1990. Amongst the heterogeneous caste/class groups within the Backwards, the economically rich and politically influential Yadavs (the so-called creamy layer) cornered most of the benefits of the 'Lalu Raj', while the larger mass of Backwards remained poor. But, they supported Lalu Prasad Yadav till 2005 because he provided them with a sense of pride and participation.

Though deterioration in governance had started setting in from the mid-1960s onwards, Lalu further hastened the process by taking a number of steps. He decided not to fill up vacant posts, despite the availability of funds. Vacancies were more common at higher levels of the public service, where there were even fewer plausible candidates from historically excluded groups[3] (Mathew and Moore 2011). The political leadership thus sent clear signals both to its own supporters ('This government is really serious about humbling the old elite') and to their upper -caste opponents ('You are no longer welcome in Bihar').

Then he centralized the whole process of budget release by deciding that all new plan schemes and even ongoing plan schemes exceeding ₹25 lakh are to be brought before the Cabinet before issue of financial sanction (Nayak and Saxena 2006). There is no such parallel provision in the Transaction of Business rules of the GOI, nor is there any such provision in other States. In Bihar, however, such plan schemes exceeding ₹25 lakh were to be approved by an

3. In 2002, for example, out of a total of 244 Bihar cadre officers of the IAS, 135 were from upper caste groups, while only seven officers came from the three largest backward caste groups (Witsoe 2007). Lalu's favourite, Mukund Prasad, was from backward caste.

Empowered Committee headed by the Development Commissioner as a first step. Then it required the approval of the Planning Minister and CM through the Chief Secretary. When the CM directs that it should be placed before the Cabinet, a Cabinet memo is circulated. Thus, the whole process delayed sanction by several months, so much so that Bihar could spend only 2 per cent of its budget in the first six months of the financial year. Despite GOI bearing the expenditure on MDM for school children, such meals could be provided only for a few months during January to March in a year because of late releases of funds. Bihar had the country's lowest utilization rate for centrally funded programmes. The state's Annual Plan expenditure was revised downwards in the course of every year between 1992–1993 and 2004–2005, sometimes by more than half.

If, during one of his many trips to villages, Lalu Prasad was asked to provide better roads, he would tend to question whether roads were really of much benefit to ordinary villagers, and suggest that the real beneficiaries would be contractors and the wealthy, powerful people who had cars (Mathew and Moore 2015).

As Secretary, Rural Development in GOI during 1997–1999, I was incharge of drinking water schemes. During these years, Bihar did not spend a single rupee on drinking water, though its annual allocation was around ₹100 crore. I called the Bihar Secretary, Debashis Gupta, who had been my student, for an informal chat. He admitted that because of fear of future enquiries, no Secretary would ever put his signatures on a file dealing with purchase of pipes, especially after the fodder scam of 1997. I suggested that he delegate these powers to the Chief Engineer, who might earn a Commission, but at least funds would be spent. Even that did not happen, and Bihar remained deprived of central assistance.

The collapse of administration was also commented by the World Bank (2005) in its report on Bihar:

> There also appears to be a breakdown of hierarchy and the loss of control by DMs, heads of departments and depart- mental secretaries over subordinate personnel. The DMs appear to be frustrated by centralization, absence of support and understanding from their superiors, and inaction on reports of malfeasance and inefficiency at subordinate levels.

Lalu also weakened the Police administration. The business of kidnapping for ransom thrived. It was inevitably aimed mainly at the higher castes, and was believed to receive high-level political support and protection, if not direct sponsorship. The state government did not generally exercise discipline over the police, but retained sufficient control that the service could be used for politically crucial tasks. We quote below from a New York Times article[4] dated 10 April 2010 about the state of affairs of Bihar during Lalu's regime:

> Criminals could count on the police for protection, not prosecution. Highwaymen ruled the shredded roads and kidnapping was one of the state's most profitable businesses. Violence raged between Muslims and Hindus, between upper castes and lower castes. Its economy, peopled by impoverished subsistence farmers struggl ing through alternating floods and droughts, shrivelled. Its government, led by politicians who used divisive identity politics to entrench their rule, was so corrupt that it required a newly coined phrase: the Jungle Raj. Lalu Prasad, a wily populist politician whose party peddles a message of lower caste empowerment, ran the state for 15 years from beneath a banyan tree. Under Mr. Prasad's watch, criminal syndicates kidnapped, extorted and robbed with impunity, protected by political leaders, or in some cases led by politicians.

When Lalu was sent to jail, the district administration cited security reasons to keep him in the Bihar Military Police guest house, instead of Beur Central Jail. Ministers and top officials, including the chief secretary and principal secretaries, would make a beeline to the guest house.[5] Even when in 1998 the Supreme Court took exception to keeping Lalu in a guest house and shifted him to Beur Central jail, the government brass continued to treat him as the big boss. 'Lalu used to call up anyone he wanted to meet and they would go with the files', recalled a former bureaucrat.[6]

---

4. https://www.nytimes.com/2010/04/11/world/asia/11bihar.html
5. https://www.telegraphindia.com/india/lessons-for-sasikala-from-lalu-s-school/cid/1518802
6. https://www.telegraphindia.com/india/proxy-rule-lessons-from-bihar/cid/1497968

Anup Mukerji, who later in 2009 became the Chief Secretary, was the first IAS officer to question Lalu Prasad for functioning as an 'extra constitutional authority'—presiding over meetings in the jail with secretaries when his wife, Rabri Devi, was the CM, who was simply a surrogate for Lalu. As a secretary-rank officer in 2000, Mukerji wrote a letter to the then chief secretary Mukund Prasad, saying: 'I will not be able to attend the meetings presided over by an extra-constitutional authority.' Working as a proxy for his wife, Lalu Prasad was in the habit of addressing and even presiding over official meetings. Mukerji mustered the courage to write such a letter when Lalu Prasad still controlled Bihar, often ordering senior IAS officers to prepare *khaini* (raw tobacco) and treating them like his orderlies. 'Mukerji became an instant hit with other IAS officers sulking in a regime which had scant respect for the system and institutions,' said a senior bureaucrat.

Mukund Prasad has been the most trustworthy official of Lalu Yadav. At various times, when Lalu could not attend to the affairs of the state directly—such as when he was in prison or gone abroad—the reins of the government were not given to some RJD politician but to Mr Prasad. Perhaps, in the history of the Indian bureaucracy, no other IAS or even ICS officer has wielded so much of power as Mukund Prasad. It is not as if Mr Lalu Yadav was only a figurehead; undoubtedly his was the final word but it was whetted by Prasad and his opinion was carefully considered and taken into account. It was clear to everyone in the bureaucracy that none could be posted or transferred and no expenditure can be made without a nod from 'Mukund Babu'. His power was immense and Lalu's faith in him was complete. Before going to jail in connection with the fodder scam in July 1997, Lalu specifically told Rabri not to sign any file without the consent of Mukund Prasad. Rabri always signed on the dotted line only after Mukund's go-ahead. Prasad has been a clean officer. Even the worst of detractors would not accuse him of financial irregularity. It was said of him that he would even fine himself if ever his bills were inflated or turned out to be wrong. In the corrupt world of Bihar government, Prasad was one of the few who could not be bribed, influenced or compromised (Verma 2002).

As was the customary practice, Rabri Devi, Mukund Prasad and other senior Bihar officials came to the Planning Commission in 2000 for seeking annual Plan funds, when I was Secretary there.

Rabri Devi looked at me and whispered something to Mukund, who nodded. It appeared as if she wanted confirmation that I was the notorious Rural Development Secretary who had bitterly criticized and run down the Bihar bureaucracy two years ago (see the next section and annexure). With a view to assuage her hurt feelings, I gave some extra funds to Bihar. However, after the official meeting, Mukund Babu came to my room and said, 'Dr Saxena, why have you given us additional money? We won't spend even the previously allotted funds.'

The overall situation in Bihar was best summed up in the Economist in 2004 (Long 2004) as:

> 'Bihar has become a byword for the worst of India, of widespread and inescapable poverty, of corrupt politicians indistinguishable from mafia-dons they patronise, caste-ridden social order that has retained the worst feudal cruelties. Chronic misrule has led to crumbling infrastructure, collapsing education and health systems and evaporating law and order.'

My response to Bihar's decline

To the best of my knowledge, GOI for a long period kept mum and did not officially respond to the pathetic situation in Bihar. However, GOI could not keep quiet when Ranbir Sena of Bhumihars in December 1997 massacred 61 Dalit labourers and sharecroppers, and soon after in retaliation CPI (ML) killed 9 upper -caste landlords in January 1998 in central Bihar. I received the following letter from the Joint Secretary, Ministry of Home Affairs, in January 1998.

> Dear Dr. Saxena,
>
> The Prime Minister has desired that the socio-economic factors responsible for the presently deteriorating law and order situation in Bihar may be discussed in a meeting of Committee of Secretaries with a view to work out short and long term strategy for increasing rural employment opportunities. A meeting of Committee of Secretaries to discuss the above subject is proposed to be scheduled very shortly.

> It is therefore requested that a brief background note for the Committee of Secretaries to meet the above objectives, in so far as your Department is concerned, may please be sent to this Ministry for onward submission to Cabinet Secretariat extremely urgently.
>
> With regards
>
> Yours sincerely
>
> (V.K. Malhotra)

Normally such letters get marked to a Joint Secretary, who then prepares a routine note with the help of his subordinates. However, I decided to dictate the background brief myself, given as annexure to this chapter, and sent it to the Home Ministry[7]. Since it concerned Bihar, I marked a copy to the Chief Secretary Bihar too. This somehow got leaked to the Press and all hell broke out soon. Never before in the history of centre–state relations in India, such a strong worded letter had gone to the Chief Secretary. My letter became the cannon fodder for all newspapers and magazines and often got coverage as front headlines. India Today[8] had the following to say on my note:

> **Union secretary N.C. Saxena pulls up bureaucrats, accuses them of behaving like politicians**
>
> **Patna:** Politicians could easily have taken strong exception to it. As far as Union Government's Secretary for Rural Development N.C. Saxena went, he was only pulling up the bureaucrats when he accused them of behaving like politicians—English-speaking ones at that.
>
> Stung by reports that the ₹1,177 crore allocated for rural development in Bihar for 1997–1998 was not reaching the poor, Saxena sent off a missive to Bihar Chief Secretary B.P. Verma last week. 'The development machinery has nearly collapsed today,' Saxena said.

7. There was no follow-up by the home ministry on my note, presumably because the Prime Minister Sri Gujral resigned in March 1998.
8. https://www.indiatoday.in/magazine/indiascope/story/19980330-union-secretary-n.c.-saxena-pulls-up-bureaucrats-accuses-them-of-behaving-like-politicians-826002-1998-03-30

> 'Many civil servants have become like politicians—corrupt, with short-term targets, narrow horizons, feudal outlook....' To add insult to injury, three days later the Patna High Court observed that most officials in the state were corrupt.

Chief Secretary Verma reacted strongly to the criticism. 'Bihar seems to have become a soft target for everybody these days,' he said. Added state Finance Minister Shanker Prasad Tekriwal: 'He (Saxena) has overstepped his brief.' The state Government will write to the Centre demanding action against Saxena.

But if Saxena has attracted brickbats, there are bouquets too. The president of the Bihar State Administrative Services Association, Shashi Bhushan Verma, feels,'There's at least one IAS officer who has the guts to call a spade a spade.'

Says the state IAS Officers' Association President Abhimanyu Singh: 'Instead of taking offence to the letter, we should do some soul-searching.'

The Times of India covered the story as:

> **Dysfunctional, insensitive, corrupt: Bureaucrat demasks Bihar bureaucracy**
>
> Perhaps for the first time the State bureaucracy has come in for scathing criticism by a central agency for inept governance and downright incompetence. The two-page letter stresses that the poor would have been perhaps better off if we could send the amount of various schemes had been sent by moneyorder directly to them bypassing bureaucracy. Right from the BDOs to many district Collectors and often some Secretaries are busy making money, or collecting money for their political masters, thereby totally distorting priorities which are set on paper. As corruption is on the increase even in higher echelons of bureaucracy, the fear in the minds of lower level officials against making money has disappeared, and corruption at all levels has become a low risk and high reward activity.

But what about the politicians? One of the Ministers reacted sharply over the language of my letter and told the Hindustan Times

(8 March 1998) that the Secretary Rural Development has gone beyond his jurisdiction by passing such subjective remarks against the state administration. However, the IAS Association of Bihar supported the contents and wrote to the state government,'there is hardly any doubt that the contents of the letter appear to echo the thoughts and sentiments of teeming millions of the poor downtrodden population'.

I also received several angry reactions from the Bihar cadre IAS officers. The most balanced but still critical of my accusations was from CK Anil, of 1991 batch who was my student at the Academy. I produce the entire letter below:

> Sir,
>
> I am to state that the paper which was written with avowed aim of 'Improving Governance in Bihar' actually turned out to be for 'denigrating the Bureaucracy of Bihar'. Of course, the paper received wide newspaper coverage and thanks to the article each of the 350 IAS Officer of Bihar Cadre have been termed as corrupt, insensitive, feudal, incompetent and agents of exploitation. It shall probably be beyond your comprehension as to how this article has contributed handsomely in demolishing the little self esteem left in the especially younger batches of IAS in Bihar Cadre.
>
> The paper is a continuation of the 'Bihar Bashing' which the state has been receiving at the hands of the media since the last several .years especially so since when Sri Lalu Prasad had been C.M. of this State. It is a typical outsider view of the mess that Bihar seems from outside – a dysfunctional anarchy.
>
> The genesis of your paper appears to be the non-utilization of funds or rather funds not reaching the actual beneficiary. As Project Director I was handling Rural Development funds and it was often a problem to release money to the Blocks and Panchayat. This was so because the BDO or the Mukhia[9] would immediately take

9. head of the village council, called sarpanch in other states

up 'n' number of schemes and distribute the total money as advance to either his own relatives who act as agents in employment Schemes or the muscle men or petty contractors of the local MLA. So the question arises how does the money get spent? Or is it all to be thrown down the drain? The District Collector or the Project Director have little control over either the BDO (who are members of Bihar Administrative Service Association, BASA) or the Mukhia who have direct links to the MLA or even the Chief Minister. If any action is proposed against the BDO it has to be sent to the Rural Development Department at Patna and it has to be pursued for a favourable outcome, otherwise the Minister usually disagrees with the enquiry report of a District Magistrate/Project Director and doesn't take any action against the BDO who further gets emboldened and organises union activities through the BASA Association and adopts a non cooperative attitude. Hence the Collector/Project Director loses face and is demotivated. Besides if he is not able to either meet the expectations of the Chief Minister for any reasons he is transferred summarily leaving the Officer holding the post of Collector/Project Directors a demoralized lot.

It shall be incorrect if we the IAS do not accept that the upright officers have been systematically marginalized by the indulgent political masters (especially CM) who expects a committed bureaucracy. Those officers who belong to the committed group enjoy better posting and they are rewarded with outstanding ACR's and foreign training etc. While the non-committed upright group in absence of proper Cadre management are sidelined in working for inconsequential departments as Rajbhasa, Reservation, Protocol etc. When these officers apply for central deputation to Delhi, as many hindrances are created as possible. All this effort is done basically to break the upright officer and to make him submissive and more committed.

It is certainly wrong to club most Collectors and Secretaries in the category of BDO who is working with only one zeal—money making. Of the 55 Districts in Bihar more than 30 are in command of direct recruited IAS Officers and not more that 20% of these have any reputation of being corrupt openly.

As far as the 40 departments run by the Secretaries to Government are concerned the departments of Excise, Food Supply, Animal Husbandry etc. have always been headed by pliable officers and the P.A. to the Ministers and Private Secretaries have been traditionally taking money uniformly on every file related to any personal or financial matters. In some cases the Secretaries to Government know about this racket but couldn't care less they have no drive in them left to stop these rackets/ scams.

The Working conditions in the State for bureaucrats are extremely difficult and political masters have vested interest in making the working conditions as unbearable as possible to make the average IAS officer succumb to the pressures of the Ministers, MLAs & the CM. Admittedly, there has been no statesman in the politics of Bihar in recent past and no politician of National Stature, resulting in lack of foresight and political will in the CM. No politician is bothered about the long term benefits of the State what they are more bothered is about how to fill in their own pockets at the expense of the State by looting/siphoning off available funds to the tune of 40 per cent or more. The Secretariat is manned by Babus who have a very strong union and the Government has no control over the clerks. No IAS Officer dare take any action against them for fear that they would go on strike. Hence the clerks do not work, they play cards/chess during office hours and the Secretary looks the other way. The IAS Officers who dare say anything against these clerks are branded as rash, tactless and ineffective officers and they get a scolding from senior officers in the bureaucracy that 'Are you trying to improve the system?'. Thus any bureaucrat with integrity, courage and political neutrality is left to fend for himself and fight alone against the political masters and the Committed bureaucrats, who never let go an attempt to victimize the officer. As a result most bureaucrats bide their time to leave the cadre on deputation etc. A typical cynicism sets in the officer by the tenth year of service and he is convinced that however hard he tries the system is not going to change substantially.

From the above at least one thing is certain that most bureaucrats are not corrupt but due to the tough working conditions we have been marginalized and accepted a diminished role for ourselves.

Yours sincerely, (C. K. Anil)

Thus the insider Anil admitted corruption at the level of BDOs and Ministers, and agreed with my description of the sad affairs of Bihar administration, but he rightly pointed out that not all IAS officers were part of the ruling mafia. They, on the other hand, were often sufferers but incapable of reversing the collapse. In retrospect, I think I should not have branded the entire IAS cadre of Bihar as corrupt or helping their political masters in making money. Many of them were at the receiving end of the chaotic conditions during Lalu days, although some like Mukund Prasad were also causing them.

The turnaround after 2005

Fortunately, Bihar under Nitish Kumar as CM from 2005 onwards lost its reputation as an exemplar of bad governance. Indeed, the pendulum started swinging to the opposite extreme, and Bihar became almost the poster child for governance reforms. The new government began to do a large number of sensible things. Political and economic confidence increased. The state economy began to perform well. People began to talk of the 'Bihar miracle'. Bihar has always been a very poor state, and in 2005–2006, its per capita income was 29.2 per cent of the all-India figure. By 2017–2018, this had increased to 42.1 per cent of the all India per capita income, which shows that while it is still very poor, its position has improved significantly.

When Nitish took charge, he came with a dramatically different approach. Lalu Yadav had 'weakened the bureaucracy and ruled through informal political networks,' said Witsoe (2013). But Nitish sought to revive the bureaucracy by operating through a 'core team' of senior IAS officers and by forcibly weakening the political class. This was a centralized, top-down model. As Witsoe writes, in key departments, even when 'Nitish distributed ministerial posts out of political compulsion, corrupt ministers were teamed with secretaries with honest reputations, constraining the influence of the former'. The bureaucracy threw its weight behind him, fearful of a possible return of Yadav. As someone who had worked at the Centre, Nitish Kumar had both an eye and memory for detail. He worked 'more like a cabinet secretary than a politician', said a senior bureaucrat.

He loosened bureaucratic rules to move important infrastructure projects along more quickly. Before, projects costing more than `25 lakh required cabinet-level approval, and piled up on the desks of senior officials as the fiscal year ticked away. Mr Kumar raised that limit to 20 crores, which led to huge improvement in infrastructure. In Kumar's first term, Bihar gave cycles to girl students. 'Extremely Backward' castes were given their own reservation quota. Kumar led a crackdown on illegal arms. Crimes like kidnapping came down. The state's cities became safer at night.

During the period 2004–2005 to 2014–2015, Bihar's income at constant prices grew by 10.1 per cent per annum (Bihar Economic Survey 2017–2018), significantly higher than the Indian average. Bihar improved on law and order, roads and power, but its performance on matters crucial for the poor—health, quality education and implementation of NREGA (described in detail in Chapter 6)—still remained abysmal.[10] Bihar's off-take of subsidized food grain through ration shops used to be very poor, less than 20 per cent of the allocation during Lalu days but has in recent years gone up to 95 per cent. Changes during Nitish's era have been best captured by Shekhar Gupta in 2015 as below:[11]

---

10. https://scroll.in/article/839031/bihar-is-struggling-to-improve-the-lives-of-the-poor-even-after-27-years-of-backward-caste-rule
11. https://www.outlookindia.com/magazine/story/gen-gana-mana-of-youth/295786

So in the poorest India, such as in Bihar circa 2005, nothing was selling on the walls because nobody had the money to buy anything. Five years of rapid growth and the return of the rule of law under Nitish Kumar, and the walls were selling branded underwear and English-medium school education. By the time of the 2014 parliamentary elections, the hottest selling items were coaching classes for IIT-JEE and medical entrance examinations.

When there was no education, the same young Biharis were happy to be in villages or migrate elsewhere in the country to work as security guards if not as casual labour. But now, having had some taste of education, they want better jobs. However, neither the quality of their education nor the mostly agrarian economy of their state can promise them anything better than a clerk's life. Here too, as one young person after another tells you, railways have frozen recruitments, so, '*bhaisaheb, aap batayein hum jaayein kahan*?'

Bihar's agriculture has improved, you now see tractors with seed-drills, poultry farms, shops stacked with fertiliser and hybrid seeds in village shops. But nothing else has imp¬roved with the economy. It is as if the villages have become a little better, or let's say less worse, but the cities have worsened greatly. Driving a couple of thousand kilometres from the west to the east in the state, you see no signs of a modern manufacturing or services economy. You can drive hundreds of kilometres and the only 'industry' you'd see is of brick kilns that pollute, consume fertile soil and provide just a few jobs at the lowest and exploitative end of the value chain.

In contrast to Mukund Prasad who advised Lalu and Rabri how to slow down Bihar's growth, Pratyaya Amrit, an IAS of the 1991 batch, did miraculous work in both road connectivity and rural electrification. Amrit was recalled by the CM Nitish from Delhi to head the Bihar State Bridge Construction Corporation Limited. At that time, the corporation was on the verge of a shutdown. The salaries were unpaid since long, which had resulted in the morale of the employees being in the boots. When Pratyaya Amrit took over the outfit, it was nose deep in debt of ₹17 crore. Astonishing enough, it registered a profit of Rs 83 crore in just three years. Pratyaya Amrit was the only IAS officer in India that Government of India picked in 2011 in the individual category for the Prime Minister's Excellence Award in Public Administration.

After reviving the moribund Bihar State Bridge Construction Corporation, Amrit was entrusted in 2014 by Nitish Kumar to get the laggard state's electricity story right. Earlier, the per capita electricity consumption was 112 per kilowatt-hour (kWh), which in three years by 2017 increased to around 360 kWh, still much below the national average of 1,200 kWh, primarily because of the lack of industrialization in Bihar.[12] Farmers throughout Bihar are able to get eight hours of power every day, which has greatly boosted agricultural production.

To sum up, Bihar's turnaround illustrates how a handful of seemingly small changes can yield big results. Political leadership plays a vital role in how a state performs; bureaucracy responds to demands from leadership. Both Lalu and Nitish were great centralizers, but one denuded the public service and the other empowered it to deliver 'development'. Goals were set by the politicians, civil servants helped them achieve these.

12. https://www.livemint.com/Politics/8GjbuWPi6q4zw2gB005U3J/Earlier-it-was-unthinkable-that-electricity-will-come-in-Bih.html

ANNEXURE

Towards Improving Governance in Bihar

During the year 1997–1998 ₹1,177 crore was available to Bihar for implementing various schemes of this Ministry. Since the number of poor families in Bihar is estimated to be 50 lakhs, allocation per family comes to ₹2,350 per annum, which is a substantial amount. The poor would have been perhaps better off if we could send this amount by moneyorder directly to them bypassing bureaucracy.

It is obvious that success in the implementation of schemes depends upon the capability of the delivery system to optimally utilize funds meaningfully. This alone will justify spending funds through the official machinery, and not remitting it directly to the poor. The moot question is: to what extent are these funds reaching the poor?

Without going into the reasons for administrative decadence in Bihar, it is an open fact that the development machinery has nearly collapsed today, more so in the secretariat and the central districts which are prone to caste violence. An unfortunate impression has gained ground that government is an arena where power and authority should be used for personal gains. Right from the BDOs to many district Collectors and often some Secretaries are busy making money, or collecting money for their political masters, thereby totally distorting priorities which are set on paper. As corruption is on the increase even in higher echelons of bureaucracy, the fear in the minds of lower level officials against making money has disappeared, and corruption at all levels has become a 'low risk and high reward' activity.

Even when the senior officer is not corrupt, he does not put his heart in the job, as he has no faith in getting support from the top. Effort does not lead to output, and output does not lead to reward.

In Bihar patronage seems the main criterion for judging officeholders. It isn't really expected that inputs will ever be used as intended, that irrigation projects will actually deliver much water to farmers, that roads will be built to handle the traffic load they were designed for, etc. The first purpose of government development activity is to provide patronage and build allegiance for those who can deliver the patronage.

State of Bihar is being treated as a private property by those who are at the top, and this culture of using executive power for private gains has become the norm. The bureaucracy serves the State but the State structure is itself getting increasingly dysfunctional and diminished. Over the years, whatever little virtues the civil services of Bihar possessed—integrity, political neutrality, courage and high morale—are showing signs of decay. Many civil servants have become like politicians—the English speaking politicians—corrupt, with short term targets, narrow horizons, feudal outlook, disrespect for norms, contributing nothing to the welfare of the nation, empty promises and no action.

Lower level bureaucracy in Bihar is worse. It has become insensitive and even hostile to the poorer sections of society. Growing activism among landless dalits and unrest at the bottom of the class/caste spectrum is met with brutal repression at the hands of rural elite and the police establishment acting in the interests of the elite. Government servants do not serve but oppress the poor and the helpless, they do not uphold the law but connive with those who cheat the state and whose only concern is their private welfare at the cost of society. They have no work ethic, no feeling for the public cause, no involvement in the future of the nation, no comprehension of national goals, no commitment to the values of modern India. They have only a grasping mercenary outlook, devoid of competence, integrity and commitment.

Rather than try to improve the delivery system, the top civil servants are compromising with the rot and accepting a diminished role for themselves by becoming agents of exploitation in a State structure which now resembles more like the one in the medieval period—chaotic, brutal, directionless and callous to the needs of the poor. In the process they have become totally indistinguishable from other rent -seeking parasites—politicians, Inspectors and Babus. Perhaps, they had not imagined that they would end up like this at the time of joining the service. Stagnation in their intellectual capabilities and a decline in self-esteem has further demoralized them. Disillusionment and corruption are thus likely to coexist in the civil services for quite some time to come.

Suggestions

What should be the role of GOI in general and this Ministry in particular to stem the rot?

Firstly, the panchayats must immediately be put in place and funds should be routed through them. Since the state government is not taking initiative in getting the stay order vacated, GOI should stop JRY grant to the state, and put their share in suspension, to be passed on to the panchayats with backlog as and when elections are held.

Secondly, there should be intensive evaluation and impact assessment of all rural development programmes in Bihar. Joint teams of senior officers from the Ministry, state government, NGOs and academics should do detailed inspections in random villages with cent per cent verification of the assets. Such reports should be made freely available to all, with a view to encourage transparency and honest reporting in administration.

Thirdly, since most funds for RD are controlled by the Ministry, we should lay down strict norms for ensuring continuity in the tenure of key officers, such as Collectors and Project Officers. A Stability index should be calculated for important posts, and a norm of at least two years be fixed, so that although government would be free to transfer an officer before two years without calling for his explanation, the average must be maintained above two years. This would mean that for every short tenure someone else must have a sufficiently long tenure to maintain the average. Just as every government order carrying financial implications has to quote the authority of the Finance Department, every transfer order must indicate in arithmetical terms how the average has been affected by the transfer in question.

Fourthly, Secretaries from this Ministry should hold periodic meetings with all Collectors and Commissioners at Patna at least once in six months to enthuse energy in the system.

Fifthly, financial procedures followed by the Bihar secretariat administration should be closely studied. Not a single rupee has been sanctioned by our Ministry for Drinking Water schemes this year, because Bihar government has not been able to finalize procedures for buying pipes for the last one year.

The general feeling among field officers in Bihar is that the secretariat is largely dysfunctional because of the long delays in financial approvals.

Some of these suggestions have often been debated in this Ministry but not put to effect because these impinge on Centre–State relations and may not be palatable to the state government.

N. C. Saxena

Ministry of Rural Areas & Employment

9 Chapter

CORRUPTION IN THE IAS: ABUSE OF POWER

'Corruption is all-pervasive, eating into the vitals of our system, undermining economic growth, distorting competition and disproportionately hurting the poor and marginalized citizens.'

-Second Administrative Reforms Commission, Government of India

Political Power for stealing

Over the decades, after having inherited very substantial powers from its colonial legacy, the State apparatus has steadily amassed functions—and more powers often in the name of the poor. The new developmental State has been bestowed a vast number of new responsibilities and vastly extended financial powers. Although the exercise of these powers is not untrammelled—there are a number of checks and balances imposed by the democratic system—the labyrinthine and obscure processes through which decisions are taken, over-regulation in many spheres of public life, the weakness of democratic institutions and the sheer monopoly which vests with the State, creates sufficient ground for arbitrary exercise of this power (Planning Commission 2001). This has led to two very major problems in the governance structures, *inefficiency* and *corruption.*[1] According to Raghuram

1. http://planningcommission.gov.in/reports/genrep/bkpap2020/15_bg2020.doc

Rajan (2012), economic reforms of 1991 left many lucrative sectors of the economy, such as oil and gas, mining and heavy industry, largely untouched, with a great deal of discretion with the GOI Ministries, which bred corruption.

Overregulation is both a cause and an effect of bloated government discretion and the single surest route to corruption. In the scarcity-ridden context of development in a poor society, the executive (both political and bureaucratic) amass large monopolistic and discretionary powers for the apportioning of resources. This results in 'rent -seeking' behaviour. With a view to prevent rent seeking, more rules and regulations are prescribed, which may further result in delays, inefficiencies and corruption. Often rules on the same subject issued at different times contradict each other, thus facilitating subjective interpretation ('show me the face and I will show you the rule'). Thus, a vicious circle is set up, non-compliance of rules leads to more rules ending up in a situation where individual politicians and bureaucrats may with the best of intention find themselves helpless in changing the 'system', and ultimately find it more convenient to join the system rather than fight it. Consequently, regulatory simplification and the resulting contraction of bureaucratic discretion, although complex and politically difficult, could raise economic efficiency, reduce corruption and also produce substantial fiscal savings at the same time.

India's failure to take appropriate structural, pre-emptive, corrective and punitive action against corruption has led to a situation where it is ranked a lowly 87 on the International Transparency Index. It should come as no surprise that the most corrupt institutions are seen to be political parties, legislators, the police, public officials and businessmen. All of them score poorly. More worrying is that even the media and the judiciary, which are generally said to be institutions that can act as watchdogs over others, have been adjudged just as corruption-ridden, and NGOs are roughly as corrupt as the judiciary.

The political system in many states is accountable not to the people but to those who are behind the individual MLAs; they are often contractors, the mafia, corrupt bureaucrats and manipulators who have made money through the political system and are, therefore, interested in the continuation of chaos and the patronage-based administration. The fact that half of the politicians in some states are either criminals or have strong criminal links and thus have no faith in the rule of law further compounds the problem.[2]

High unaccounted for election costs, and the need to accumulate illegitimate funds, have further accentuated the client–patron relationship between the holders of state power and those seeking favours, and the bureaucracy has become a tool to transfer resources from people to politicians. According to Association for Democratic Reforms (ADR), 75 per cent of the income of India's six major parties comes from undocumented sources (ADR 2014). It is no surprise that a UP Minister has openly asked his staff to 'steal a little, but don't rob the people'.

Gill (1999) describes the situation in UP as follows:

> Such abuse of authority invariably tells even on the young officers, many of whom join the services with a degree of idealism. For instance, it is believed that quite recently, a young IAS officer was posted to a lucrative district of UP as Collector and within forty-eight hours of taking charge, instructed by the state's top political authority to deliver a sum of ₹70 lakhs in cash directly to the minister. He was flabbergasted and muttered that he was the wrong man for this kind of job. On a visit to that town the next day, the 'spurned' politician humiliated him in public and promptly transferred him out of the post he had barely assumed! This being just a typical example of the kind of treatment meted out to honest officers in the early years of their career, it is not surprising that in due course the fire of idealism gets doused by the polluted waters of flagrant

2. Vaishnav (2017) suggests that one reason 'criminal' politicians are prevalent in India is because they are highly skilled in catering to their constituents and are viewed as credible.

> corruption and even the most sincere officers stop resisting. First, they turn a blind eye to petty corruption among subordinates, justifying the illegal gratification received by the junior bureaucracy with reference to their meagre salaries. From there, it is just one small step to accepting a gratification for oneself.

Due to an enormous increase in political corruption, the leader of the civil society movement against corruption, Anna Hazare, had received the reverence normally reserved for holy men, for demanding action against senior politicians who have indulged in alleged corrupt activities. The country cannot realize its true potential unless it increases the risks of indulging in corrupt activities, by making its legal regime more effective. It is as much about widening the net as about increasing the conviction rate for corruption.

It must be admitted that even in our colonial past, honesty at lower levels was as rare as it is now. The British appeared to believe that as long as the man at the top was honest, corruption at lower levels would not really do much damage and would remain confined within manageable limits. As corruption today is increasing even in the higher echelons of bureaucracy, the fear in the minds of lower -level officials against making money has disappeared. People in the past looked upon functionaries at strategic levels as an organized band of exploiters. In the not so recent past, senior Class I officers were not considered a part of this mafia. Rather, they were looked upon by the people as saviours from the tyranny of lower-level functionaries, and were never considered corrupt. Of late, the distinction seems to have got blurred in public perception, if not totally eliminated. Corruption at the top has emboldened lower-level officials who now openly exploit the masses with impunity. Decades back, a junior engineer would construct a house with his ill-gotten wealth in the interior of the city so as to hide it from the eyes of his bosses, but today he might construct it right in front of the Circuit House and request the Engineer-in-Chief to inaugurate it!

How I helped a Minister in making money?

A case of blatant corruption is described below.

While working as Secretary, Rural Development, in GOI I wrote the following letter in 1998 to the Chief Secretary, UP, which is self-explanatory:

> My dear Ravin,
>
> Two days back, I had gone to deliver a lecture at the IIPA, New Delhi for vertically integrated programme of Indian Forest Service Officers (all belonging to UP cadre and working in different districts of UP). During discussions, they complained that in many districts in UP, the Employment Assurance Scheme[3] (EAS) funds are 'auctioned' by Collectors and DRDA authorities. Since EAS funds are not earmarked for any particular department and the nature of work is such that projects can be prepared by many departments, such as PWD, Agriculture, Horticulture, Soil Conservation, Forests, Minor Irrigation, etc., there is an informal 'bidding' among these departments, and whichever department is able to offer the highest amount of bribe to the Collector, is able to get EAS funds for the project. The bribe money is around 30 per cent of the total funds, according to the participants in the Course. It was also alleged that this money is shared with local politicians, intermediaries and officials of DRDAs. This does not include bribes and commissions which have to be shared internally between different officers of the department that gets the contract. The general feeling among the participants was that between 50–60 per cent of EAS funds are thus spent

3. This was a centrally sponsored scheme to generate rural employment, akin to NREGA.

on bribes and corruption and the real benefit to the people is thus reduced at least by 50 per cent.

Since these are very serious allegations, levelled by officers working in the field, I thought I would bring it to your notice. You may like to organise technical teams to do cent per cent verification in a few randomly selected blocks.

Yours sincerely,

(N.C. Saxena)

Sri R. S. Mathur

Chief Secretary, Govt of Uttar Pradesh, Lucknow

This letter somehow got leaked to the press and was published as the front page top news in the Pioneer dated 10 February 1998, with the shocking headlines, **'Corrupt officers auction public funds'**. Hitting hard on the system, the article said, 'This is an auction no one has heard of. The auctioned item here is public funds running into several thousand crores meant for the use of the rural poor. Both the auctioneers and the bidders are same: bureaucrats and politicians.' The article also quoted from CAG's report, 'the practice of fund auctioning was prevalent in other states as well. In an exhaustive investigation carried out last year, the auditors found that district collectors, BDOs and local politicians have been lining their own pockets with the project funds'.

The Chief Secretary set up an enquiry committee, and after that I lost interest in the case. Till one day, I learnt that the UP Minister incharge of the EAS funds was praising me in an informal chat with a friend of mine, and wanted more officers in the IAS to be like me. This was somewhat puzzling as the Minister did not have a good reputation as regards integrity. When probed, I learnt that the enquiry had led to suspension of eight officers of the Agriculture and Soil Conservation departments, but within a month the suspended officials were reinstated by the Minister who collected a bribe of Rs 5 lakhs from each one of them. So my tirade against corruption made the Minister richer by 40 lakh Rupees!

With growth and increase in per capita income, the experience of other countries is that petty corruption declines, though 'grand' corruption at the Ministerial level may still continue. In India, however, there is no evidence that the grassroots corruption at the sub-district level has shown any trend of getting inconsequential. Liberalization and market friendly reforms have failed to curb petty corruption in India (Gupta 2017). This is because of many reasons. There is acute shortage of supervisory officers (discussed in Chapter 5), which makes the lower-level officials rule the roost. Then, deregulation has made almost no impact at the state level, as discussed in Chapter 5. A simple operation of converting *prosopis* (a shrub occurring everywhere in states such as Gujarat and Tamil Nadu, which, the more you cut, the more it grows) into charcoal, which can give employment to thousands of people, requires four different permissions!

When I had to 'bribe' the CM

State bureaucracy has misused its powers under the Essential Commodities Act and the Indian Forest Act to enact Rules that merely harass the common citizen and enable both politicians and government servants to enrich themselves. We describe below how women were prosecuted and jailed in Odisha in 1995 for keeping brooms in their homes!

Forests are State property and all products growing in forests are owned by the State. The State's control extends even to the designated forest products (such as kendu[4] or mango kernel) growing on private lands and non-forest common lands. Three of the most economically important MFP items (kendu leaf, sal seeds and bamboo) are nationalized and brought by law under the direct control of the State parastatals. In addition, until March 2000, the Odisha government exercised control over many other MFPs through administrative orders, generally to create public monopolies up to 1985, and after that the State encouraged private leases. Thus, for about 15 years (1985–

4. Called tendu in other central Indian states. It is used for making bidi, local cigarette.

2000), the MFP policy in Odisha was a source of political patronage rather than a support for people's livelihoods.

Until 2000, even the State agencies entrusted with the objective of giving a 'fair' price to gatherers exploited the poor. In principle, they worked with multiple objectives—to maximize their profits, to protect the interests of the gatherers as sellers, and to satisfy the conflicting demands by industry and other end users. In practice, a hierarchy of objectives developed—industry and other large endusers had the first charge on the product at low and subsidized rates; revenue was maximized subject to the first objective which implied that there was no consistent policy to encourage value addition at lower levels (local processing was in fact discouraged for many commodities, such as kendu and hill brooms; criminal cases were initiated against those who tried to process or store these MFPs); and the interests of the poor gatherers was relegated to the third level. The performance of these parastatals was hardly satisfactory. They were confronted with growing liabilities and huge staff, and opted to limit their role by becoming rentiers. Thus the way the scheme worked in actual practice was that the poor were taxed to support an inefficient government organization.

Other Indian states have also passed similar laws and orders, but the number of items covered by state intervention up to March 2000 was particularly high in Odisha. Second, although many States supplied subsidized raw material to the industry, Odisha went far ahead, and gave the industry monopoly rights of collection, especially during 1990–2000, amounting to a near-surrender of state control over forests. These orders smacked of favouritism, and a lack of probity and openness. The gatherers were required to sell MFPs to the company's agents at preset prices. Although in theory a State- or district-level committee fixed the price for each item, in practice there was no check on the price paid by the monopolists to the gatherers. State monopoly provided room for private monopoly, and aided and abetted market imperfections, besides pouring money into the coffers of bribe takers at all levels.

A study (IFAD 2000, 2002) revealed that the actual price received by the forest dwellers varied from 1/4 to 3/4 of the minimum price fixed by government. Monopoly and poor regulatory monitoring adds to overuse of resources in areas close to habitation. Because of the uncertainties created by law and the fear psychosis in the minds of gatherers, most MFPs were sold by gatherers without any processing or value addition, even when the MFPs concerned were not nationalized.

In 1995 when I visited Raygada (Odisha) I discovered to my horror that some women had been prosecuted and jailed because they had kept brooms in their houses! According to Odisha's policy at that time, the processing of hill brooms could only be done by a government parastatal called Tribal Development Cooperative Corporation (TDCC) and its traders. Gatherers could collect hill brooms, but could not bind these into a broom, nor could they sell the collected item in the open market. Thus, the poor are prevented from both, doing value addition through processing and the right to get the best price for their produce. In one particular case, assurance was given by the Collector of Raygada to a women's cooperative society that it would be allowed to collect and market hill brooms, so that the primary gatherers, who are mostly poor tribal women, could get the benefit of higher prices in the market. The Society started functioning, but without a valid licence. After the Collector's transfer, rather than helping them with processing and finding the best price, the state government machinery decided to launch prosecution against the women and their organization at the instance of TDCC. Their stocks were seized, and even after a court order for release, the full stock was not released, causing a huge financial loss to the women.

I took it as a personal challenge to get this law changed. For four years I kept on writing to various secretaries in Odisha, but as expected, nothing happened. I was told by the Odisha Development Commissioner, L. D. Mishra, an expert on labour issues, that the state government was annoyed with me because I wrote an article in the newspaper condemning the Odisha government for its anti-tribal policy. My response was that the state government could seek action against me by complaining to GOI, as publishing an article without government permission is not allowed, but why punish the poor hapless *adivasi* women?

Ultimately, I had to do what all Indians do to bend government in their favour—resort to bribing! I bribed the then CM with ₹50 crore! I was Secretary, Planning Commission and when the CM came to us for funds, I said 'Sir, please get this law changed, I will give you ₹50 crore extra in your plan outlay this year as advance, and the same amount next year after my work is done.' He said yes. He himself was a tribal and he empathized with the issue. So the oppressive law was changed in March 2000, and 67 MFPs were de-nationalized, and freed from government control. The fact that during the formulation of this new policy the CM of Odisha Mr Giridhar Gamang was a tribal must have improved the acceptability of the new policy with bureaucracy. In fact, soon after the meeting, the CM announced that the system of royalties and long-term leases in MFP trade would be abolished and that MFPs would be put to free trade. Actual orders were, however, issued after the elections in March 2000 when Naveen Patnaik took over as the new CM.

Although deregulation reduced corruption, withdrawal of government left tribals at the mercy of traders. What is needed is a policy of minimum support price for tribal products combined with freedom to sell to anyone in the open market, a policy that is followed for wheat and paddy. We have discussed this in chapter 7.

Nexus between different actors

Politicians are able to use the bureaucracy as a giant patronage machine, because political control over appointments and transfers enables politicians to draw large rents from bureaucrats, and to place their supporters in key offices. Min and Golden (2014) show that electricity theft in Uttar Pradesh was substantial and varied with the electoral cycle of the state during 2000–2009—in years when elections to the State Assembly were held, electricity theft was significantly greater. Their interpretation of these results is that power theft exhibits characteristics consistent with the politicians doling out favours to local elites to win elections—incumbent legislative members of the state assembly are more likely to be re-elected as power theft in their locality increases.

Politicians are able to win elections through patronage and by building coalitions based on narrow interests. Patronage in India tends to be geared towards advancing the interests of individuals or narrow groups rather than towards bringing results for the broader constituency. This is a classic description of what political scientists call a 'clientelistic state'. Clientelism and patronage are rife and voters are mobilized more on the politics of caste, regional or religious identity than on the politics of accountability and initiatives that bring long -term benefits to the public as a whole. Consequently, the state and its apparatus, including the bureaucracy, are treated not so much as a means of generating public goods but as a means of generating benefits for the particular group that controls the state (GOI 2009).

Raghuram Rajan (2008) in his paper,'Is there a threat of oligarchy in India?', describes the nexus between politicians and business as follows:

> "The poor need the savvy politicians to help them navigate through rotten public services. The politician needs the corrupt businessman to provide the funds that allows him to supply patronage to the poor and fight elections. The corrupt businessman needs the politician to get natural resources cheaply.

But as commented by Jaffrelot et al. (2019), the businessman in question not only needs access to natural resources, but also needs loans for his investments. The huge NPAs of the public banks today partly stem from this mechanism, as the country's rulers can help friendly businessmen get loans from the public banks, even if the projects supporting their applications are not terribly convincing and even if they are running heavy debts—because the rulers in question will get something in return (possibly a fraction of the loans) in order to pay for their next election campaign.

The percentage of businessmen-turned-MPs in the Lok Sabha jumped from 14 to 26 per cent between 1991 and 2014—when 143 of the 282 BJP MPs belonged to this category, a record. This reflects the win-win equation between parties and businessmen. On the one hand, parties do not have to pay for the election campaigns of these rich candidates and, on the other hand, these businessmen-turned-MPs get access to the corridors of power. This also helps in developing nexus between the business houses and senior officials. We quote below from Jaffrelot's brilliant paper (2018):

> Businessmen-turned MPs not only learn about the laws that Parliament is making to regulate their activities (possibly influence them), but they also come to know the bureaucrats who will implement these rules. They may even recruit them after retirement. A former chairman of the LIC, Sebi and the National Stock Exchange and a former finance secretary were part of Kingfisher's Board of Directors. Similarly, bureaucrats of the Gujarat State Petroleum Corporation, an ex-head of the Gujarat Maritime Board and a former Union home secretary have joined the Adani group.
>
> The business houses benefit from the expertise and connections of senior bureaucrats. This means those who aspire to start a private sector career after retirement may not deal with private companies with a complete sense of independence when in office—all the more so as the cooling-off period can be waived on request, as evident from the way the last foreign secretary of India joined the Tata group immediately after retirement. Incidentally, the same argument can be extended to public servants (including judges and bank directors) who aspire for a government appointment (as governor for instance) and may, therefore, lose some of their independence.

Another example of nexus between a serving bureaucrat and a leading business house was hinted by Jawahar Sircar, who retired as Secretary, Ministry of Culture, GOI, in his paper[5] quoted below:

> "Senior civil servants—even of the regular variety—have been known to alter government policies to suit certain business interests, even if this causes losses to the exchequer. A disturbing piece of news that one hopes is not true is of a just-retired Secretary of the Human Resources Development ministry, who drafted the controversial rules to accord the 'centre of excellence' tag to even unborn universities. It is reported that he is currently employed by the same business leviathan that stands to benefit from this rather illogical rule. The media says that the government has been unduly kind in granting special permission to this favoured bureaucrat to serve his new employer before the quarantine period was over. Orwell's dictum comes to mind, that 'all animals are equal, but some animals are more equal than others'. After all, the business house is so close to the centre of power.

Jawahar hastens to add that such 'breaches' of conduct are rare amongst regular civil servants, but may multiply if Joint Secretaries are recruited through lateral entry from the private sector. He sounds a word of caution against such lateral entry, 'An occasional breath of fresh air is surely desirable, if one is sure of the quality of "professionals", not just their loyalty.'

There is a reverse trend as well: if businessmen become MPs and MLAs (even ministers), politicians also become businessmen. As a result, the functioning of the state is affected. Why should rulers invest in government hospitals, schools and the police work if they have privately invested in clinics, private schools and security firms?

---

5. https://www.thehinducentre.com/the-arena/current-issues/article 24459377.ece

It is common knowledge that most training colleges offering a Bachelor of Education (B Ed) degree are owned or supported by the politicians. Teachers in secondary and upper-secondary education must have this degree, which is typically a postgraduate qualification. Common perception is that one can buy this degree by paying a bribe of 5 lakh rupees without attending a single class! According to Anil Swarup (2019), Secretary, GOI, in the Department of School Education and Literacy, of the total 18,000 colleges offering BEd and DEd courses, many guaranteed a degree without attendance or internal assessments, of course for a fee. Some even guaranteed employment as part of a 'package deal'.

Some corrupt IAS officials who were convicted

Akhand Pratap Singh—protected by four CMs

Though the IAS has become more politicized than it was five decades back, it does not follow that the majority have become corrupt. As stated earlier, the percentage of those who have stashed black money under their pillows may not be more than a quarter of the total. Some colleagues put this number even lower at 15 per cent. It is likely that a much larger number indulges in peccadilloes. Many have not only remained clean but are quite concerned about the general reputation of the service going into mud because of the conduct of a few. Tired of its notoriety for political patronage system, in 1996 the UP IAS association attempted a contentious clean-up and voted to identify the three most corrupt bureaucrats amongst themselves, offering the administration details of their crimes. Interestingly over time, despite their names being made public and communicated to government, two[6] of them, Akhand Pratap Singh and Neera Yadav, rose to the highest position and became Chief Secretaries in UP! Common perception in the UP cadre was that the CM deliberately chose them to head the civil service as they would be pliable to political pressures. 'The political class has subjugated the IAS. This is because politicians need civil servants to make

6. The third died.

money. They pick and choose the weakest. And UP has the worst politicians in India,' says T. S. R. Subramanian (2004), former Union Cabinet Secretary, also a former Chief Secretary of the state.

However, the publicity that this episode of naming the most corrupt ones generated in the media was an important factor why both were later booked for corruption.

Akhand and I came from a similar lower-middle-class small-town back-ground, and worked as colleagues first at Lucknow in the Industries Department, and then as Collectors in the same division. I recall our meeting at Agra over a glass of beer in early 1976 when both of us were convinced that the Emergency that was imposed by Mrs Indira Gandhi in June 1975 would continue forever. Since I had a terrible weakness for writing and publishing critical papers[7] against government, I feared that government would imprison me or throw me out, so I decided to run away from active administration and sought a posting at the Mussoorie IAS Training Academy. Akhand, on the other hand, chose to become integral part of the corrupt system, but was not lucky enough to escape unscathed.

The bureaucracy-politician nexus is best revealed with all its ramifications in the case of Akhand Pratap Singh who was voted as the most corrupt officer in the state. First, a demand into his assets was turned down by the then chief Minister Kalyan Singh. Then, Rajnath Singh, the succeeding CM, refused a probe by the CBI. Rajnath Singh's successor Mayawati not only turned down another request for a CBI probe but also closed the vigilance enquiry against him as well. Her successor Mulayam Singh went further and appointed Akhand as the chief secretary in 2003 and

7. I even wrote a small piece in 1977 against the then prime minister for describing Fakhruddin Ali Ahmed as a 'nationalist' Muslim, arguing that she would not have said so if the late president was a Hindu. My criticism was not justified as Mrs Gandhi was referring to his participation in the Indian freedom movement, which was opposed by followers of Jinnah. In 1985, I wrote an article titled 'Wrong Move' on the government's forest policies in the *Illustrated Weekly of India* criticizing my own boss, T. N. Seshan, who was then the Union Environment Secretary.

later granted him an extension with the approval of the Central government. Thus, four CMs belonging to different political parties shielded Singh.

Akhand Pratap Singh was arrested by the CBI for allegedly amassing wealth disproportionate to his known and legitimate sources of income.[8] Vijay Shankar Pandey, a 1979 batch UP cadre IAS officer who had spearheaded the first-ever in-house anti-corruption signature campaign in the country, welcomed the CBI move. 'It is a welcome move and it will send the right message to all those who think that they can get away with murder,' said Pandey. 'Deterrence is the only way to curb corruption in high positions. The former chief secretary's arrest will compel the corrupt to think ten times before indulging in illegitimate practices,' he added.

CBI officials carried out simultaneous raids on various premises owned by Singh and his immediate family members on 21 March 2005. Singh allegedly owns as many as 42 properties worth a whopping ₹120 crore. According to a CBI source, 'Singh had gold-plated taps in his bungalows in various cities across the country.' With the help of his son-in-law, a senior official in the Income Tax Department, Singh allegedly fudged tax returns and even forged documents to cover up his corrupt ways.[9] Thanks to his influence and money power, Singh managed to evade arrest for over two years, even though the Lucknow bench of the Allahabad High Court had turned down his plea for a stay against his arrest.

Singh was indicted by the Supreme Court in 2003 and had to resign from his post as Chief Secretary. He was charged by the CBI in 2007 with fraud, forgery and acquisition of wealth disproportionate to his known sources of income.

Neera Yadav's largesse benefited politicians of all hues

As regards Neera Yadav, she was found guilty by a CBI court in a Noida land allotment scam of 1993–1995. She was sentenced in 2008 to three years in jail. This is what Sharat Pradhan wrote[10] about her:

---

8. http://www.rediff.com/news/2007/sep/25up1.htm
9. Ibid.
10. https://m.rediff.com/news/jan/15up.htm

- Motilal Vora and Romesh Bhandari may lead diametrically opposite lifestyles, but the two governors (past and present) of Uttar Pradesh have one thing in common. Both appear to be equally averse to the idea of curbing rampant corruption at the highest levels of the state bureaucracy. And their apparent reluctance to give the statutory nod to the Central Bureau of Investigation to probe a multi-billion rupee land scam involving a senior lady IAS officer proves the point.
- The CBI director's letter reveals how the officer bypassed all norms when it came to obliging those who mattered with allotment of lucrative plots in NOIDA.
- The son of then chief secretary Mata Prasad, who sat on the file on which Vora had ordered a vigilance probe, received a residential plot in a prized NOIDA sector. Two of Mayawati's brothers were awarded residential plots in the township.
- According to the CBI, Bharatiya Janata Party leader Lal Kishinchand Advani was a recipient of her alleged largesse. One of Advani's kin secured a plot in NOIDA as did Samajwadi Party leader Balram Yadav, a former minister in the Mulayam Singh Yadav cabinet and currently accused of involvement in the multi-million rupee ayurved scam.
- Many VIPS bought petty kiosks or tiny shops—juice stalls, paan-beedi shops—to fulfil the eligibility criterion for NOIDA plots. Asks a young IAS officer, 'Can you imagine a top bureaucrat's wife being certified as running a juice stall or chairman of the state electricity board running a tailor's shop?'
- Neera Yadav obtained four NOIDA plots for two daughters, her husband and herself. On one plot

measuring some 500 square metres in NOIDA's most expensive sector, a palatial bungalow is currently under construction. The CBI, it is learnt, estimates its cost at about ₹7 million.

It is also alleged that the IAS officer owns property in Bulandshahar, Ghaziabad and Lucknow, besides Bangalore and Bombay. Significantly, the CBI director's letter claims Yadav—whose husband Mahendra Singh Yadav quit the IPS to become a BJP MLA—owns real estate in London and Glasgow as well. Soon after *The Pioneer* broke the story, Neera Yadav accused some of her colleagues of having received similar allotments from her predecessors at NOIDA.

She also addressed a press conference where she declared that 'I am being framed simply because I happen to be a backward'. This declaration took a bizarre turn when one correspondent reminded her that before she married Yadav she belonged to a Brahmin (Tyagi) family.

In December 2010, Yadav was sentenced to four years' rigorous imprisonment after being convicted of misusing her official position to fraudulently allot land in Noida to Flex Industries, owned by industrialist Ashok Chaturvedi. She thus became the first IAS officer of Uttar Pradesh to have been convicted of corruption charge. On 2 August 2017 the Hon'ble Supreme Court of India reduced her sentence from three to two years' imprisonment in the Noida land allotment scam.

She had earned the dubious distinction of being the country's first IAS officer to be removed from the Chief secretary's post by the Supreme Court on charges of corruption in 2005. Neera Yadav held

> the post of Chairman-cum-Chief Executive Officer (CCEO) of NOIDA for the period from 10.01.1994 to 08.11.1995. Her husband Mahendra Singh (ex-IPS) had been a BJP minister in the state before joining the Samajwadi Party.'

The IAS couple who slept over ₹3 crore cash

Both Arvind and Tinoo Joshi of the 1979 batch were my trainees at the IAS Academy, and the readers can certainly blame me too, if my students were found wanting in upholding the desired ethical standards. This story is particularly sad because Arvind's father, who retired as DGP of the Madhya Pradesh police, enjoyed an impeccable reputation for honesty. Both Arvind and Tinoo had done their MBA together from an Australian University, were selected for the elite IAS the same year and were allotted the same Madhya Pradesh cadre. They lived happily ever after until Income Tax officials turned up at the sprawling D-19 bungalow in the posh Char Imli area of Bhopal at the crack of dawn in 2010 and slapped a disproportionate assets case against the serving IAS couple.[11]

A trunk filled with currency notes—the lock of which had to be broken after Joshis refused to provide the keys—prompted officials to requisition note-counting machines. ₹3.04 crore was recovered as cash kept under their mattress and the box. A thorough search of the house revealed documents that indicated that the couple owned 25 flats, 387 acres of agricultural land and seven non-agricultural plots—at places ranging from Bhopal to Delhi to Assam—estimated to be worth ₹360 crore and more. Some ₹8.5 lakh in US dollars, British Pounds and Euros were also seized and so were crates of expensive foreign liquor.

Their 78 bank accounts were frozen and properties attached while a notice for recovery of ₹135 crore by way of income tax was slapped on them in 2012. Their assets were 4,000 per cent more than what they earned as salary together, claim investigators. Fellow IAS officers point out that Arvind Joshi could not have

11. https://www.outlookindia.com/website/story/the-tale-of-two-joshis-from-bhopal/293206

prospered without the patronage of the political leadership, which kept him posted in the same department for five years. While Tinu was a deputy secretary in the PMO in 1988–1989, her husband was a joint secretary in defence ministry during the 1999 Kargil war. It was around that time when a major deal for purchase of light helicopters was signed and he is believed to have made his millions during that period. They were both dismissed from service in July 2014 by the government.

Practical Tips on Reducing Corruption

Reducing corruption is not easy, particularly once it becomes a part of the system. A multi-pronged approach encompasses most recommended policies which are the following:

- Reduce opportunities for corruption by deregulation and privatization, and placing greater reliance on competition to ensure low prices and good quality of products and services.
- Improve administrative procedures to reduce the opportunity for corruption by increasing accountability, transparency and the role of the citizen's voice.
- Strong punitive action against the corrupt, including immediate compulsory retirement of officials whose record and reputation is tainted, and prosecuting those against whom there is evidence of corruption.
- Establish the Lokpal and strengthen powers of the state vigilance departments, the Lokayukta, and the anti-corruption branch of the state police, enabling them to effectively initiate and pursue investigations independent of government direction.
- The guaranteed protection of civil servants who expose corrupt practices. Governments should in each department institute annual awards for recognition of the contribution made by such persons in exposing wrongdoings in the government.
- Fast tracking criminal cases against corrupt politicians and public servants and confiscating their properties and ill-gained wealth.

- People with criminal backgrounds should be barred from fighting elections. Publishing paid news should be an electoral offence, and punishment must be severe.
- Make Civil Service e-governance friendly Research on e-Seva in Andhra Pradesh illustrates potential positive impacts. In case of e-Seva (earlier known as the TWINS project) after the successful implementation of the pilot, private sector partners were involved to give citizen-centric services. The government supported the system with physical infrastructure and acted as the regulator. This project has won the confidence of citizens and has made government more creditable, responsive, efficient and transparent.

Bhoomi is a Government to Citizen project on land records implemented by Karnataka. Studies (Ahmad 2006) show that 78 per cent of users found the system easy to use; 66 per cent could use kiosks without help. Seventy-nine per cent of the people did not have to meet any officials for their work except the kiosk operator in comparison to the manual system, where 19 per cent had to meet at least one official and 61 per cent had to meet 2 to 4 officials. Errors in documents were reduced substantially from 64 to 8 per cent. Cost of service to the farmers came down considerably as 84 per cent of the users had to make only one visit to get service and there was an 85 per cent improvement in the implementation of mutation requests. The most important benefit was reduced levels of corruption which came down from 66 per cent to less than 3 per cent. Overall, the project saved farmers ₹806 million in bribes.

Factors behind Singapore's success

How is it that Singapore has been so successful in building up an efficient civil service? This is because of the successful implementation of the following five policies: (a) the adoption of anti-corruption measures; (b) selective recruitment of the 'best and brightest'; (c) competitive pay; (d) massive computerization leading to transparency and greater con-sumer satisfaction; and (e) linking promotion and pay increments with both potential and actual output of the public servant.

While these policies promote individual excellence, attention has also been given to maximize institutional outcomes through (a) delegation of authority for operational decisions to autonomous agencies, while retaining the power of oversight with central agencies; (b) instilling in organizations a sense of pride and ownership of their outcomes through training and ethical movements; (c) linking performance measurement systems of institutions with incentives and awards for innovative practices; and (d) leading by example which transmits strong values and principles of good governance socially rather than formally throughout the organization.

It must be noted that the city-state's situation is evidently very different from many developing countries. In coordinating the supply of trained personnel to meet the needs of the expanding economy, Singapore has one distinct advantage when compared with other countries. Its small geographical size and compactness (supported by an excellent communication infrastructure), besides lowering transaction costs associated with monitoring bureaucratic behaviour, allow for efficient planning, cohesive decision making, channelling of information, and deployment of personnel within and between the government and private sectors. Another is the virtuous circle through which resources for bureaucratic reform (such as civil service pay increases) have both contributed to, and been generated by, Singapore's remarkable economic ascent.

In addition to rules and procedures, the performance of an organization is also influenced by its culture, which is created by and springs from the beliefs, values and assumptions of the founders of the organization. The early generations of leaders in Singapore, such as Lee Kuan Yew, Goh Keng Swee and Rajaratnam, strongly believed in building up an effective civil service based on integrity, meritocracy and result orientation that would facilitate economic growth and social development. Overtime, these values were internalized by the civil service, and since then have stood as guiding principles for its policies and programmes.

Culture has also influenced the relations between state and the people. The success of the paternal culture that has developed in Singapore as regards how people view government is to some extent aided by the ingrained Asian values of respect and trust towards authority. The fact that two generations back most Singaporeans were immigrants with no sense of identification with the state and its politics, but at the same time hard working, rugged, pragmatic and concerned with their own economic development, has also helped in the evolution of state– people relationships.

Finally, Singapore has emerged virtually as a one-party democracy. This permits the government to be more involved in administration than with politics. Its main concern was and continues to be the management of Singapore, rather than how to manipulate voter behaviour in its favour. No other democracy can afford to announce, as the ruling party in Singapore does, that it will 'do what is right, not what is popular' (Saxena 2011).

Corruption: A 'Low-risk and high-reward' activity

Amongst the many challenges facing the civil service in India, corruption remains one of the most pervasive and the least confronted. There are several well-recognized causes of corruption. One is *monopoly*. There has been a steady accretion of functions and powers of the state in the post- Independence period, with hardly any review of these functions. The monopoly functions of the state are often exercised through cumbersome rules, regulations and procedures which render decision-making sufficiently opaque and difficult, thus relegating an extraordinary range of ordinary day-to-day functions exclusively in the domain of professional touts and the public officials accustomed to dealing with them.

Corruption flourishes because of two elements in our culture of governance. The first is the lack of transparency. We must use information technology extensively to bring in transparency. Some success has been achieved in states such as Andhra Pradesh. The second element is delay. This delay is also partly because of the tendency of our public servants not to take decisions. While the corrupt are prepared to take even the most brazenly illegal decisions propelled by the viagra of the right amount of bribe, many honest public servants contribute only delay by not taking decisions at all. After all, we had a Prime Minister who had reportedly said that not taking a decision was a decision in itself!

Many civil servants are under the mistaken impression that there is a negative correlation between high salaries and corruption; in fact, the example of Singapore is often quoted to justify their demand for higher emoluments. However, the facts are that throughout the first 20 years of Singapore's independence salaries remained modest, and yet corruption was eliminated due to strong political will. Salaries started increasing in Singapore from 1985 onwards in order to stop the exodus of senior civil servants to corporate sector. Second, salaries of classes C and D in India are at least three to four times the market wages, as discussed in Chapter 5. Corruption in India is not need-induced, it is because of greed, and the perception that no harm would be done to them. It is a 'low-risk and high-reward' activity.

10 Chapter

CIVIL SOCIETY: SUBSTITUTE FOR BUREAUCRACY, OR JUST TROUBLE SHOOTERS?

Advocacy groups and civil society

Several changes in policy can be attributed to policy advocacy done by the civil society organizations. The best example is the Right to Information Campaign in Rajasthan that not only has led to passing of a law but has vastly improved sharing of information by the government with the general public. I was also associated with the drafting of this legislation, as acknowledged by Aruna Roy in her recent book (2018). Another would be the introduction of hot cooked MDM in schools and expansion of ICDS programme due to a public interest litigation (PIL) filed by the People's Union for Civil Liberties (PUCL). Interestingly, most recommendations of the PUCL's petition were readily accepted by the government. The fact that two retired IAS officers, Mr Sankaran (a super idealist civil servant, see Chapter 3) and I, were Supreme Court Commissioners in this case facilitated collaboration with the government. PUCL in collaboration with the Right to Food Campaign played an extremely important role in pressing for the passage of the Right to Food Act, passed in 2013. Another success was the Campaign for Survival and Dignity, a coalition of more than 200 grassroots and activists' organizations from across the country that was instrumental in the legislation of the FRA in 2006 (Harriss 2017). The Anna Hazare's anti-corruption movement in 2011 had magical impact on the psyche of the young in Delhi, contributing significantly to the AAP's electoral victory in Delhi. Aman Biradiri Campaign against violation of human rights in Gujarat drew the attention of everyone to mass killings of Muslims in the 2002 riots. And last, civil society as members of the controversial NAC immensely contributed to several rights-based legislations creating legal entitlements for the poor, such as right to employment, food and forest lands.

The relationship between civil society and bureaucracy in India is a complex one, characterized by mutual suspicion and hostility. While civil society regards bureaucracy as inherently insensitive, oppressive, inefficient, parasitic and corrupt, the image of civil society amongst government officers is that of trouble shooters and wasters, and totally dependent on foreign funding. The fact that many civil society activists today, unlike their predecessors 40 years ago, no longer have an austere life-style and are well-paid professionals opting for social work as a mainstream (and frequently globalized) career adds to such an impression. Several bureaucrats think that if an activist frequently travels abroad and is well paid, he or she must be a hoax. This is unfair. We should judge them by their deeds and output and not by their life styles.

The most independent of civil society avoid being dependent on government for funds and prefer to engage in the less glamorous role of working with the people, empowering them and building their capabilities. Unfortunately, there are not many of these who are both professionally competent and financially independent. Some of them operate in close collaboration with their international counterparts and raise issues such as globalization, climate change etc.

There was uproar in the country in 2013 following an Intelligence Bureau report, identifying several-foreign -funded NGOs and accusing them of negatively impacting economic development. The report revealed that a significant number of Indian NGOs, funded by foreign donors, were using people-centric issues to create an environment which often stalled development projects. The report was clearly one sided, as raising people's voice against firing by state authorities on unarmed tribals and peasants that has been resorted to on many occasions in recent years in central and eastern India can by no means be considered an anti-national activity.

However, dependence on foreign donors has many problems. It often excludes smaller NGOs who cannot talk fluently in English. It is not just language, but knowing the 'right' buzzwords, and technical terms and skills (e.g., how to write up log frames and complicated funding applications). Even not having the skills and/or money to produce glossy applications, reports and documentation can force organizations to divert funds to pay for computer-literate graduates from the cities, who could deploy the right language and skills, but who are less aware of local conditions, and perhaps less motivated (Mawdsley et al. 2000).

Civil Society and the National Advisory Council

As is well known, when the new Congress -led government came to power, an NAC was set up under the chairpersonship of Mrs Sonia Gandhi 'to oversee the implementation of the National Common Minimum Programme of the Government'. However, in March 2006 Sonia Gandhi resigned from the post of chairpersonship of the NAC after a controversy arose on the question of whether holding the post of the chairperson of the NAC amounted to holding an office of profit. The NAC functioned without any chair for two years and was dissolved in March 2008.

Contrary to popular perception, the first NAC was not dominated by the civil society activists. Except for Aruna Roy and Jean Dreze, other members[1] could hardly be described as 'activists'. In fact, some members within the NAC had opposed the National Rural Employment Guarantee Act (NREGA), which was passed by the government in 2007. The fact that the left political parties were active members of the ruling coalition, and issues that the NAC took up were already part of the ruling coalition's manifesto facilitated smooth processing of NAC's recommendations within the Ministries. Our recommendations on Right to Education and Right to Forests, and on setting up a National Mission on health

1. C. H. Hanumantha Rao, agricultural economist; Jayaprakash Narayan, IAS (retd), who later set up a political party; Dr V. Krishnamurthy, former secretary, industries, GOI, and former chairman in several PSUs; Sam Pitroda, former chairman,Telecom Commission; A. K. Shiv Kumar, special adviser, UNICEF; Madhav Chavan, CEO of Pratham, which does excellent work in spreading and evaluating elementary education; Jairam Ramesh, MP; and D. Swaminadhan, former member, Planning Commission.

were readily accepted by the Ministries. A 'Right to Information Act' (RTI) aimed at creating transparency in governance was passed by the Indian Parliament in 2005. One of the recommendations of the NAC relating to women's land rights (described in detail in Chapter 7) resulting in a landmark change in granting inheritance rights to women in 2005 hardly received any publicity.

Prime Minister Manmohan Singh was personally not in favour of safetynet programmes such as NREGA, and this must have been the reason why NAC was not reconstituted soon after the Congress formed the government in 2009. However, adverse publicity that the ruling Congress party suffered in 2009–2010 due to several corruption scandals must have been a factor that led him to reluctantly agree to revive the NAC in March, 2010 to '*provide policy and legislative inputs to Government with special focus on social policy and the rights of the disadvantaged* groups'.

Both Dr Manmohan Singh and Dr Montek Ahluwalia (Deputy Chairman, Planning Commission from 2004 to 2014) were better known for their commitment to neoliberal reforms rather than to concerns of the disadvantaged peoples. It was only Sonia Gandhi who tried to temper hard market fundamentalism with compassion and equity, and this I believe was her most valuable and least acknowledged contribution to Indian public life.[2]

Rights-based development

Thanks to Mrs Gandhi's inspiring leadership and commitment of NAC members, the period 2004–2014 saw the enactment of prominent laws related to civil, political, economic and social rights in India. The enactment of each of these legislations was driven by social movements that emerged in the Indian context, and in one way or another made a case for the extension and expansion of Constitutional Rights in India. In addition to creating rights of the people for information, employment, education, forests, inheritance, an initiative towards social security of unorganized sector workers was taken under the Unorganised Workers Social Security Act, 2008. A 'National Food Security Act' was passed in 2013, the provisions of which are to be implemented in rural and urban areas. However, passing such laws is not enough as

2. https://scroll.in/article/print/863057 (accessed on 10 July 2019).

people do not have the time or resources to knock on the doors of overcrowded courts manned by overburdened judges.

Unlike the first NAC, this time there were many more civil society activists enrolled as members, and our recommendations on the food security and communal violence Bill were viewed by the con- cerned Ministries with suspicion. Though the first draft of the food security Bill was submitted to the Ministry in 2011 itself, it was delayed by more than two years due to Prime minister's hesitation on fiscal worries. The Act was finally passed in 2013 because of pressure from Mrs Gandhi, but after reducing the number of priority households from 10 to 2.5 crore and entitlement to subsidized food grains from 7 to 5 kg per unit. NAC's recommendations on the communal violence Bill[3] were rejected by the Home Ministry. NAC was a more effective institution in its first term than in its second, with the bureaucracy in the central government sometimes hostile to the legislations proposed by NAC 2.

I too had internally resisted some proposals of the NAC 2, but was generally overruled due to pressure from other members. Fearing that NAC is becoming too radical and impractical, I decided to openly oppose such recommendations in a short op-ed, published in the Indian Express, dated 2 January 2013, which is reproduced below:

The power of populists and naysayers

The growing influence on policy issues of activists who call themselves 'civil society' is a worrying trend and needs to be objectively analysed. Two recent policy pronouncements will illustrate how government seems to be yielding to their pressure.

It is well established that absenteeism of teachers and poor quality of outcomes in government

3. It assumed that only religious or linguistic minorities and people from the SCs and STs could be the victims of communal violence. On a TV debate in 2013, while I defended the bill, Rajiv Pratap Rudy from the BJP opposed it. After the debate, while having tea, Mr Rudy told me, 'Saxena Sahab, we will be very happy if you get this Bill passed. We will sweep the Hindu votes in our favour and win the elections on this plank itself '.

schools is the main factor behind the popularity of private schools with poor infrastructure that cater to the needs of the underprivileged. The management pays pittance to the teachers but such schools are still attracting students because of better teacher attendance, personal attention to each student and testing of their homework by the teachers, faster scholastic learning, and in some places greater emphasis on English. Often they run under a banyan tree or in a dilapidated building. However, the Right to Education Act insists that such schools would be closed down if they do not have an all-weather building consisting of at least one classroom for every teacher and an office-cum-store-cum-head teacher's room; barrier-free access; separate toilets for boys and girls; safe and adequate water facility to all children; kitchen for mid-day meals; playground; library; and qualified teachers.

Shutting down private schools that do not meet the required norms and standards will place an additional burden on Sarva Shiksha Abhiyan (SSA) funds at a time when the overall demand for primary education is still greater than supply. This is particularly so in urban areas that cater to migrants and slum dwellers. At the very least, the answer lies in improving the quality of infrastructure and outcomes in government schools and not in shutting down the private schools, thereby denying access to education to the deprived sections. However, the lobby of 'fundamentalists' in the education sector is so strong that these schools are under threat of being de-recognised under law.

A more recent example of the civil society influence on drafting of laws can be seen in the

Land Acquisition Bill. A close examination of its clauses would reveal that acquisition of even one acre of land would take at least two years and the proposal will have to pass through about a hundred hands. The delay is caused mainly because the bill seeks to establish several committees adorned by activists and 'experts'. To begin with, Social Impact Assessment would be carried out by a committee, and its report would be vetted by an Expert Group. In addition, there would be an R&R Committee, of course a State Level Committee and a National Monitoring Committee to pontificate over the reports generated by the junior committees.

As land cost is insignificant (between 1 to 5 per cent of the project cost), a simpler solution would have been to increase compensation several fold, and make land available to the project in a few months' time. However, landowners cannot ask for more than the recorded price (it is common knowledge that it is often less than one-third of the actual price) in urban areas and not more than double in rural areas. The bill is anti-farmer and anti-growth, but certainly pro-civil society!

Barring a few exceptions, many of these NGO activists think with their hearts and not with their brains. They are populists and cater to a constituency of 'habitual seminar participants'. One can easily predict their stand on any development issue. For instance, they would never say that profits are legitimate or that industry is creating jobs, or that agriculture has shown vast improvements in Gujarat. They believe in development being a 'zero-sum game' where the poor can benefit only when the rich are losing out. Both cannot win, according to them. Ramachandra Guha rightly called them the ‘No No People’. In the past, they criticised the Green Revolution, in the 1980s their target was farm forestry, and now their target is infrastructure, dams, power plants, direct cash transfer schemes, UID, PPP, etc. Reality for them is either black or white, never grey. Everywhere, they see a conspiracy engineered by the World Bank/ IMF or the ‘neo-liberal state’.

They pick up facts selectively, or distort them. They are people in a hurry looking for quick-fix solutions. Like journalists who only write but do not read, they too only talk but have no time for comprehensive analyses of such facts that do not support their biased views. Their favourite pastime is to hog media space and run down government. No wonder, their image amongst bureaucrats is that of wasters, dependent on foreign funding. Interestingly, their differences and rivalries with each other are at times quite open. Competition for funds, professional jealousies, differences in operational traditions and the desire to be seen everywhere, are common maladies that restrict inter-NGO collaboration.

The Planning Commission should critically examine their contribution before they acquire permanent space for themselves in all social ministries.

The writer is member,
National Advisory Council’

This article caused a great deal of furore, both within and outside the NAC. Tavleen Singh who had been consistently criticizing NAC, wrote:

An NAC insider speaks up

If you have read this column more than once, you would know that I have a deep distrust of the NGO sector. This is because the NGOs I have encountered in long decades of covering politics and governance have turned out nearly always to be frauds. The biggest frauds are those who claim to be working to save the environment and alleviate rural poverty but sadly nobody told Sonia Gandhi these things and so she allowed NGOs to make up her kitchen cabinet. And, believe me when I tell you that Sonia's kitchen cabinet has been more powerful than the Prime Minister's cabinet in recent years. The truth is that the NGOs who became Sonia's main advisors are mostly people who have their hearts in the right place (on the left) but their economic ideas in a muddle. So in the name of removing poverty, they are given to devising massive welfare schemes without noticing that these rarely work because their size and centralised nature make them an administrative nightmare.

Nobody had the courage to tell India's de facto prime minister this till last week when a member of the NAC, Shri N C Saxena, wrote an article in this newspaper admitting that the Right to Education Act would end up closing excellent private schools and that the new land acquisition bill would make land impossible to acquire. He said of NGOs that 'they pick up facts selectively, or distort them'. This from the man[4] who closed down the Vedanta project in the Niyamgiri hills and thereby started the rot in the investment climate. When investors realised that major projects could be closed after huge investments had been made, they started to flee especially because the Environment Ministry became a handmaiden of the NAC.

Gurcharan Das, another liberal in the category of Tavleen, appreciated my stand, and wrote to me,

> ‘What you have said is courageous and very important. It seems to me that no group in contemporary India has done as much damage to the cause of rational policy making than this well

4. I chaired a government committee on the Niyamgiri Bauxite project, arguing that it had violated government laws and guidelines. This led to the closure of the project, though the Supreme Court upheld my stand.

> meaning tribe, beginning with its failed attempt to stop the green revolution in the 1960s.

Vimala Ramachandran, who has contributed immensely on reforms in education, wrote to me:

> 'I really liked your article in Indian Express today, and agree wholeheartedly! It is not only that thousands of poor children have no option but to attend private schools with little or no infrastructure and poor teachers; if all children were to seek admission in government schools there would be no place! Instead of trying to shut down these poor schools, what we should focus on in RTE is to ensure the quality of government schools improve and the capacity expands - so that people - on their own - will then migrate to government schools. The solution does not lie in shutting down private, but improving government schools. Thank you for making the point so forcefully.'

These anecdotes should in no way be seen as belittling the contribution of NAC and civil society to legislate for the marginalized. Such legislations, also called rights-based development, put pressure on the bureaucracy to improve implementation of such laws. Often our efforts to empower them through legislation made little impact on the ground because of the indifferent attitude of both bureaucracy and social media. Chapter 7 describes the fate of one such law for women. Similarly, the government passed the NAC drafted law, the Prohibition of Employment as Manual Scavengers and their Rehabilitation Act, in September 2013, but complementary action towards solid waste management has still not been completed. However, the efforts of both, Dr Bindeshwar Pathak through his Sulabh concept for building and managing public toilets in India since the 1970s, and activist Bezwada Wilson who founded a group in 1994, Safai Karmachari Andolan, to campaign for the demolition of illegal 'dry latrines' and the abolition of manual scavenging are in themselves sufficient evidence to appreciate the positive contribution of civil society in promoting inclusive development.

Civil Society members of the NAC, though aware of my differences with them on matters of detail, always considered me as one on 'their' side. When the Prime Minister did not renew the membership of three NAC members in 2012, which included Harsh Mander,[5] whom I admire most for his deep commitment to the poor and disadvantaged, I decided to send a strong protest letter to Mrs Sonia Gandhi. The letter and her response are at the annexure for record.

Summing up

Despite these shortcomings, policymakers in the government should appreciate the strengths of the NGO delivery system. Since the 1990s, India has witnessed the rise of several governmental programmes in which the NGOs have been assigned an important role. The best examples of these programmes, in which both government and NGOs act as facilitators, are the mass campaign for literacy, Watershed Development Programme, Joint Forest Management, micro-finance, polio eradication, and now Skill Development. The major difference in these programmes from the past has been their focus on empowerment through mass mobilization, motivation and organization, with information on rights, laws and schemes, and through training. Because the philosophy of empowerment runs counter to the established image of government as a coercive institution, such efforts are not very well understood by the bureaucracy, especially at the lower levels. One would like to end this chapter by offering a few suggestions to improve the effectiveness of NGO intervention, and for maintaining their credibility. Firstly, there must be several sources of funding available for NGOs, so that they are not dependent on the whims of the government alone. Secondly, the Foreign Contribution (Regulation) Act provisions must be simplified so that NGOs, especially new and smaller NGOs can access donor funds easily. Thirdly, income tax laws should be modified in order to encourage voluntary contribution from industry for noble causes. This has been achieved to some extent by introducing the concept of CSR through legislation.

5. The prime minister thought that these three members are pushing reforms with which he did not agree.

Fourthly, donors should implement projects jointly with NGOs and government staff in such a way that NGOs are not placed in a subordinate role to junior government staff. If the project is carefully designed, joint implementation may combine their respective strengths and improve relations between them. To give an example, the Slum Networking Programme of the Ahmedabad Municipal Corporation (AMC) had paired technical staff from the AMC with NGOs. Not only did 28,000 poor households gain access to a suite of services, but municipality staff developed strong, constructive relationships with their NGO partners. The NGOs motivated community members to participate in the project, facilitate the collection of community financial contributions, resolve bottlenecks or conflicts during implementation, and provide a menu of community development services that correspond with the organization's resources and skills. The critical role of the NGOs gave them substantial influence in their relationship with the municipality staff; over time, this close working relationship has evolved into mutual respect, innovation collaboration and a deepening commitment to the project.

Finally, civil society, too, should take adequate steps to weed out the undesirable amongst them, by evolving a rating system similar to the one being followed in the corporate world. This will reduce patronage of the government and reduce wastage of scarce public resources. NITI Aayog could perhaps initiate such a rating system.

ANNEXURE

Annexure

29th June, 2012

Dear Mrs. Gandhi,

Greetings and trust this finds you in good health.

I am writing to you because I am quite perturbed by the recent changes that have been made in the NAC. The composition of the National Advisory Council, is admittedly, government's sole prerogative. This letter, therefore, is not a note in dissent but written more in the spirit of conveying my anguish at the changes. I must also, at the outset, state that I whole-heartedly welcome the two new members who are joining the NAC, and since I have worked very closely with one of them, I know that their membership will further strengthen the NAC.

As acknowledged in its Charter, the NAC always had a special focus on social policy and rights of the disadvantaged groups. The Council under your able leadership has, since its inception, emerged as a beacon of hope for the social justice agenda. Over the past two years, NAC members, despite opposition from various quarters from government and elsewhere, have worked as a cohesive team. In the current NAC we have been able to come up with three legislations on the right to food, against communal violence, and on land acquisition. This is in addition to a host of other policy measures on a range of issues affecting the most marginalised sections of the country.

The members whose terms have not been renewed, viz. Prof. MS Swaminathan, Harsh Mander and Madhav Gadgil contributed a great deal to the deliberations of the NAC and helped shape the agenda despite facing a lot of public criticism on many counts. They stood up and defended (with the rest of the NAC) the decisions of the NAC, as a collective, notwithstanding privately held differences on the various issues that we worked together. In many ways, they had emerged as the public face of the NAC. They are also perhaps, the most respected members of Indian civil society and doyens of their respective fields. Harsh was particularly involved in almost all the working groups set up by the NAC, and worked day and night ignoring his other commitments to draft single-handedly various policy documents and bills, which if implemented, would have empowered the 'Aam Aadmi' enormously. Not including Harsh and the other two in the think tank gives an impression that government is not keen on pro-poor reforms.

I believe in the principle that no individual is indispensable and that the institution is more important than the individual. The NAC could have continued to benefit from the three members' scholarship, experience and wisdom, even as the two new members were added to it, in the two positions that were vacant.

I therefore find the inexplicable non-renewal of the three distinguished colleagues from the NAC extremely de-motivating. Many of us have been fighting against injustice all our lives. Now that I see unjust action – pushing out the three members who were most committed to the poor and hungry – it would have been cowardly if I had not sent you this protest.

I request you to forward my letter to Prime Minister.

best regards,
NC Saxena

Mrs Gandhi's response dated 4 July 2012

Dear Dr. Saxena,

I have received your letter of 29 June 2012 regarding the reconstituted National Advisory Council.

Dr. MS. Swaminathan, Dr. Madhav Gadgil and Shri Harsh Mander served with great distinction in the NAC. You are right that during their two terms, they provided valuable input towards setting the agenda and achieving many of the NAC milestones. Non-renewal of their membership for a third term is in no way a reflection on their many qualities nor does it diminish in any way our recognition for the contribution they made to the Council.

Our work is such that the NAC has to remain dynamic. Like many other organizations it must be infused with new thinking and fresh ideas. Reconstitution and change in membership is inherent to this.

We must look forward to the NAC's third year, and I hope that with your support we will continue to contribute meaningfully to our pro-poor agenda.

With good wishes,

Yours sincerely, (Sonia Gandhi)

Chapter 11

IAS UNMASKED: IN DIRE NEED OF SYSTEMATIC REFORMS

The first two decades after Independence are considered to be an ideal period for Indian administration because of trust and mutual respect that existed between politicians and the IAS. Hierarchical administrative discipline was not disturbed down the line till then due to subdued political interference, which unfortunately started growing and gnawing at professionalism from the 1970s onwards. Chapter 2 narrates several examples of that trust, such as between the CM of Madhya Pradesh and his Chief Secretary, the iconic Mr Noronah. Even when there were policy differences, such as between Morarji Desai as CM of undivided Bombay and his Chief Secretary, these did not affect normal functioning of the government. However, if one judges the performance of administration from the eyes of a common citizen, one wonders if the administration in those days would get more than 3 out of 10 marks. Was poverty getting reduced during those two decades? Did an ordinary citizen have access to primary health and education? Was it easy to get a ration card or get grievances addressed in a reasonable time? Were decisions taken in a transparent manner or with people's involvement? Wasn't police and tehsil staff oppressive and corrupt? The IAS formed a kind of an exclusive club, constantly praising their service, but oblivious to the concerns of the common person.

The focus at the district level in those days was on revenue collection, law and order and providing emergency relief during floods and drought and so on. Because welfare funds were limited, there was hardly any expansion of the existing primary education or health, though absenteeism amongst government doctors and teachers was minimal. Administration ran smoothly, because of internal culture which is best summed up in a phrase, '*Huzur ka iqbal hai*', meaning 'discipline is maintained because of awe of authority'. Efficiency in the IAS was always very narrowly defined. It meant aloofness from politics and rigid adherence to rules; 'public satisfaction' was an insignificant part of their job assessment.

Despite their high integrity, hard work and motivation, senior civil servants even in the past were dedicated to the public service only in the abstract. That somehow failed to translate into service to the individual citizen. The system seemed to be running for the convenience, first and foremost, of civil servants themselves. The customer in India was always '*kasht se mar*'. That is, he was harassed so much by the maze of rigid rules that he died several deaths before his legitimate prayer was heard. Interestingly the stories of trust in Chapter 2 describe how the seniors permitted the juniors to break rules, but the seniors did not set up committees to simplify rules and controls that came in the way to realize fast results, so that achieving the desired outcomes becomes routine. With the expansion in the number of government servants, especially at lower levels, the system became too big, costly and slow, and was not even able to put its own house in order (judged by a large number of writs and cases filed by government servants on issues of seniority and promotions). Today it is not able to provide even a patchy service to the citizens. Growing criminalization and corruption amongst politicians and the desire amongst some IAS officers to stick to positions of power has further distracted administration away from the people.

We have described in detail in the previous chapters how India's performance on social indicators is dismal; it would improve only when governance reforms that are needed are implemented. These should aim at making the system outcome oriented, outcomes should be measured regularly, reporting of data should be honest, flow of funds should be smooth down to the village level, design of flawed schemes should be improved, bureaucracy should be more sensitive to the needs of the disadvantaged groups and people's participation should be encouraged.

One of the main reasons why systemic reforms have not been taken up earnestly is the lack of stable tenure for IAS officials, as described below.

Posted for weeks, collecting weekly bribes

Appointments and transfers are two well-known areas where the evolution of firm criteria can easily be circumvented in the name of administrative efficacy. Even if the fiscal climate does not allow fresh recruitment on a large scale, a game of musical chairs through transfers can always bring in huge rentals to corrupt officials and politicians. As tenures shorten both efficiency and accountability suffer. In UP, the average tenure of an IAS officer in the last 20 years is said to be as low as six months.[1] In the IPS, it is even lower, leading to a wisecrack that 'if we are posted for weeks all we can do is to collect our weekly bribes'.

According to a report published in the *Times of India* dated 1 January 2014,[2] some of the frequently transferred officers include 1982 batch Himachal Pradesh cadre officer Vineet Chaudhary (transferred 52 times in 31 years), Assam–Meghalaya cadre officer Winston Mark Simon Pariat (50 times in 36 years), Kusumjit Sidhu of the Punjab cadre (46 transfers) and Haryana cadre officer Keshni Anand Arora (45 transfers), in addition to the much-talked about Ashok Khemka of the Haryana cadre (50 transfers in 23 years). Khemka became very wellknown publicly as a result of his exposure of corruption in departments in which he was posted, as already discussed in chapter 3.

Transfers have been used as instruments of reward and punishment, as tools for controlling and taming the bureaucracy. There is no transparency, and in the public mind transfer after a short stay is categorized as a stigma. Officers who are victimized are not in a position to defend themselves. Internally, the system does not call for any reaction to explain one's conduct, while externally public servants are debarred from going public to defend themselves.

---

1. On one particular day in April 1970, there were three district magistrates in Fatehpur (UP); Dhesi had the house, Bagla had the charge, and I had the luggage.
2. http://timesofindia.indiatimes.com/india/68-of-IAS-officers-have-average-tenures-of-18-months-or-less/articleshow/28203370.cms

Frequent transfers and limited tenures are playing havoc with public organizations. Robert Wade (1985)[3] has argued that the Indian state is not better at promoting development because of the corruption-induced transfer mechanism and its effects on bureaucratic initiatives. With every quick change in the head of the office, a funereal air is noticeable and down the line the respect for authority is whittled away. Rapid changes erode the mandate of the Department or organization. There are two other consequences. The incumbent himself is not sure of how long he will stay. This affects his attention to detail, capacity to master the situation, and he begins thinking, even incrementally, about how to change things and improve them. Since he is not too sure of what has to be done, the preference is to opt for whatever was tried out in the past and seemed to have sufficed. In the process, changes which may have been initiated by a predecessor are either disregarded or thought of as being disruptions. Most public organizsations do not possess the 'memory' which will absorb change and continue it even under adverse circumstances. Second, there are even more deleterious consequences down the line. Other staff in the organization do not extend the commitment so necessary for change to be institutionalized. Their assessment is that everything new is only temporary, and that it is different from the ordinary way of doing things represents the foibles, or the prejudices (at worst) of the incumbent, to be forgotten immediately on the departure of the officer concerned. An attenuated hierarchy, which distorts intent and initiative, further impels the status quo (Saxena 2016b).

The topic of reducing political interference is a sensitive one, for the right to transfer government servants is clearly vested within the political leadership under Article 310 of the Indian Constitution, which maintains that civil servants serve at the 'pleasure' of the ruling authorities. Yet, few would disagree that this power is often abused by both government servants and politicians—the former in seeking prime postings, and the latter for a variety of legitimate and illegitimate reasons. The prime concern of the political executive now is not to make policies but to manipulate jobs and favourable postings for their constituents. Managing service providers is

3. Wade documents that the cost of getting transferred to a desired post in the cadre of superintendent engineer in the irrigation department in Odisha was 40 times the average monthly salary for the position.

the prime concern of politicians rather than improving service provision. This means a high degree of centralization at the level of the State government and little accountability.

While presiding over a meeting of the Planning Commission in 2001, Prime Minister Vajpayee lamented that the problem with poor states was that they did not have any industry. I made a cheeky remark, 'Sir, these states have a flourishing transfer and posting industry.' He looked angrily at me for making fun of his tribe.

While working in UP as Secretary, Food and Civil Supplies, a department known for rampant corruption, the Chief Secretary once asked me how come I had a smooth relations with my Minister. I said, 'we have a very good distribution of work amongst ourselves; I look after policy and he looks after establishment.' However, as discussed later in this chapter, new policies without sufficient political and administrative support make little impact.

GOI's initiatives that remained only on paper

The Second Administrative Reforms Commission of 2008 recommended[4] that all senior posts both in central and State governments should have a specified tenure. The task of fixing tenures for various posts should be assigned to an independent Civil Services Authority. This is already being done in GOI for Secretaries in the Ministries of Home, Defence and Finance, as well as for Cabinet Secretary. However, none of the State Governments have made the tenure of higher ranks of the civil services (e.g., Chief Secretary and DG of Police) stable, say, for a fixed period of at least two years. This is despite the Supreme Court's specific direction of ensuring stable tenure for senior positions in police and civil administration.

In January 2104, GOI amended the IAS (Cadre) Rules 1954, mandating that an officer in a cadre post in the state government would hold the office for a minimum specified period and can be transferred before this only on the recommendation of a Civil Services Board comprising the Chief Secretary as its chairman, and other senior officers of equivalent rank as its members. Many State

4. http://darpg.gov.in/darpgwebsite_cms/Document/file/Decision10.pdf, and http://darpg.gov.in/darpgwebsite_cms/Document/file/decision15.pdf

governments[5] have notified new rules[6] in tune with the GOI law, prescribing the minimum tenure as two years for senior IAS officers, but cleverly keeping the Chief Secretary outside the purview of these Rules. Thus, the Chief Secretary will continue to be at the mercy of the political bosses. This has made the GOI Rule for steady tenure ineffective even for other State officials, as the practice in the States is that after the CM decides on transfers (which may be before the expiry of two years of tenure and purely based on political or monetary considerations), the Chief Secretary and other members of the Civil Service Board are made to sign their approval with a back date. GOI must insist that the Chief Secretary and the DG (Police) have a stable tenure, so that they can then independently and objectively decide on the tenure of others through the statutory Civil Services Boards.

It may also be mentioned here that many transfers are initiated at the request of the officer himself, and this tendency will also get curbed with effective implementation of new laws. The hankering after posts is linked quite often to the 'trappings' of the post—free vehicles, house and so on. It is clear that to a large extent these are dictated by the nature of jobs and should also constitute an element in determining how to categorize posts. One should follow the example of Singapore where the salary package for government servants includes cash in place of perks. No one is entitled there to subsidized housing or government vehicle, and this increases transparency and accountability. One could begin this practice in the GOI with the retired government officers who are re-employed in various sinecure jobs. They should just get salary but no government car or accommodation in Lutyens' Delhi.

It is not correct to assume that there would be political resistance to the idea of stability of tenure. Many CMs would welcome this proposal, as they are often pressurized by their MLAs to resort to frequent transfers, and with a change in procedure which is laid down by GOI, they would be able to resist the pressure in a better manner. 'We are caught in a cycle,' says Subramanian, who

5. Andhra Pradesh, Chhattisgarh, Haryana, Himachal Pradesh, Jammu and Kashmir, Jharkhand, Karnataka and Uttarakhand.
6. persmin.gov.in/DOPT/Acts_Rules/AIS_Rules/Revised_AIS_Rules_Vol_II_Updated_Upto_31Oct 2011/Revised_AIS_Rule_Vol_II_IAS_Rule_02.pdf (accessed on 10 July 2019).

averaged one transfer a year when he was a bureaucrat in UP. 'Chief ministers are scared of their own MLAs. MLAs are controlled by vested interests at the local level, and they in turn want weak and corrupt officials.'

Many countries such as Japan and Singapore do not pursue the practice of annual transfers. If an employee is corrupt or inefficient, the traits would get displayed wherever the employee is posted. What we require is effective supervision and the prompt commencement of disciplinary action against such employees instead of shifting them to another place.

In addition to addressing the problems caused by external environment we need to look at some of the maladies afflicting the attitudes and work ethics of the top civil service, the IAS, which is supposed to provide leadership at the State and district levels.

Maladies affecting the IAS leadership

Lack of domain knowledge

A high degree of professionalism ought to be the dominant characteristic of a modern bureaucracy. The fatal failing of the Indian bureaucracy has been its low level of professional competence. The IAS officer spends more than half of his tenure on policy desks where domain knowledge is a vital prerequisite. However, in the present environment of short tenures and obsession with status and perks, there is no desire in a young civil servant to acquire knowledge or improve his skills. Development administration that requires qualities of innovation, methodical and rational thinking and a clear focus on outcomes gets a low priority. IAS officers systematically under-invest in skill acquisition because loyalty to powerful politicians, as opposed to merit-based advancement, offers an alternative path to career success (Vaishnav and Khosla 2016).

An average IAS officer is generally status quoist and wishes to stick to positions of power, rather than aim to improve outcomes for the common man. The very desire to write IAS after his name shows status consciousness and an attempt to feel exclusive and important. Jawahar Lal Nehru used to feel indignant at this practice. He did not realize that the mystique of the service is, after all, the new class's only passport to the select circle of the elite. It was, therefore, unrealistic of him to ask civil servants not to flaunt the three magic letters on their name plates, visiting cards and letter heads. As Sunanda K. Datta Ray put it, 'the reincarnated Heaven-born service would be a far less attractive career without this constant reminder of having arrived'.

The IAS officer, more so his wife, is highly conscious of his seniority which gets determined by the year he enters the service. Just as an IAS officer considers himself superior to the officers of all the other services, however, senior, experienced and competent they may be, within the IAS, seniority determines respect and dominance. No wonder that the civil list which contains the names of all IAS officers arranged in the strict order of seniority, which even the gods cannot change, becomes the Bible for them. It is said that in the house of an IAS officer, one would find only three books—the railway timetable, because he is always on the move, a news magazine, because that is his level of interest, and of course, the civil list. An important factor which contributes to the surrender of senior officers before political masters is the total lack of any market value and lack of alternative employment potential.[7] Beyond government, they have no future, because their talents are so few. Most IAS officers thus end up as dead wood within a few years of joining the service and their genius lies only in manipulation and jockeying for positions within government (Saxena 2010a).

This kind of orientation and craze for power is also reflected in the way IAS officers grade their jobs. For instance, in GOI the Ministries of Home or Defence are considered far more important than the Ministries dealing with land or forests. This is best reflected in a verbal request made by T. N. Seshan in 1986, who was then Secretary in the Ministry of Environment and Forests, to B. G. Deshmukh, who was then Cabinet Secretary. In his first meeting with the Cabinet Secretary, Seshan pleaded

> Sir, I will be in the run for the post of the Cabinet Secretary at the appropriate time. The UP lobby, however, is bent upon obstructing me and therefore PK Kaul did not give me an important ministry. I

7. Of late, some retired officers are being hired by the private sector, not so much for their professionalism, but for their ability to influence government in favour of the hiring company.

> would therefore request you to keep my name in mind whenever either the Home Ministry or the Defence Ministry Secretaryship falls vacant and try to fix me there. (Deshmukh 2004)

Although the unofficial hierarchy of jobs varies from state to state, certain common points can be noted. Posts in the Finance, Industry and Commerce Departments occupy a very high rank. These enable the IAS officer to enjoy freebees from the industrialists, and well-paid Directorships after superannuation. As a posting in the Ministry of International Trade involved frequent foreign trips, it was once known as the 'Ministry of Sons and Sons-in-law', as it was packed with the relatives of senior IAS officers (Bagchi 2007). The Next in the list would be posts which carry a lot of patronage and influence like a district charge, the Departments of Home, Establishment, Excise, etc. The lowest rank goes to jobs where excellent performance would directly benefit the poorest, such as Tribal and Social Welfare, Land Reforms, Urban Slums, Minorities Welfare and so on. Similarly, posts that require studying reports or fondness for acquiring new knowledge, such as Planning Boards, Evaluation Directorates or Training Institutions are considered punishment postings or dumping grounds for unwanted officers. Very few IAS officers know why Bangladesh is doing better than India on health, sanitation and gender indicators, or how Thailand reduced child malnutrition in about 10 years from 50 to 25 per cent in the 1980s. Apathy towards reforms is also due to perception that the system does not have a 'collective will' to encourage radical changes, an issue that we take up later in this Chapter.

Lack of concern for the poor

This kind of orientation has serious implications. The IAS officer is not so much worried of a transfer *per se*, as he is worried of being transferred to a job which everyone else considers to be an unimportant one. He would use all kinds of pulls and pressures—both administrative and political—to avoid it. If it does not work he proceeds on long leave; in fact, that is the only time he takes earned leave. The punishment to an officer for annoying the authorities would be a posting in the tribal districts or other backward areas. No one realizes that in the process the *adivasis* and people of the backward area get punished for being saddled with an officer who has no interest in continuing there.

An officer in the late 1960s was posted to Banda, a backward district of Central India, but his only recollection of the two years stay was that the district was full of pre-historic statues and how excitedly he used to look forward to unearthing and obtaining such antiques. Not only did the illegality of his action not bother him, but he did not notice at all the poverty of the people, their indebtedness and intense oppression. Another young IAS officer in the late 1970s was asked to assess the extent of bonded labour in Mirzapur in eastern UP, but his report was that the incidence of bonded and child labour was negligible. When an NGO was asked to do a survey in the same district, the situation appeared to be radically different.

A by-product of this attitude is that in this milieu proper career planning is impossible. In this age of specialization, a healthy personnel policy would mean that many officers specialize in sectors where good administration is needed most, such as Welfare of Weaker Sections, Tribal Development, Administrative Reforms, Skill Development, Training and so on. Unfortunately, due to the unwillingness of the IAS officers to work on such 'condemned' posts, the development of the state suffers. On the other hand, because of the pressure which the IAS lobby exerted on the state governments, the number of commercial corporations increased several fold in the 1980s and 1990s, each demanding monopoly of controls[8] and budgetary support from the State. Despite this, or may be because of this, several states have remained industrially backward.

Fast promotions create redundant posts

Due to the control that the IAS and the IPS lobbies exert on the system, a large number of redundant posts in the supertime and superior scales have been created to ensure them quick promotions. Often a senior post has been split, thus diluting and diminishing the scale of responsibilities attached with the post. For instance, in some States against the post of one chief secretary, there are many officers now in equivalent but far less important posts drawing the same salary. In one State, previously where one officer used to be

8. How these controls harmed the poor women in Odisha is discussed in Chapter 9.

the Secretary of Medical and Health, now there are five officers doing the job of one, four are incharge of health, family planning, medical and medical education, respectively, whereas the fifth one, as principal secretary, oversees the work of these four secretaries! Two decades back, there was only one IGP in Punjab, controlling the entire police force. Now there are 16 IGs, and to supervise their work there are 14 DGs and Additional DGs! The ministries in GOI dealing with State subjects have seen tremendous expansion; the Agriculture Ministry has 23 officers of the rank of joint secretaries and above!

Deshmukh (2004) describes the situation in Bihar as follows:

> ‘Now consider the scenario in Bihar. Every new Chief Minister would have his favourite as the new Chief Secretary. At one time, there were about 8 to 10 IAS officers drawing the pay of a Chief Secretary only because their juniors were appointed as Chief Secretaries at one time or the other. There were so many ex-Chief Secretaries that it was jokingly said that they could even form an Association of Chief Secretaries. The result of this on the civil service morale in Bihar does not need any elaboration.

This inverted pyramid (too many people at the top and too few in the middle and lower rungs) has apparently been created to avoid demoralization due to stagnation, but the net result has been just the opposite. First, it leads to cut-throat competition within the same rank of officers to get into more important slots. The old camaraderie has given place to a rat race. Instances are not lacking when officers wanting a plum job—say a foreign posting—have gone to the Press denigrating their competitors. Second, this no-holds-barred competition is then exploited by politicians in playing up one against the other, leading to officers becoming more pliable. The lure of after-retirement sinecures further increases the number of those who would be willing to crawl when asked to bend. Third, for officers in marginalized positions, the government seems remote, heartless and more unjust now than ever before, which results in their demoralization. Many have gone to the Tribunals and Courts for promotions and postings, a phenomenon that was unknown 40 years ago. Obsession amongst civil servants with what they can get from the system rather than what they can give is not conducive to achieve high professional standards.

There are too many meaningless posts in the all -India Services, their number should be drastically reduced, so that only such posts where people can contribute meaningfully are retained. GOI should also reduce the number of Boards and Commissions it has created, each wanting IAS officers to serve them. In case such Boards have to be created, they should hire officials from the open market (retired IAS officers could also apply), but they should not be given any subsidized government housing or vehicle. In any case, posting in such commissions is regarded as a punishment posting by the peer group!

After the first 15 years in service, an average officer spends at least 50 per cent of his time doing useless work on posts that call for no challenge. CMs in India have got used to be waited upon by a horde of politicians jockeying for power, and they have developed a mindset of meting out similar treatment to civil servants—keep half of them under-utilized to make them pliable. The Indian government must be the only organization in the modern World where half of the top management is deliberately and consciously forced to waste its time on useless posts, both at the central and the State levels. Working much below their capability results in stagnation and low self-image, and many officers ultimately become 'dead wood'. The suggestions are:

- Retire 25 to 50 per cent of the officers at the age of 52 to 55, as it is done in the Army;
- Drastically reduce the cadre as well as ex-cadre posts, especially in the supertime and above, leading to slower promotions;
- Encourage officers to join NGOs, educational and research institutes during mid-career. The DOPT should play a more active 'placement' role by maintaining a list of officers who wish to be out of the service for a temporary period, and liaise with the desirous NGOs and other institutions;
- Increase the period an officer can be out of the system from five to seven years, without losing his seniority and

- Many posts in the government should be earmarked to permit lateral entry of people from NGO/professional institutions at various levels to bring in a fresh outlook.

Perverse incentives are not the only factor undermining the effectiveness of bureaucracy. Its composition is also skewed. For instance, in most States, about 70 per cent of all government employees are support staff unrelated to public service—drivers, peons and clerks. Key public services—education, health care, police and judiciary—are starved of people, whereas many wings are overstaffed. This aspect has already been discussed in Chapter 5. Efforts should be made to identify surplus staff, set up an effective re-deployment plan and devise a liberal system for exit. There should be incentives for clerks and educated class IV staff to become teachers and constables.

Internal Reforms Needed

Civil Service Accountability

As a consequence of its colonial heritage, as well as of the hierarchical social system, administrative accountability in India was always internal and upwards, and the civil service's accountability to the public has been very limited. With politicization and declining discipline, even internal accountability stands seriously eroded today, while accountability via legislative review (as State Legislatures hardly meet) has not been sufficiently effective. But strengthening internal administrative accountability is rarely adequate by itself, because internal controls are often infructuous—especially when the social ethos tolerates collusion between supervisors and subordinates.

'Outward accountability' is, therefore, essential for greater responsiveness to the needs of the public, and thus to improve service quality. Departments such as the Police and Rural Development, which have more dealings with the people, should be assessed annually by an independent team consisting of professionals such as journalists, retired judges, academicians, activists, NGOs and even retired government servants. These should look at their policies and performance, and suggest constructive steps for their improvement. The system should be made more open so that the civil service can gain from the expertise of outsiders in the mode of donor agency evaluations of projects. It is heartening to note that GOI has already started doing so for some of its flagship programmes, such as elementary education (SSA) and health (NHM). Petitions under the Right to Information Act (RTI) have also empowered citizens, but its use is still dominated by civil servants on personnel issues of appointments and promotions.

Priorities for enhancing both internal and external civil service accountability should also include improved information systems and accountability for inputs; better audit; face-to-face meetings with consumers and user groups; publishing budget summaries in a form accessible to the public; a stronger performance evaluation system; scrutiny and active use of quarterly and annual reports; and selective use of contractual appointments.

One way to bring in accountability is to start the system of holding public hearings in matters pertaining to the works handled by each office. Prominent social workers and NGOs should be associated with this exercise for more productive results. The teams would undertake surveys of the quality of service delivery in key areas: scrutinize policies, programmes and delivery mechanisms. Civil servants' views on work constraints and reporting fraud and corruption should be elicited. The reviews conducted should also form the basis of time-bound changes and improvements which should be monitored.

Needless to say that such comprehensive reforms need for their sustenance strong political and administrative will from the top. In their absence, reforms remain only on paper. Accountability has to be induced; it cannot be decreed by fiat. Accountability is a result of a complex set of incentives, transparency in processes and decision -making, and checks and balances at various levels of government. Thus, the seniors in the government departments have to put their weight behind new accountability systems and review them from time to time.

Administrative reforms in many countries, notably New Zealand and Singapore, have aimed at limiting the area of functioning of politicians and civil servants, and construct boundaries. Whereas politicians decide social goals and outcomes, civil servants are responsible for outputs that would lead to achieving the goals. The civil servant enters into a performance agreement with the minister every year, and the civil servant's performance is based on production and delivery of outputs as described in the performance agreement. In return, the civil servant gets total autonomy for managing his organization.

Is this paradigm workable in India? The administration already has a lot of power, discretion, and hence opportunities for rent seeking, whereas the new autonomy and flexibility will give limitless opportunities to the civil servant for corruption. Therefore, the New Zealand model is feasible in India only when parallel reforms for transparency, accountability and reduction in corruption are carried out, which all require strong political will. On the contrary, there is a feeling amongst civil servants in some states that honesty, impartiality and concern for public welfare are no longer being demanded of them by the elected representatives. Due to this perception, even when the senior officer is not corrupt, he is not committed to reducing corruption in his organization, as he has no faith in the stability of his tenure or in getting support from the top for anti-corruption drive. The cynical view is that the politicians' need for money is greater than that of civil servants, and therefore honest administration is not in their interest and politicians have to coerce officials for their share in the loot.

Therefore, in addition to delineating the functions of politics and administration, it is important to reduce the powers of government, as well as reduce their discretion and increase transparency at every level. Citizens must have an oversight role in anti-corruption efforts. The focus of this section is on suggesting how external pressure can be brought to bear on the system so that flouting the rules and ignoring public welfare becomes increasingly difficult for both the political class and bureaucracy.

Improvement of M&E systems

At present, officials at all levels spend a great deal of time in collecting and submitting information, but these are not used for taking corrective and remedial action or for analysis, but only for forwarding to a higher level, or for answering Parliament/ Assembly Questions. The data collected are not normally subjected to any regular checks. There is a failure of the ministries in verification of their correctness and almost total absence of accountability procedures. Although some Ministries do concurrent evaluation and engage professional organizations in preparing impact studies, such reports are hardly read by the policymakers, and no corrective action follows from the examination done in the reports. Ultimately, the process of hiring a professional for an impact study degenerates into another patronage activity, where favourites are chosen, and the quality of the report is a secondary consideration.

This was also echoed by the Finance Minister in his Budget Speech on 28 February 2005:

> Robust economic growth has thrown up many new challenges, among them the need to put in place effective monitoring, evaluation and accounting systems.... I think we do not pay enough attention to outcomes as we do to outlays; or to physical targets as we do to financial targets; or to quality as we do to quantity... Government ...intends to strengthen evaluation.... This needs to be supplemented by independent evaluations conducted by research institutions.

Emphasis is laid only on the initial or current expenses. After five years, little is done or monitored. Secondly, when money has been allocated for a particular activity in a particular area, it is assumed that the work in question has been done, and that it was sufficient. This ignores the fact that either of the above assumptions could be wrong. The primary monitoring activities have to do with fiscal accountability. While it is necessary, it should not be allowed to overshadow the need for technical and resource monitoring and planning work accordingly. At present, there is great pressure on the field staff as a whole to account for funds utilized, but not in terms of longer-term results, because those are not monitored. Thus, financial planning is divorced from physical planning.

In some cases, academic institutions are asked to review the schemes. Their approach emphasizes rigour, but often its completion requires years and policymakers lose their patience with their work. There are also reports by professional consulting organizations, especially on centrally sponsored schemes. However, the Ministries look upon giving of funds to consulting organizations as a patronage activity. Little interest is taken in ensuring the quality of the report or in following up on their recommendations.

The physical aspect of information is normally not subjected to any regular checks. One needs to discuss in what manner physical monitoring can be strengthened. There is a failure of the ministries in verification of their correctness and almost total absence of accountability procedures. Although some ministries do concurrent evaluation and engage professional organizations in preparing impact studies, such reports are hardly read by the policymakers, and no corrective action follows from the examination done in the reports. Ultimately, the process of hiring a professional for impact study degenerates into another patronage activity, where favourites are chosen, and the quality of the report is a secondary consideration.

Absenteeism to be Monitored

A World Bank study (Keefer and Khemani 2012) showed that the bulk of expenditures in education and health typically flow to the salaries of teachers and health workers, yet rampant absenteeism and shirking by these service providers means that no services are effectively provided in many cases. That is, governments use these resources to provide (targetable) jobs rather than (less targetable) high quality services. The system exists for the service providers but not for service provision. Field investigations in rural areas of Indian states, particularly in the north, reveal that teacher absenteeism is endemic, with almost two-thirds of the teachers employed in the sample schools absent or not teaching at the time of the investigators' unannounced visits. A study quoted by Keefer and Khemani (2003) recounts how a village school in UP can be non-functional for as long as 10 years due to teacher absenteeism and shirking, without any collective protest being organized. Another World Bank study (2008) found that the average rate of teacher attendance was 65 per cent in UP but the average rate of teacher activity (i.e., active engagement in teaching-related activities) was only 27 per cent. No more than a third of the teachers were actively teaching during survey visits.

Similarly, rural health care in most states is marked by absenteeism of doctors/health providers, inadequate supervision/monitoring and callous attitudes. A study by the Planning Commission (2009) described the physical availability of staff at the Community Health Centres (CHCs - These operate at the sub-district or block level) as follows:

Figure 11.1: per cent of medical staff actually present at CHCs as a ratio of sanctioned and recruited strength

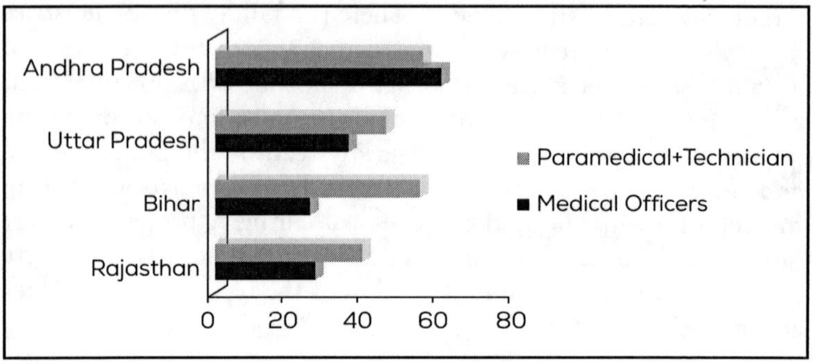

Source: Planning Commission (2009)

Thus Andhra Pradesh has the best record, whereas Bihar has dismal attendance, just 24 per cent, in respect of medical doctors at CHCs. If the Medical Officer is not present to monitor the attendance of those operating under him/her (including not just paramedical staff but also technicians, pharmacists and others) in Public Health Facilities, it is more likely that they, too, will abscond from their duties.

Long-term absenteeism is reinforced on a daily basis by the skewed incentives of a significant disparity in remuneration between the public and private spheres. Consequently, large numbers of medical staff ostensibly serving in the public health system are really devoting significant tracts of their time and energy to informally serving the private system, more or less openly, and at times even using government facilities to see patients on a private basis and charge accordingly. On the other hand, Tamil Nadu has an effective system to ensure that doctors employed by the government actually serve in rural areas, which other states may like to study and incorporate in their policy.

As regards solutions, one idea that has been tried in rural Udaipur in Rajasthan is the use of cameras with tamperproof time and date functions (Narayan and Mooij 2010). Teachers were required to take their own pictures, along with students, at the start and close of each school day. Together with other measures (a bonus in addition to the base salary contingent on presence, and a fine in case of absence), the experiment led to a decline in the teacher absence rate from 44 per cent to 27 per cent in a period of 27 months. The test scores of students also improved.

All ministries/departments should collect quantitative data on the absenteeism of both service providers and service receivers (students in classrooms, or women turning up for institutional deliveries) as it throws a great deal of light on the quality of service. Through a carefully designed methodology backed by technology, it is quite possible to measure the performance of all service -providing agencies, such as police stations, health and anganwadi centres (meant for children below six), panchayats and so on, and to what extent they are responsive, efficient and participative.

Shift focus from input controls to monitoring of outcomes

The root cause of the implementation problem is that the government (both politicians and bureaucrats) is neither adequately focused on nor accountable for social outcomes—the health status of the people, learning by students—and do not hold personnel providing the service accountable either. Incentives to public providers are not such that anyone feels responsible for better or worse outcomes. The policymakers have insufficient means of influencing the incentives facing service providers. This weakness of administration hurts the poor and denies them basic services.

A few years ago, I visited a rural school in district Singhbhum, Jharkhand. I wrote on the black board a two -digit subtraction (31 minus 18), and asked the class V students to do it. Then, I went round the desks and found that hardly half of the students could do it correctly. The Next day, when I met the District Collector, I asked him if he or his team monitored quality of learning. He said,

> "Sir, you are the first person to be asking me this question. Government has never asked this, they only want to know if I have spent the allotted budget, or the number of teachers appointed, and the new classrooms built. There is no column in my format about the quality of learning.

One way to make outcomes more of a motivating factor in service delivery is to generate and disseminate information regarding progress in services. Parents and patients should know what they are entitled to and have a place to lodge complaints when they are not received. Public officials should know whether the public is satisfied or not. Providers and policymakers should know (and be constantly learning) about what works. This requires outcomes to be more regularly measured and their determinants analysed. One critical role of the state government, when panchayats and departments have the primary responsibility for the delivery of publicly-funded services, is to be an independent source for this measurement. Initially, measurement of outcomes may just be for information and for the sake of openness. Over time, such measures could be used to hold districts and departments accountable for improvements—perhaps to the extent of conditioning fiscal transfers to panchayats based on progress. It is in the experimentation that such flexibility allows that solutions to the problem of implementation can be found. Lessons learned will help all districts and panchayats improve their performance.

Check inflated and incredible reporting

Equally, state governments do not discourage reporting of inflated figures from the districts, which again renders monitoring ineffective. As data are often not verified or collected through independent sources, no action is taken against officers indulging in bogus reporting. For instance, in UP the number of fully immunized children that was being reported by the state government in 2008 was almost 100 per cent, but independent assessments put the figure of fully immunized children in UP at less than 40 per cent. Such cases of flagrant over-reporting should not go unpunished; otherwise honest reporting would be discouraged.

As the data on performance (immunization and malnutrition are good examples) on health indicators are fudged, there is no accountability for the district health staff towards achieving results. No mechanisms have been put in place in any State in India to check blatant underreporting (Ramani 2019). Data on some other indicators (IMR and maternal mortality rate) are collected once in eight years and are never used to hold individual officers accountable for slow decline of the index. This is despite the fact that too much of data are collected in government at all levels, but only for upward submission and hardly for analysis or taking corrective action.

The practice of fudging data is so widespread in all the States, presumably with the connivance of senior officers, that the overall percentage of severely malnourished children, in case of 0–3 years according to the data reaching GOI from the states is only 2 per cent, as against 9.4 per cent reported by Unicef (2014) in their survey (Table 11.1). The field officials are thus able to escape from any sense of accountability for reducing malnutrition. Figures from some states show their children to be as healthy as in Denmark and Sweden!

Table 11.1: per cent of severely malnourished children in 2013-14 according to

	State Government	UNICEF
Andhra Pradesh	0.8	4.7
Gujarat	0.8	10.1
Jharkhand	0.5	16.0
Orissa	1.4	11.0
Uttar Pradesh	0.8	12.9
West Bengal	0.7	8.9
India	2.1	9.4

Source: UNICEF (2014)

One district head, when confronted with this kind of bogus figures, told me that reporting correct data is 'a high-risk and low-reward activity'! The sad story of fudging of data by the field staff got a great deal of publicity when the census report in 2011 brought forth the startling revelation that about 3.5 crore rural toilets built in the last 10 years at the individual household levels were missing. In some states, the number of missing toilets was more than 60 per cent, as in Madhya Pradesh, UP and Tamil Nadu.[9] While looking at these inflated figures for Maharashtra in a one-to-one meeting with the state secretary, I could not help shouting,'Vandana, all your data is bogus!' She retorted, 'Sir, don't call it bogus, this is advanced statistics! This is what we will achieve after 10 years, but since we are very fond of the sanitation programme, we report it right now in advance!!'

9. https://www.indiatoday.in/magazine/cover-story/story/20141013-clean-india-modi-govt-toilets-missing-defunct-india-805413-2014-10-02

Similarly, there are no indicators for assessing the quality of programme outcomes. For instance, one would like to know how many newly constructed toilets are being used, and what impact has it has had on people's health and hygiene. Results from a late 2018 survey (Gupta et al. 2019) in four states—Bihar, Madhya Pradesh, Rajasthan and UP—show that although rural latrine ownership increased considerably during 2014–2018, open defecation remains very common; approximately 40 to 50 per cent of rural people in these states defecated in the open in late 2018. This is reduced from about 70 per cent of rural people in the 2014 survey. Much of the reduction in open defecation is a result of new latrine construction: nearly 6 in 10 households that did not own a latrine in 2014 acquired one by the 2018 survey. However, the fraction of people who own a latrine, but who nevertheless defecate in the open, did not change between 2014 and 2018: it was about 23 per cent in both years.

Most states have a computerized ICDS monitoring system, but the available information is not used for taking corrective and remedial action or for analysis. For instance, each anganwadi centre (ICDS clinic) reports on the number of malnourished children category wise, but these figures are neither verified independently by the States nor being used for assessing the effectiveness of the programme.

Sachin Pilot, who was then a young MP, while trying to understand how ICDS functions in the districts observed (Economic Times, 11 February 2008):

> “As a part of a group of MPs working on the issue of malnutrition, we visited several states, especially remote tribal areas, to see how these centres were being run. I was surprised to see that the anganwadi worker who manages the centre with almost no help has to keep 18 registers updated! It is another matter that sometimes the number of children at such centres is less than the number of registers.
>
> “During another visit, we discovered that all data of children at the centre for the past five months, weight, vaccinations, health records etc., were filled

> in with pencils. On probing further, I found it was done so that in case of an official inspection, the figures could be erased and 'correct' data inserted to make the centre's performance look good!

The situation can easily be corrected by greater transparency of the district records that should be put on a website, and by frequent field inspections by an independent team of experts, nutritionists and grassroots workers. The Ministry of Women and Child Development at the Centre should also pull up the States for not recognizing and reporting almost 90 per cent of the severely malnourished children.

Pratham, a voluntary organization, has evolved a simple test in education at a low cost which judges the extent of learning in primary schools. Their findings show that the actual learning levels of students are abysmally low. However, the States do not accept Pratham findings.

It is not enough that the central government departments and the state governments use professional and academic organizations to undertake impact studies from time to time. Their findings must be publicized and discussed with key stakeholders so that improvements in design and delivery can be effected at the earliest. Governments should also put on their websites the findings of the impact studies, and distribute these in workshops they organize. Dissemination of results is critical for use.

I failed in the absence of 'collective will'

If I was to sum up my findings on the IAS in just one sentence, I would say, 'Individually they are very bright, but collective performance needs scaling up.' Even when radical policy reforms are introduced, their implementation remains a non-starter, because it is just next to impossible to bring a very large number of active stakeholders in the states to understand and agree with the spirit of the reform, unless, of course, there is strong political and bureaucratic support at several levels to that reform.

Let me give a few instances how some policy changes that I initiated made little impact in the field because of a lack of commitment to reforms on the part of senior state government officials.

Forest Policy, 1988

Forest policy in India since the early 20th Century was to use forests for timber and industry, and forest dwellers were seen as a burden. From the early 1970s, when increased fuel prices led to greater pressure on forests for collecting fuelwood, government encouraged local farmers to produce fuelwood and fodder outside government forests on farm and common lands through a programme called 'social forestry'. This programme was actively supported by external donors too, such as Swedish International Development Agency, World Bank and Department for International Development.

In a one-to-one meeting sometime in late 1985 with the then Prime Minister, Rajiv Gandhi, when he asked me[10] what I thought of the forestry sector, my response was:

> 'Sir, in a mixed economy, where both government and private sectors work, it is generally the government sector that looks after the livelihood needs of the people, whereas market needs are met by the private sector. However, in forestry it is just the opposite. It is strange that in forestry this distribution of responsibility is not being followed, and the reverse is being attempted. Government forest lands are meeting the commercial needs of the economy and private farm lands and common lands are being asked to produce fuelwood and fodder.

The Prime Minister looked puzzled but asked me to send him a note on the subject. This is how the new forest policy took shape. Announced in 1988, it was 180 degrees different from the past policy. According to this, forests are not to be commercially exploited for industries, but they are to conserve soil and the environment, and meet the subsistence requirements of the local people. It discourages monocultures and prefers mixed forests. The focus has shifted from 'commerce', and 'investment' to ecology

---

10. I was joint secretary in the ministry of environment and forests, and the PM held the forest portfolio.

and satisfying minimum needs of the people[11] providing MFPs, fuelwood and fodder and strengthening the tribal–forest linkages.

Such a radical policy shift could take place because of the support of the then Prime Minister, Rajiv Gandhi. However, his successors took no interest in its implementation. There was also no consultation with the state governments while drafting the new policy. In fact, many senior forest officers in the states had serious reservations about the implementability of the new policy on the ground.

The 1988 policy failed to make any impact in the field and states did not change the working of forests which continued to be timber oriented. Large areas of government forests continued to be under the control of private paper industries in Orissa and Maharashtra. While visiting one forest depot in district Nayagarh, Orissa, in 1995 I discovered that 33,60,000 pieces of bamboo were supplied to industry at 15 paise a piece, whereas the local artisans got only 350 pieces at Rs 4.30 per piece, which was almost 25 times the price at which it was sold to industry. Despite clear instructions in the new policy that tribal requirements of MFP would be given highest priority, MFP policies in the states are often dictated by the desire to maximize state revenues, and not maximize welfare of gatherers, who are often tribal women. The revenue interest of Orissa can be judged by the fact that during the period 1989–2001, the State Government earned revenues of Rs 752 crore from kendu leaves (KL). The total wages earned by KL pluckers during the same period was only `387 crore. The high incidence of royalties on KL needs to be contrasted with the royalties collected on a major mineral, where labour is organized, for example, royalty is Rs 30 per tonne on bauxite, but a whopping Rs 12,000/tonne on KL!

Thus, states remained indifferent to the new 1988 Policy, and forest management strategies continued to be markedly biased in favour of commercial and industrial exploitation, with little attention paid to the interests of gatherers. Ultimately, GOI had to enact a new law (FRA) in 2005 to undo the historical injustice

11. Para 4.3.4.3 of the 1988 policy reads as follows: The life of tribals and other poor living within and near forest revolves around forests. The rights and concessions enjoyed by them should be fully protected. Their domestic requirements of fuelwood, fodder, minor forest produce, and construction timber should be the first charge on forest produce.'

done to the Adivasi forest dwellers. The fact that almost all IAS Secretaries incharge of forests have no professional knowledge of how forests impact upon the lives of the poor and are totally dependent upon the advice of professional foresters may explain why the implementation of the 1988 policy did not receive their attention and remained a forgotten chapter. My successors in the GOI Ministry, too focused more attention on participation through Joint Forest Management (JFM) rather than insisting on fundamental changes in the silvicultural practices that formed the core of the new 1988 policy. JFM too, despite initial hype, degenerated into a departmental activity, in which the Forest Department kept controls within itself by bossing over the people, 'I will manage, you will participate' (Saxena 1997).

Sanitation Policy, 1999

The other policy with which I was associated refers to rural sanitation during my tenure as Secretary, Rural Development, in GOI, 1997–1999.

GOI started way back in the 1970s many social sector programmes in poverty alleviation, drinking water, health, nutrition and so on; however, up to 1986, there was no such central sector programme for sanitation. The 1981 Census revealed that rural sanitation coverage was a meagre 1 per cent, and open defecation was the norm even for well-to-do families. For the first time in 1986 a new Central Rural Sanitation Programme was introduced by GOI for the construction of household toilets in rural areas with huge subsidy element, which was in 1998 `3,000 per toilet available to all. This resulted in the construction of a large number of toilets mostly by contractors and hence of poor quality, but these were hardly used for want of felt need, and gradually became dysfunctional.

As Secretary Rural Development in 1997, I was convinced that high subsidy brings in contractors, whereas the focus should be to create felt need to use toilets through an awareness -raising campaign. Since sanitation is a public good and subject to externalities, the effort should be to mobilize the entire community. I was keen to totally withdraw the subsidy, which encouraged contractors, but Minister was not agreeing. Ultimately, I was able to persuade him to agree to 'no subsidy regime' for the general population, and reduced subsidy from `3,000 to only `500 for the BPL households. The new restructured policy called 'Total Sanitation Campaign' (TSC) provided enhanced budget for Information, Extension and Communication (IEC) through NGOs and so on to promote community-led and demand driven household involvement.

However, the states did not like reduction in subsidy, and even funds for IEC were not effectively utilized. Often these were given to some NGO who would publish publicity material that remained undistributed and dumped to a junk room. Or, the NGO would organize a lavish function where a high official would cut the ribbon followed by sumptuous tea, but with no impact on behavioural change of the ordinary villager. The number of toilets reported to have been constructed in a year fell by 25 per cent from 8,03,260 in 1998–1999 to 5,96,380 in 2002–2003. State Secretaries informally admitted that not even 10 per cent of the toilets constructed during the low subsidy regime were in existence 10 years later, as there was no superstructure and only a single pit was constructed. Thus, my policy had neither political support, nor could I convince the state bureaucracy to concentrate on generating felt need, and encourage self-construction by the households rather than depend on subsidy and contractors. Obviously, the state Secretaries and I were not on the same page, they were quite comfortable with the subsidy induced construction by contractors. My tenure as Secretary too ended[12] soon after the new Policy was decided, and perhaps my successors were not convinced of the need for low subsidy regime in toilet construction.

Gradually under pressure from the states the amount of subsidy kept on increasing, and it became ₹12,000 per toilet in 2014. The entitlement to subsidy was also increased from 35 to 85 per cent of the households in stages. According to the states, sustainability of the low -cost toilets constructed was a major issue and therefore they were in favour of higher subsidy to construct more durable toilets. Fortunately, because of a high priority given to this programme by the Prime Minister in the last six years and excellent administrative leadership of Param Iyer, both construction and usage have improved, but safe disposal of excreta is still an issue.

---

12. The circumstances under which my transfer to Planning Commission took place in 1999 is narrated in Chapter 2.

These two case studies of failure clearly demonstrate that a change in policy alone is not sufficient to achieve results, unless the entire IAS field machinery is convinced of the merits of the new policy, willing to come out of the 'status quo' mentality, and assume leadership role in publicizing and enforcing the new policy in the districts.

Capacity building and training

Reforms suggested in this chapter can be internalized only through high priority to capacity building through training. Most training programmes, however, aim at enhancing the knowledge and skills of individual officers, but do not focus on collective capability of the entire organization. Trainees may learn new skills, but the environment in which they function allows them no time nor provides any incentive to apply those skills. Also, organizational performance does not depend on individual calibre only. Individual performance itself is shaped by organizational culture. Therefore, training should be geared and directly linked to improving the effectiveness of the entire organization.

Several changes will be necessitated if collective performance is to improve. First, training needs assessment should be more group oriented, should involve the top management and should pinpoint other deficiencies of the organization in implementation, which may relate to policy, procedure, man-management or organizational culture. Second, the shift in objectives would imply that all levels are trained within a given period. Third, this will lead to preparation of a long-term training plan as a component of HRD. Fourth, training should include on-the-job training, short workshops, orientation courses and visits to places where excellent work has been done by previously trained people. Fifth, trainees should be a mix of civil servants, politicians, NGOs and so on at least in some courses so that harmonious relations develop between different groups of people involved in development.

Therefore, ideally speaking, one should identify a few key departments or cadres whose performance is to be enhanced through training courses, and link institutional training with other aspects of personnel management. This would mean that one will do a baseline survey on the performance of that department/ cadre and will do surveys from time to time to examine how their performance has changed through training. The report will obviously suggest improvements in other aspects of personnel management, such as transfer and placement policy, promotions, accountability, transparency and so on. It should also suggest pragmatic changes that can be brought in the functioning of these departments through training. Training Needs Assessment should follow this report.

Staff posted at the training institutions should be not only excellent teachers but should have done well in the field too, so that they carry credibility. This would happen only when career as a trainer is seen as bringing long -term personal and professional benefits, and when adequate incentives are given to good officers to join the training institutions. The officers and staff posted to research and training assignments should be given suitable honorarium and free accommodation etc. as an incentive to attract good talent. Opportunities should be available to them for enhancing their own knowledge and training skills. Training institutions must recruit at least a part of their staff on contract from the open market who can bring with them new ideas and new culture. They may also take experienced people from recognized NGOs or from government on a fixed contract. Since these people know that they have to seek a fresh job after a few years, they cannot afford to stagnate. However, the new approach and policy will work only if all concerned, state governments at the highest levels, give full backing to strengthening training institutions. In the absence of the desire to locate the best, it is feared that these contract jobs may be filled up with retired and useless people.

Action on some of the new ideas can begin easily. For instance, preparing case material and documenting success stories will not only improve the training content, but it will also create an atmosphere of optimism that something positive is being done through administration. If this material is prepared by senior officers, or even by professionals with full sense of ownership by officers, it will also inculcate positive values amongst them, so necessary to fight against cynicism that is all -pervasive in government today.

Most training institutions are poorly funded, and they lack necessary equipment, audio-visual aids, case studies, training material and funds for preparing new material or for taking trainees to field visits in other states. However, confronting only these deficiencies in physical infrastructure and software will not be enough. One has to examine the broader issues that marginalize the impact of training, and then evolve a strategy.

Many central departments and state governments tend to look at training as a stand-alone activity to be performed at the residential training institutions. However, training should be seen as an integral part of personnel management, and should be linked to recruitment, career and promotional avenues, human resource development and general environment of governmental functioning. Without improvement in these related sectors, the efficacy of training would be limited. At present, most of the time, field officials are busy doing routine jobs, such as looking after senior officers or politicians, filling up useless formats, attending meetings or seeing endless files. One needs reforms in these sectors, such as in maintenance and movement of files, where political will is not a constraint.

Blind faith in training as an instrument of change amounts to an almost wilful mis-recognition of the malaise afflicting government. Training alone would not affect attitudes rooted in entrenched, often corrupt, interests (such as private practice for doctors). Nor would it reform institutional structures that were not accountable or transparent. Arrogance in government servants is a result of both untrammelled powers and ignorance. Therefore, pressure needs to be mounted in favour of more transparent and accountable structures.

Training institutions should also create short- to medium -term fellowships for serving officers, who could come to such institutions for pursuing studies in their chosen field and write a monograph.

Lateral Entry

IAS officers working in GOI often come in touch with experts who have the necessary domain knowledge. Such experts in the past have been inducted at senior positions in the government, such as Dr Manmohan Singh, Bimal Jalan, Lovraj Kumar, Vijay Kelkar, Montek Ahluwalia, Rakesh Mohan, Jairam Ramesh and Arvind Subramanian. Russi Mody from the Tata Group headed Air India back in 1993, and in 2002, former BSES CMD R .V. Shahi was made Power Secretary for five years. Let us hope this practice will continue in the future too, as they bring in fresh and vibrant ideas, expose the top civil service to competition, and promote better policy formulation based on expert domain knowledge. Their presence in high positions brings central government IAS officials under peer group pressure to learn their subject to be able to converse with the professionals and specialists on equal terms.

Unfortunately, IAS officers working in the states hardly come across people who can inspire them either ethically or intellectually. They are surrounded by politicians, traders and similar other fellows seeking due or undue favours. Desire to learn and improve performance is limited in the states. One can only hope that they are exposed to innovative ideas through effective training programmes. In the ultimate analysis, the key to understanding governments' underperformance is not the personal attributes of civil servants but the environment under which they operate that does not promote excellence.

Summing up

Civil service reform is an issue of critical importance and one which has engaged the attention of the GOI since well before Independence. Since Independence, about 50 Commissions and Committees have been set up at the level of the Union Government to study and make recommendations on what can be broadly characterized as administrative reforms. As a result of the deliberations and recommendations of these Commissions and Committees on different aspects of public administration, some incremental reforms have been effected. These include the creation of a separate Department of Administrative Reforms in the Union and State Governments (which, unfortunately, is considered a punishment posting by most IAS officers), setting up of the Indian Institute of Public Administration, setting up of the Central Vigilance Commission, Constitution of Lokayuktas in States, strengthening of citizens' grievance redressal machinery, drawing up of citizens charters, focus on training and capacity building of civil servants, restructuring of the recruitment process and modifications in the performance appraisal system.

The reforms which have been put in place are essentially 'soft' reforms, which have not seriously addressed the issues of lack of accountability and outcome orientation, corruption, and collusion within the Government. Many of the recommendations involving basic changes have not been acted upon and, therefore, the framework, systems and methods of functioning of the civil services based on the Whitehall model of the mid-nineteenth century remains largely unchanged. Yet, all these Reports have been dealt with in a routine manner, with cursory Action Taken Reports being prepared, filed and forgotten. The prodigious research and intellectual efforts of these Committees, not to mention the administrative and financial resources expended on them, have been largely wasted. As the Second Administrative Reforms Commission noted, 'the Indian reform effort has been unfailingly conservative, with limited impact...Civil service reform in India has neither enhanced the efficiency nor the accountability of the Civil Service in any meaningful manner.'

Many policy reforms suggested in this book, such as a stable tenure, would require strong political support. In some rogue states, political pressures for distribution of patronage are so intense that there is no time or inclination for the ministers and bureaucrats to do conceptual thinking, design good programmes, weed out those that are not functioning well and monitor programmes with a view to improve the effectiveness of delivery. One can only hope that these states would learn from the positive example of other states where the CMs have overcome the anti-incumbency factor by improving governance, and thereby achieving inclusive growth.

Civil service reforms must be aimed at improving transparency, accountability, honesty, efficiency and sensitivity in public administration at all levels. The solution to the problem of corruption has to be more systemic than any other issue of governance. Merely shrinking the economic role of the State by resorting to deregulation, liberalization and privatization is not necessarily the solution to addressing the problem. All such procedures, laws and regulations that breed corruption and come in the way of efficient delivery system will have to be eliminated.

Reforms designed to reduce corruption and improve outcomes may have a better chance of success if there is free media and electoral competition with open elections. Free media and elections transmit demands for change and can be useful in holding politicians and officials to account. On the other hand, it can also be argued that significant improvement in the functional capability of the state often takes 10 to 20 years, if not more, which is clearly beyond the life-cycle of a single government for most democratic countries. Therefore, the argument that implementing reforms in autocratic regimes is easier than in democratic regimes (given the limited opposition forces, and less dependence on electoral cycles) is quite appealing keeping in view the success achieved in Vietnam, South Korea, China and Singapore.

We must also remember that we are not talking about creating a bureaucracy on a clean slate ab initio. We have inherited a bureaucratic system which has its own compulsions and culture. Our challenge today is how, out of this, we shape a new bureaucracy and in that sense 'create' a bureaucracy that works. We are somewhat like the managers of a fitness club knocking people into shape. We have to be content with incremental reforms that can be sustained over a long period.

A good civil service is necessary but not sufficient for good governance; a bad civil service is sufficient but not necessary for bad governance (Schiavo-Campo et al. 1997). Thus, a dilapidated civil service has been a key factor in Africa's economic decline. Conversely, a strong civil service is one of several reasons why in several east Asian economies, especially Japan, Singapore and South Korea, authoritarianism has coexisted with excellent economic performance. It can be argued that the link between authoritarianism and economic decline, so evident in Africa, has been inoperative in these Asian countries largely because of their strong civil service. Greater responsiveness and openness can legitimately be demanded of public administrations in many East Asian countries. Clearly, civil service systems in most East Asian countries cannot be considered a problem; they are, rather, an important part of the solution to these countries' other problems (Saxena 2010b).

Unfortunately, in many Indian states, politics has become a business. Politicians put pressure on the system with a view to maximizing private gains. Governance reforms are intractable under such 'kleptocracy' that exploits national wealth for its own benefit and is, by definition, uninterested in transparency and accountability. A pliable and unskilled civil service is actually desirable from its point of view— public employees dependent on the regime's discretionary largesse are forced to become corrupt, cannot quit their jobs and reluctantly become the regime's accomplices. Providing financial assistance to such states by the Central Government without linking it with performance and reforms will be a waste of resources. Niti Aayog's efforts to improve governance by publicizing interstate performance on key indicators is a laudable step. Let us hope the Aayog evaluates states on transparency, public satisfaction and integrity too.

The strengths of the IAS lie in its extraordinary pool of skills and talents, its field experience, its extensive networking, its appreciation and overview of the functioning of government at the cutting edge, its understanding of delivery systems for development, awareness of the formal and informal socio-economic networks in the field, its 'can deliver' attitude, its role in national integration, and its ready adaptability to new and unfamiliar situations (Das 2010). We need to make the Service more outcome oriented and accountable for results.

REFERENCES

Administrative Reforms Commission. 2008. 'Public Order.' *Fifth Report of the Second Administrative Reforms Commission.* New Delhi: Government of India.

ADR (2014): Analysis of Total Income of National Parties between FY 2004-05 and 2011-12, Association for Democratic Reforms, at http://adrindia.org/research-and-report/politicalparty-watch/combined-reports/analysis-total-income-national-parties-be (accessed January 12, 2019).

Ahmad, R. (ed.). (2006). *The role of public administration in building a harmonious society: selected proceedings from the Annual Conference of the Network of Asia-Pacific Schools and Institutes of Public Administration and Governance (NAPSIPAG).* Asian Development Bank.

AI 2019: Changes in open defecation in rural north India: 2014-2018, Accountability Initiative, Delhi, at https://accountabilityindia.in/sites/default/files/pdf_files/Changes%20in%20open%20defecation.pdf

AI 2019a: Samagra Shiksha GoI, 2019-20 (Pre-Budget), Budget Briefs, Accountability Initiative, Delhi

AI 2019b: PMMVY & JSY, GoI, 2019-20 (Pre-Budget), Budget Briefs, Accountability Initiative, Delhi

AI 2016, Budget Briefs, volume 6, Issue 5, Feb, Accountability Initiative, Delhi

AI 2015, Fund Tracking Survey (PAISA), December, Accountability Initiative, Delhi

Aiyar, Yamini, 2009: Fostering Participation and Accountability in Local Governance: Current Experience, Future Challenges, New Delhi

Alphons, KJ 1996: Making a Difference, Penguin

APPU, PS, 2005: The All India Services: Decline, Debasement and Destruction Economic and Political Weekly February 26

ASER 2018: Annual Status of Education Report, PRATHAM, New Delhi

ASER 2022: Annual Status of Education Report, PRATHAM, New Delhi

Bagchi, Sanjoy 2007: The Changing Face of Bureaucracy, Rupa & Co

Baig, M.R.A. 1974: The Muslim Dilemma in India, Vikas, Delhi

Banerjee, Partha Sarathi (2008): *The Party and the Panchayats of West Bengal*, Economic & Political Weekly, June 14

Bardhan, Pranab K. *Globalisation, Democracy and Corruption: An Indian Perspective*. Frontpage, 2015.

Benbabaali, D. (2008). Questioning the role of the Indian Administrative Service in national integration. *South Asia Multidisciplinary Academic Journal.*

Beschel Jr, R. P. (2003). Civil service reform in India: perspectives from the World Bank's work in three states. *State-Level Reforms in India: Towards More Effective Government*, 233-55.

Besley, T., R. Pande and V. Rao (2005): 'Participatory Democracy in Action: Survey Evidence from South India', Journal of the European Economics Association, 3(2-3), pp: 648-657

Bhanumurthy N R, Manish Prasad, and Richa Jain, 2018: Public Expenditure, Governance and Human Development, The Case of Madhya Pradesh, Economic & Political Weekly, APRIL 7, vol 53, no 14

Bourgon Jocelyne 2011: A New Synthesis of Public Administration: Serving in the 21st Century, School of Policy Studies and McGill-Queen's University Press, Kingston

Buch M.N., 2005: Why India Needs A Strong And Impartial Civil Service, in Bhattacharya P.(edited), Readings in Public Administration—I, Administrative Training Institute, Calcutta

Chand, Vikram, ed. 2006: *Reinventing public service delivery in India: Selected case studies*. Sage

Chaturvedi, BK 2014: Governance: Civil Service & Politician Interface, Yojana, Delhi

CPR 2018: Budget Briefs, Vol 10/ Issue 1, Sarva Shiksha Abhiyan (SSA), GoI, 2017-18, Centre for Policy Research, New Delhi

CRISIL 2018, States of Growth, Mumbai

Dab, J. K., Medinipur, P., & Bengal, W. (2014). The menace of criminalization of politics: challenges to indian democracy. Council of edulight, 180.

Das, S. K. (2010). *Building a world-class civil service for twenty-first century India*. Oxford University Press.

Deshmukh, B. G. (2004). *A cabinet secretary looks back*. Harper Collins Publishers India

Deshpande D. and A. Kapur, 2018: Unpacking the Processes of Achieving Open Defecation Free Status: A Case Study of Udaipur, Rajasthan. Accountability Initiative Working Paper, Centre for Policy Research, New Delhi.

Dev, S. Mahendra 2016: The Problem of Inequality, WP-2016-029, Indira Gandhi Institute of Development Research, Mumbai December

Eckholm, Eric, 1979, Planting for the Future: Forestry for Human Needs, Worldwatch Institute, Washington

Gaikwad, V. 1981. Community development in India. In: R. Dore and Z. Mars (eds), Community Development: Comparative Case Studies in India, the Republic of Korea, Maxico and Tanzania. Croom Helm, London.

Ghosh Arun 1998: Bureaucracy and Bureaucrats of a Bygone Era, Economic and Political Weekly, February 21.

Gill, S. S. (1999). *The pathology of corruption*. HarperCollins Publishers India.

GOI 2007: XI Five Year Plan, Planning Commission

GOI (2008): *Impact Assessment Of Nirmal Gram Puraskar Awarded Panchayats*, Department of Drinking Water and Sanitation, New Delhi

GOI. 2009. Government of India, Department of Administrative Reforms, Civil Service Day 2009, Panel Discussion, Theme Papers.

Gopal Krishna, 'Indian Muslims in the Nation Formation Process,' in Gopal Krishna (ed.), Contributions to South Asian Studies 2, (Delhi, Oxford, 1982) : 117.

Guha, Ramachandra 2018: Liberals, sadly, Indian Express, March 24

Gupta, Aashish, Nazar Khalid, Devashish Desphande, Payal Hathi, Avani Kapur, Nikhil Srivastav, Sangita Vyas, Dean Spears, and Diane Coffey. 2019: *Changes in Open Defecation in Rural North India: 2014-2018*. No. 12065. Institute for the Study of Labor (IZA),.

Gupta, Akhil 2017: Changing Forms of Corruption in India, Modern Asian Studies, May 24

Gupta, Shalini (2012): Food Expenditure and Intake in the NSS 66th Round, Economic & Political Weekly, January 14, vol xlvii no 2

Haksar PN (2005), The Pot and the Kettle, in Bhattacharya P.(edited), Readings in Public Administration—I, Administrative Training Institute, Calcutta

Hari K. S. and Neelambar Hatti 2015: Poverty and Inequality in India: An Exploratory Analysis, Social Science Spectrum, Vol. 1, No. 4, December, pp. 249-261

Harriss, J. (2016). What Are the Prospects for a Social Democratic Alliance in India Today?. *Reinventing Social Democratic Development: Insights from Indian and Scandinavian Comparisons*, Copenhagen.

Himanshu 2018: India Inequality Report 2018, OXFAM, Delhi

IFAD (2002) Final Appraisal Report, Second Orissa Tribal Development Programme, Rome

IFAD (2000) 'Draft Formulation Report: Second Orissa Tribal Development Programme', Rome

IFPRI, 2022: Global Hunger Index: IFPRI, Bonn

ILO 2018: Global Wage Report 2018/19: What lies behind gender pay gaps, ILO, Geneva

Jaffrelot, Christophe 2018: The new corruption, Indian Express, September 19

Jaffrelot, Christophe and Kalaiyarasan A 2018: Margins of New India, Indian Express, November 27

Jaffrelot, Christophe, Atul Kohli, and Kanta Murali, eds. 2019: *Business and Politics in India*. Modern South Asia

Jaffrelot, C., & Gayer, L. (2012). *Muslims in Indian cities: trajectories of marginalisation*, Columbia University Press.

Jayal, Niraja Gopal (2006) 'Engendering Local Democracy: The Impact of Quotas for Women in India's Panchayats', Democratization, 13:1,

Keefer, P., & Khemani, S. (2003). The political economy of public expenditures. World Bank, Washington, DC.

Kohli, Atul 2010: Politics and Redistribution in India, in R Nagaraj (edited), India, Poverty Reduction and Policy Regimes, NRISD Geneva

Krishna, Anirudh (2006): 'Politics in the Middle: Mediating Relationships between the Citizens and the State in Rural North India,' in Herbert Kitschelt and Steven I Wilkinson (eds), Patrons, Clients and Policies Patterns of Democratic Accountability and Political Competition, Cambridge: Cambridge University Press

Kumar, Arjun (2016): India's Residential Rental Housing, Economic & Political Weekly, June 11, vol lI, no 112

LANSA 2017: Implementation of the ICDS in Chhattisgarh and Uttar Pradesh (India): A Systemic Study, Research Brief 06, June

Lieten G. K. and Ravi Srivastava. 1999. Unequal Partners: Power Relations, Devolution and Development in Uttar Pradesh. New Delhi: Sage Publications

Liu, Yanyan and Christopher B Barrett (2013): Heterogeneous Pro-Poor Targeting in the National Rural Employment Guarantee Scheme, Economic & Political Weekly, March 9, vol xlviii no 46

Mawdsley, Emma Gina Porter and Janet Townsend, 2000: How Can Southern NGOs Have More of an Influence on the Development Agenda?, November, Global Policy Forum, New York

Mander, Harsh (2018): 'Pehlu Khan, One Year Later,' Indian Express, 21 April, https://indianexpress.com/article/opinion/columns/pehlu-khan-rajasthan-cow-lynching-5145631/

Manor, James (2002). Democratic decentralisation in two Indian states: Past and present. The Indian Journal of Political Science, 63(1), 51–71

Mathew, Santhosh, & Mick Moore (2015). The Purposeful Destruction of State Capacity in Bihar, India. In I. Jamil et al. (eds.), *Governance in South, Southeast*, and East Asia (pp. 229-243). Springer, Switzerland

Mathew, Santhosh and Mick Moore, 2011. 'State incapacity by design: Understanding the Bihar story.' *IDS Working Papers*, no. 366 (2011): 1-31.

Mathur, B P 2014: Reforming Public Services: Embracing A New Management Philosophy, Yojana, Delhi

Mathur, Ravindra S 2019: Craft of Politics Power for Patronage, Manas, Delhi

Min, Brian and Miriam Golden. 'Electoral cycles in electricity losses in India.' *Energy Policy* 65 (2014): 619-625.

Mitra, Chandan. 1998: *The corrupt society: the criminalization of India from independence to the 1990s*. Viking Penguin.

MTA 2000, Mid-term appraisal of the 9th Plan, Planning Commission, New Delhi

Mukerji, Siddhartha (2018): *The 2015 Gram Pradhan Elections in Uttar Pradesh: Money, Power, and Violence, Economic & Political Weekly*, June 16

Narayan, K. and J. Mooij (2010): 'Solutions to Teacher Absenteeism in Rural Government Primary Schools in India: A Comparison of Management Approaches', *Open Education Journal*, 3(1), 63-71

Nayak, Nandini, and Naresh C. Saxena (2006): 'Implementation of ICDS in Bihar and Jharkhand.' *Economic and Political Weekly*: 3680-3684.

NFHS 2017: National Family Health Survey–4, Ministry of Health & Family Welfare, GOI

Niehaus, Paul, Antonia Attanassova, Mariane Bertrand and Sendhil Mullainathan (2013), 'Targeting with Agents,' American Economic Journal: Economic Policy 5.1: 206-238.

NITI 2018: Healthy States, Progressive India, NITI Aayog, Delhi

Oxfam 2018: India Inequality Report 2018: Widening Gaps, New Delhi

Panagariya, Arvind, Pinaki Chakraborty and M. Govinda Rao (2015): Growth and Development of States in India, Oxford University Press, New York

Parkinson, B. K. (1967). Non-economic factors in the economic retardation of the rural Malays. *Modern Asian Studies*, 1(1), 31-46.

Piliavsky, A. and Sbriccoli, T., 2016. The ethics of efficacy in North India's goonda raj (rule of toughs). *Journal of the Royal Anthropological Institute*, 22(2), pp.373-391.

Planning Commission (2001): *Mid-term Appraisal of the 9th Plan*, Planning Commission, New Delhi

Planning Commission (2009): *A Primary Evaluation of Service Delivery under the National Rural Health Mission (NRHM): Findings from a Study in Andhra Pradesh, Uttar Pradesh, Bihar, and Rajasthan*, Kaveri Gill, Working Paper 1/2009 – PEO, May

Planning Commission (2012): Twelfth Five Year Plan, , volume 1, Government of India

Planning Commission 2008: Eleventh Five Year Plan, , volume 1, Government of India

Planning Commission 2001: Approach Paper, X Plan

Planning Commission 2011. Evaluation of the ICDS, New Delhi, at http://planningcommission.nic.in/reports/peoreport/peo/peo_icds_vol1.pdf

Potter, David C. 1986: *India's Political Administrators: 1919-1983*. Oxford University Press, USA.

Pritchett, Lant. 2009. Is India a Flailing State?: Detours on the Four Lane Highway to Modernization. HKS Faculty Research Working Paper Series RWP09-013, John F. Kennedy School of Government, Harvard University

Puri, Raghav (2012): 'Reforming the Public Distribution System: Lessons from Chhattisgarh', Economic & Political Weekly, February 4, vol xivii no 5

Radhakrishna, R. (2015), 'Well-being, inequality, Poverty and Pathways out of poverty in India', Economic and Political Weekly, Vol.50, No.41

Rai, Vibhuti N. 2016: Hashimpura 22 May, Penguin

Rajan, Raghuram (2012), The Next Generation of Reforms in India, Speech at a Function to Re-release a Book of Essays in Honor of Dr. Manmohan Singh, New Delhi, April 14.

Rajan, Raghuram 2008: Is There a Threat of Oligarchy in India? Speech to the Bombay Chamber of Commerce on its Founders Day celebration, September 10th

Ramani, V. 2019: Fixing Child Malnutrition in India: Views from a Public Policy Practitioner, The Hindu Centre for Politics & Public Policy, Chennai

Rao, C. S., & Kumar, D. S. (2017). Decentralisation and Participatory Planning by Pris in Telangana: A Study of Grama Jyothi Programme. *Journal of Rural Development*, 36(4), 569-593.

Rao, Govinda M, U A Vasanth Rao, 2008, Expanding the Resource Base of Panchayats: Augmenting Own Revenues, Economic & Political Weekly January 26

Rao. V and Paromita Sanyal (2009): 'Dignity through Discourse: Poverty and the Culture of Deliberation in Indian Village Democracies', World Bank Research Working Paper, No. 4924, World Bank.

Rodinson, Maxime 1974: Islam and Capitalism, Allen Lane, Penguin, London

Roy, Aruna, (2018). The RTI Story: Power to the People, Roli

Sarma, EAS, 2012: Economic & Political Weekly, April 14, 2012 vol xlviI no 15

Saxena N.C. 2003: Livelihood Diversification and Non-Timber Forest Products in Orissa: Wider Lessons on the Scope for Policy Change? ODI London

Saxena, Naresh Chandra 2011, Challenges Before a Resurgent Bihar: Livelihood Options and Development Possibilities, Journal of Social and Economic Studies, Vol. XXI, No. 2

Saxena, N.C. (2003). From monopoly to de-regulation of NTFPs: Policy shifts in Orissa (India). *The International Forestry*

Review, 5(2), 168-176. Retrieved from http://www.jstor.org/stable/43739891

Saxena, N.C. (2011): *Singapore Public Service and National Development, Ministry of Foreign Affairs, Singapore*, at http://www.mfa.gov.sg/content/dam/mfa/images/media_center/MFA_CSC_UN DP_book/Virtuous_Cycles.pdf

Saxena, N.C. 2004: Outlays and outcomes, in Seminar, Issue no. 574, at http://www.india-seminar.com/2007/574/574_naresh_c_saxena.htm

Saxena, N.C. 2010: The IAS Officer – predator or victim, Commonwealth & Comparative Politics, Vol. 48, No. 4, November 2010, 445–456

Saxena, N.C. 2013: Why Have Some Done Better Than Others, Inclusion, July-September, Delhi

Saxena, N.C. 2016: PMGSY vs MGNREGS; Why Some Programmes Do Better?, Inclusion, Jan – March, Delhi

Saxena, N.C. 2016a: Governance Reforms in India, in Olle Törnquist and John Harriss edited, Reinventing Social Democratic Development: Insights from Indian and Scandinavian Comparisons, Copenhagen

Saxena, N.C. and Farrington, J. (2003), 'Trends and Prospects for Poverty Reduction in Rural India: Context and Options', *Working Paper*, London: Overseas Development Institute

Saxena, N.C., 2010: Capacity Development Strategies to Support Decentralization in Asia, Global Event Working Paper, UNDP, New York

Saxena, N.C., 2015: Socio Economic Caste Census, Has It Ignored Too Many Poor Households? Economic & Political Weekly, July 25, vol L, 30

Saxena, N. C. (1997). *The saga of participatory forest management in India. Centre for International Forestry Research*, Bogor.

Saxena, N.C. 1989. 'Public Employment and Educational Backwardness Among the Muslims in India' in Moin Shakir (ed.), Religion, State and Politics in India, pp. 155-99. Delhi: Ajanta Publications.

Schiavo-Campo, S., de Tommaso, G., & Mukherjee, A. (1997). Government employment and pay in global perspective:

a selective synthesis of international facts, policies and experience. *Policy Research Working Paper*, (1771).

Sekher Madhushree and Suchandrima Chakraborty 2016: Politics of Public Policies in India: Explaining the Institutional Internalization of Inequality in Policy Legislation ICDD The International Center for Development and Decent Work University of Kassel, Germany

Sen, P. (2005). 'Of calories and things: reflections on nutritional norms, poverty lines and consumption behaviour in India'. *Economic and Political Weekly*, 22 October.

Sen, Probir : Pre-requisites for Excellence – What made the ICS the service it was, TERI, Delhi

Sharma, Atul 2012, Politicisation of Civil Services: A case study of Uttar Pradesh, 1996-2006, A summary of the thesis Ch. Charan singh University, Meerut

Shukla, Abhay and Shweta Marathe 2017: The Malnutrition Market, Let Them Eat Paste, Economic & Political Weekly, June 24

Srivastava, Ravi S. (2004): Anti-poverty Programmes in Uttar Pradesh: An Evaluation, Planning Commission, New Delhi

Subramanian, T.S.R. 2004, Journeys through Babudom and Netaland — Governance in India: Rupa

Sud, Inder. 2010. 'Governance for a Modern Society,' in Harinder Kohli and Anil Sood (eds.), *India 2039: An Affluent Society in One Generation*. New Delhi: Centennial Group.

Sukhtankar, Sandip, and Milan Vaishnav. 'Corruption in India: Bridging Research Evidence and Policy Options (SSRN Scholarly Paper No. ID 2685819).' *Rochester, NY: Social Science Research Network*, https://papers. ssrn. com/ abstract2685819 (2015): 1-79.

Swarup, Anil (2019): Not Just a Civil Servant, Unicorn, Delhi

Teltumbde, Anand 2018: The New Normal in Modi's 'New India', Economic & Political Weekly, Vol. 53, Issue No. 31, 04 Aug

UNICEF 2014. *Rapid Survey on Children, 2013-14*, New Delhi

UNICEF 2021. *The State of World's Children 2021*, New York.

UNICEF. 2007. *Evaluation of ICDS in Bihar*, Patna.

Vaishnav, Milan and Saksham Khosla 2016: The Indian Administrative Service Meets Big Data, Carnegie Endowment for International Peace, September 01

Vaishnav, Milan. 2017. When Crime Pays: Money and Muscle in Indian Politics. Yale University Press

Verma, Arvind 2002: 'The Politician and the Bureaucrat', <http://www.viewsunplugged.com/VU/20020214/reflection_mukund1.shtml>,

Verma, Ravindra Kumar 1991: Caste and Bihar Politics Economic and Political Weekly, May 4,

Wade, Robert. (1985): The market for public office: Why the Indian state is not better at development. *World Development* 13.4, 467-497.

WDR 2006: World Development Report: Equity and Development, Washington

Witsoe, J. (2007). *Challenges and opportunities facing India's poorest state*. https://casi.sas.upenn. edu/iit/witsoe.

Witsoe, J., 2013. *Democracy against development: Lower-caste politics and political modernity in postcolonial India*. University of Chicago Press.

World Bank (2005). *Bihar: Towards a development strategy.* Washington, DC: World Bank.

World Bank (2008): *Public Participation, Teacher Accountability, and School Outcomes*, November, New Delhi

World Bank (2012): *Democracy, Public Expenditures, and the Poor, by Philip Keefer and Stuti Khemani*, World Bank Policy Research Working Paper 3164

World Bank 2003: Civil Service Reform in India, Perspectives from the World Bank's Work in Three States, Robert P Beschel Jr. at http://documents.worldbank.org/curated/en/211271468033290495/pdf/714880WP0State0el0Reforms0in0India0.pdf

World Bank 2006: India - Public Financial Management and Accountability in Panchayati Raj Institutions (Rural Local Governments), Synthesis Study, Report No. 38557-IN, Financial Management Unit South Asia Region

World Bank 2013: India, Land Governance Assessment National Report, Delhi

World Bank 2014: The Anatomy of Failure, An Ethnography of a Randomized Trial to Deepen Democracy in Rural India, Policy Research Working Paper 6958

WSP (2001): *Why Some Village Water and Sanitation Committees are Better than Others: A Study of Karnataka and Uttar Pradesh (India)*, Water and Sanitation Program, World Bank, Delhi